MODERNISM AND SUBJECTIVITY

MODERNISM AND **SUBJECTIVITY**

How Modernist Fiction Invented
the Postmodern Subject

ADAM MEEHAN

Louisiana State University Press   Baton Rouge

Published by Louisiana State University Press
Copyright © 2020 by Louisiana State University Press

DESIGNER: *Mandy McDonald Scallan*
TYPEFACE: *Whitman*

Portions of chapter 1 were first published, in somewhat different form, in "Specters of Ideology in Joseph Conrad's *Nostromo*," *Studies in the Novel* 50, no. 3 (2018): 359–77, and are reprinted with permission of Johns Hopkins University Press.

Portions of chapter 3 were first published, in somewhat different form, in "Repetition, Race, and Desire in *The Great Gatsby*," *Journal of Modern Literature* 37, no. 2 (2014): 76–91, and are reprinted with permission of Indiana University Press.

Library of Congress Cataloging-in-Publication Data
Names: Meehan, Adam, author.
Title: Modernism and subjectivity : how modernist fiction invented the
    postmodern subject / Adam Meehan.
Description: Baton Rouge : Louisiana State University Press, [2020] |
    Includes bibliographical references and index.
Identifiers: LCCN 2019040538 (print) | LCCN 2019040539 (ebook) | ISBN
    978-0-8071-7218-6 (cloth) | ISBN 978-0-8071-7358-9 (pdf) | ISBN 978-0-8071-7359-6
    (epub)
Subjects: LCSH: English fiction—20th century—History and criticism. |
    Subjectivity in literature. | Modernism (Literature)—English-speaking
    countries. | Postmodernism (Literature)—English-speaking countries.
Classification: LCC PR830.S82 M44 2020 (print) | LCC PR830.S82 (ebook) |
    DDC 823/.91209353—dc23
LC record available at https://lccn.loc.gov/2019040538
LC ebook record available at https://lccn.loc.gov/2019040539

The paper in this book meets the guidelines for permanence and durability of the Committee on Production Guidelines for Book Longevity of the Council on Library Resources. ∞

CONTENTS

Acknowledgments | vii

INTRODUCTION | 1

Chapter 1
THE INTERPELLATED SUBJECT | 23
Specters of Ideology in Joseph Conrad's *Nostromo*

Chapter 2
THE VOID OF SUBJECTIVITY | 48
Sublimation and the Artistic Process in Conrad,
Joyce, and Woolf

Chapter 3
THE SUBJECT IN PROCESS | 85
Repetition, Race, and Desire in *The Great Gatsby*

Chapter 4
SPATIALIZED SUBJECTIVITY | 106
Los Angeles and the Post/Modern Subject in
Fitzgerald, West, and Huxley

Chapter 5
THE NEGATION OF SUBJECTIVITY | 145
Méconnaissance and the Other in Beckett's *Murphy*

CODA | 163

Notes | 169
Works Cited | 181
Index | 193

ACKNOWLEDGMENTS

Like any significant project, this book would not have been possible without the help of many people along the way. I would especially like to thank my advisers and colleagues who read early drafts of the book in its various forms, including Carlos Gallego, Jerry Hogle, Suresh Raval, Ed Dryden, Brent Gowen, Pete Figler, Ryan Winet, and Jerry Won Lee. Special thanks goes to Stephen Ross for an enlightening conversation at the 2015 MLA convention in Vancouver that helped shape the book's main argument and for his subsequent support and guidance as I developed the proposal. I would also like to thank my colleagues at SUNY Westchester Community College. Although I was only with you briefly, I learned a great deal from you and look back fondly at our time together. My colleagues at Palomar College are also owed a great debt of gratitude for their unwavering support and for being wonderful people. I am profoundly grateful to be a part of such a wonderful community.

I would especially like to thank James Long at LSU Press for his continuing interest in and support of this project. One could not ask for a friendlier, more responsive, or more encouraging editor. His guidance has helped me produce a better book. I would also like to thank the editorial board at LSU Press; the anonymous reader who provided very helpful feedback on the first draft; Catherine Kadair, managing editor at LSU Press; and copyeditor Joanne Allen.

None of my achievements would be possible without the support of my parents, who always made sure that I had what I needed and who gave me the freedom to make my own decisions even when they may have seemed bizarre or illogical. Most of all, infinite rewards are owed to my wife, Nicole, who has made so many sacrifices to support my career and our relationship, and to my daughter, Hadley, for reminding me that work can wait.

MODERNISM AND SUBJECTIVITY

INTRODUCTION

The central argument of this book is that conceptions of subjectivity commonly attributed to postmodern theory had already been articulated in modernist fiction before 1945. This contention raises a number of questions, such as, Which conceptions of subjectivity are being considered? How does one define *postmodern theory*? And why include only fiction, and not poetry, drama, or other artistic forms? These and other questions will be addressed below, but I would like to begin by confronting a perhaps more pressing concern: why publish a book about modernism and subjectivity *now*? After all, according to some critics, subjectivity has been outstripped as a categorical descriptor. As far back as 1991, an essay collection coedited by Jean-Luc Nancy asked the question "Who Comes After the Subject?" Nancy asked readers to consider whether "the critique or deconstruction of interiority, of self presence, of consciousness, of mastery, of the individual or collective property of an essence" had "simply obliterated its object [subjectivity]" (4). He pointed out that "the inaugurating decisions of contemporary thought—whether they took place under the sign of a break with metaphysics and its poorly pitched questions, under the sign of a 'deconstruction' of this metaphysics, under that of a transference of the thinking of Being to the thinking of life, or of the Other, or of language, etc.—have all involved putting subjectivity on trial" (5).[1] Indeed, since the turn of this century the emergence of new, reimagined, and/or reinvigorated disciplines like queer theory, disability studies, affect studies, cognitive studies, and environmental studies has meant a further pivot away from the broad-based theories of subjectivity that dominated the latter half of the twentieth century toward more individualized and politically inflected understandings of personal identity.

And yet we might point to a spring 2017 special issue of *Cultural Critique* entitled "What Comes After the Subject?" (a direct response to the collection mentioned above) as an indication that for all the effort to overthrow the subject, its specter still lingers. The editors write in their introduction that "the renaissance of theories of subjectivity—as exemplified by the work of Alain Badiou, Jacques Rancière, and Slavoj Žižek—suggests that at the very least the declaration of the subject's death was premature" (Haines and Grattan 16). The persistence of subjectivity can be seen across disciplines, including philosophy, history, anthropology, sociology, and psychology—or, if one prefers, in what we have come to call *critical theory*, which incorporates elements of these and other disciplines. There is also an enduring interest among literary scholars in exploring representations of subjectivity, as seen in the recent work of Renée Dickinson, Susan Harrow, Josephine Park, Nancy Ruttenburg, Tamar Katz, and others. Although it is true that many scholars across the humanities have jettisoned subjectivity in favor of newer formulations, I contend that the time is ripe for a revisionary look at how notions of the subject evolved in twentieth-century literature and theory—and this is the task I undertake in this book.

After all, regardless of how we feel about the concept *now,* one can make a strong case that subjectivity was *the* defining intellectual preoccupation of the twentieth century. Consider that one of the major intellectual events to take place at the onset of the twentieth century was the publication of Sigmund Freud's groundbreaking *The Interpretation of Dreams* (1899), which brought the study of the unconscious mind into mainstream society. Shortly thereafter, in the sciences, Albert Einstein published "On the Electrodynamics of Moving Bodies" (1905), which outlined his special theory of relativity and showed that all observations are relative to one's frame of reference. In the arts, modernist literature was gaining momentum across Europe and post-impressionism was leading Virginia Woolf to famously write that "on or about December 1910 [the month of the first postimpressionist exhibition] human character changed" ("Character in Fiction" 421). In philosophy, the seminal nineteenth-century work of Kierkegaard and Nietzsche evolved into a fully articulated existentialism that peaked during and shortly after World War II. And this all in just the first half of the century. The second half saw the rise of postmodernism, which was driven by a prevailing skepticism toward grand narratives and claims of certainty or objectivity that even included for some a distrust of so-called scientific facts. In short, across the intellectual landscape of the twentieth century one finds a disparate but prevailing fixation upon the singularity of individual experience and the difficulty, if not impossibility, of ever transcending one's own subjective perception of the world. This preoccupation undoubtedly reaches its apex in the age of postmodernism.

As for the designation *postmodern theory*, I admit that it is not wholly satisfactory, but one struggles to find a more apposite way to encapsulate the outpouring of theoretical work across the humanities in the second half of the twentieth century—that time now generally referred to as *postmodern*, though that descriptor itself brings along its own contentious history. In using the designation *postmodern theory*, I follow Steven Best and Douglas Kellner, who in their 1991 book of that name use the term to encompass not only theories of postmodernism as such, like those advanced by Jean-Francois Lyotard, David Harvey, or Fredric Jameson, but also the work of intellectuals across many disciplines that has been influential in forming the postmodern zeitgeist. These would include scholars of postcolonialism, gender studies, queer theory, poststructuralism, post- and neo-Marxism, psychoanalysis, and other adjacent fields. In short, *postmodern theory* is an inclusive, perhaps even vague term, but one that will nonetheless have a familiar ring for most anyone in the humanities. It is also useful for our context, in fact, *because* it is problematic, as the artificial barriers that have been erected between modernism and postmodernism are the essential targets of our critique.

We run into similar problems when we try to explain *subjectivity*. Most readers will know that *subjectivity* describes the state of being uniquely experienced by every individual, or *subject*. But like *postmodernism, subjectivity* is a fraught term with a complex history and scads of iterations. Peter Zima gives us a good sense of this problem in his book *Subjectivity and Identity: Between Modernity and Postmodernity* (2015): "The greater the number of commentators who express their opinion on a given term, the greater the danger that the term will ultimately defy all attempts at definition. *Subject* is one such term whose vague, shifting character stems primarily from the academic division of labour, which endows this ambiguous signifier with a different meaning in each discipline: grammatical subject, legal subject, literary protagonist, or even the subject of history. It is immediately apparent that there are a number of different levels at play here (language, law, literature, history as world affairs) which are far from homogeneous" (1).

Indeed, conceptions of subjectivity have been and continue to be heterogeneous, and so in using the term one assumes the inherent risk of lapsing into meaningless generality. Jonathan Rée playfully acknowledges this fact when he writes that "twentieth-century approaches to subjectivity are dominated by the anxiety not to be Descartes" (206). This characterization certainly rings true as we consider how understandings of subjectivity evolved from a stable (Cartesian) self in the Victorian era, to a conflicted ego in the work of Freud, to a fragmented personality after World War II, to a linguistic construct in the latter decades of the twentieth century. This is, of course, only the broadest of outlines, and one that obviously ignores the nuances and complexities of how ideas about the subject cut across various contexts and disciplines, but it captures the basic "structure of feeling," to borrow a phrase from Raymond Williams. However, as our argument must rest on something more solid than a structure of feeling, I would like to take a moment to explain why this book reduces this timeline even further by employing the terms *modernism* and *postmodernism* before describing its particular framing of subjectivity and explaining why it suits this project.

Closing the Postmodern Divide

Modernism and postmodernism are the defining literary periods of the first and second half of the twentieth century. This is a reductive view, to be sure, given the sheer number of the century's innovative movements—imagism, futurism, magical realism, expressionism, and so on. But these and other isms are generally categorized as ancillary movements within the binary schematic of modernism and postmodernism. This binary is inherently problematic, for reasons we will go on to explore, but it has nonetheless persisted. I thus use it *because* it is problematic, and not in spite of it. Although this project is not concerned with periodization per se, I am interested in the more particular ways in which postmodernism's dominant influence on academic thought in the latter part of the twentieth century (re)shaped our appreciation of modernism.

In order to understand how and why postmodernism affected ideas about modernism, let us first consider how much the field we now call modernist studies has evolved in the recent past, beginning with Michael Levenson's seminal book *A Genealogy of Modernism* (1984). Levenson describes the term *modernism* as "at once vague and unavoidable." "Anything more precise would exclude too much too soon," he maintains, "anything more general would be folly. As with any blunt instrument, the best that can be done is to use it for the rough tasks and to reserve the finer work for finer tools. As a rough way of locating our attention, 'modernism' will do" (vii). But *modernism* has not done, and the subtitle of Levenson's book, *A Study of English Literary Doctrine, 1908–1922*, suggests one of the major reasons why: until quite recently the canonical studies of modernism were published by predominantly Anglo-European critics and tended to focus on an exclusive set of Anglo-European writers. This led many critics, both within and outside the field, to view it as "a sort of monolithic ideological formation" (Nicholls vii). Many began to see the seemingly capacious term *modernism* as a smokescreen for the so-called high modernism of Joyce, Eliot, Pound, and a small subset of Anglo-European writers. Although there was a general understanding that modernism encompassed several decades and a vast corpus of cultural production, it seemed as though a handful of names consistently dominated the field's scholarly production. And so while modernist criticism flourished throughout the latter part of the twentieth century and into the twenty-first, it also accrued a stigma that critics have only recently begun to shed.

Damage was also done to the modernist brand when it was overshadowed by the expansive influence of the postmodern age. "By this point in the early twenty-first century," John T. Matthews remarked in 2013, "students of culture rarely encounter terms like 'modern,' 'modernist,' and 'modernity' without a familiar prefix: '*post*modern,' 'postmodernist,' 'postmodernity'" (282). Consequently, students today are probably likely to describe postmodernism more accurately than modernism. This might be a result of historical proximity (postmodernism feels less remote because it is more recent), but it also has to do at least in part with the fact that in the heyday of postmodernism's popularity critics often attacked modernism as a misguided conservative enterprise that postmodernism had rightfully overthrown. Regardless of the particulars, the fact remains that the specter of *post* now inevitably haunts modernism, which has left the latter to battle for legitimacy. One of the primary ways it has done so is by becoming more inclusive and moving away from its conventionally singular and "monolithic" moniker. In his landmark book, *Modernisms: A Literary Guide* (1995), Peter Nicholls explains his attempt to address these challenges: "When I began work on this book, postmodernism was in its heyday. The plural form of my title—Modernisms—thus had something of a polemical intent, since so much of the debate about the 'post' hinged upon what Marjorie Perloff has called a 'straw-man modernism,' one characterized primarily by its commitment to reactionary 'grand narratives' of social and psychic order" (vii). This "straw-man modernism" has had the dual effect of legitimizing postmodernism as a descriptive aesthetic category while simultaneously minimizing modernism's heterogeneity and intellectual sophistication. I would like to expand upon Perloff's appellation here in order to help frame my own reading of modernist fiction in relation to the so-called postmodern divide, a concept that minimizes the many revolutionary achievements of modernism—and modernist fiction, in particular.

Although the bourgeoning field of modernist studies has certainly chipped away at the problem of straw-man modernism, there remains a prevailing notion that while modernism's experiments with stream of consciousness, the subjectivity of individual experience, and the notion of fragmented identity were important, they were ultimately limited by writers' desire to restore some notion of a lost order (the archetypal illustration of this being T. S. Eliot's epic 1922 poem *The Waste Land*). Postmodernism, on the other hand, is commonly thought to revel in and celebrate ambiguity and fragmentation. One of the best examples of this characterization is Ihab Hassan's diagram of modernism and postmodernism in his 1987 book *The Postmodern Turn* (91–92).

Hassan's diagram epitomizes the efforts of theorists to magnify postmodern stylistic and narratological experimentation by manufacturing binaries that vastly oversimplify the variety and nuance of modernist expression or, perhaps worse, simply categorize as "postmodern" traits that appear in many modernist works. The right-hand column is replete with choice terminology from late twentieth-century theory and criticism; the left-hand column, by contrast, reads like an archetype

↕	⟷
Modernism	**Postmodernism**
Romanticism/Symbolism	"Pataphysics"/Dadaism
Form (conjunctive, closed)	Antiform (disjunctive, open)
Purpose	Play
Design	Chance
Hierarchy	Anarchy
Mastery/Logos	Exhaustion/Silence
Art Object/Finished Work	Process/Performance/Happening
Distance	Participation
Creation/Totalization/Synthesis	Decreation/Deconstruction/Antithesis
Presence	Absence
Centering	Dispersal
Genre/Boundary	Text/Intertext
Semantics	Rhetoric
Paradigm	Syntagm
Hypotaxis	Parataxis
Metaphor	Metonymy
Selection	Combination
Root/Depth	Rhizome/Surface
Interpretation/Reading	Against Interpretation/Misreading
Signified	Signifier
Lisible	*Scriptible*
Narrative/*Grand Histoire*	Anti-narrative/*Petite Histoire*
Master Code	Idiolect
Type	Mutant
Genital/Phallic	Polymorphous/Androgynous
Paranoia	Schizophrenia
God the Father	The Holy Ghost
Metaphysics	Irony
Determinacy	Indeterminacy
Transcendence	Immanence

Reproduced from *The Postmodern Turn: Essays in Postmodern Theory and Culture*, by Ihab Hassan (Columbus: Ohio State University Press, 1987), 91–92, by permission of Ohio State University Press.

of Perloff's straw-man modernism. While one may certainly find such characteristics in various modernist texts, the left-hand column looks undeniably reductive next to the other, whose terms (arguably *all* of them) could just as well be applicable to any number of modernist texts. To be fair, Hassan acknowledges the problematics of his own formulization, confessing openly that "the dichotomies this table represents remain insecure, equivocal. For differences shift, defer, even collapse; concepts in any one vertical column are not all equivalent; and inversions and exceptions, in both modernism and postmodernism, abound" (92). But while he does make this concession, he goes on to insist that "still, I would submit that rubrics in the right column point to the postmodern tendency, the tendency of indetermanence [a Hassanian term that combines *indeterminacy* and *immanence*], and so may bring us closer to its historical and theoretical definition" (92).The frequent reference to Hassan's table in discussions of post/modernism testifies to the fact that such dichotomies, however tentative, tend to ossify and become reinscribed as critical doxa. The fact that it remains relevant in discussions concerning the uncertain relationship between modernism and postmodernism reflects not so much its validity as its convenience, and I would caution that drawing such rigid distinctions, even tentatively, creates obstacles that keep us from meaningfully engaging important continuities and evolutions between the two movements.

In arguing against such distinctions as artistic categories in the chapters that follow, especially in relation to the "postmodern" views of subjectivity that I sketch above, I will pay particular attention to several of Hassan's post/modern juxtapositions. His association of centering with modernism and dispersal with postmodernism is particularly problematic, as it does not hold weight against the many depictions of decentered subjectivity that will be explored below and that can be found across many modernist texts. I will also challenge his framing of metaphor and metonymy, particularly in chapter 3, where I focus on the important role of metonymy in F. Scott Fitzgerald's *The Great Gatsby* (1925), both in a narratological and a psychological context. Using a Lacanian psychoanalytic framework, I show how *Gatsby* conceives subjectivity as radically decentered and fragmentary. Nick's suggestion early in the novel that perhaps we ought to view "personality" as "an unbroken series of successful gestures" (6) implies an identity that is not singular but dispersed among a series of individual actions. I will also challenge Hassan's distinction between signifier and signified by highlighting modernism's preoccupation with the imprecise and problematic nature of language. This extends as well to Hassan's distinction between determinacy and indeterminacy, which underappreciates the extent to which many modernist writers and texts resist teleological thinking and instead openly embrace uncertainty.

A similar critique can be leveled against another notable postmodern critic, Brian McHale, who draws comparable distinctions between modernism and postmodernism. One of his most notable postulations is that "the dominant of modernist fiction is *epistemological*," while "the dominant of postmodernist fiction is *ontological*" (*Postmodernist Fiction* 9–10). As I will go on to demonstrate, however, each of the novels that I analyze as part of this project foregrounds primarily ontological concerns—and one could find numerous examples of other modernist texts that do the same. Like Hassan, McHale offers his own set of qualifications, and he in fact begins his book *Postmodernist Fiction* (1987) by questioning the accuracy of the term *postmodernism* itself: "'Postmodernist?' Nothing about this term is unproblematic, nothing about it is entirely satisfactory. It is not even clear who deserves the credit—or the blame—for coining it in the first place: Arnold Toynbee? Charles Olson? Randall Jarrell? There are plenty of candidates. But whoever is responsible, he or she has a lot to answer for" (3). He goes on to speak of the many "constructions of postmodernism," perhaps implying the possibility of *postmodernisms,* in the vein of Nicholls's *modernisms.* The very fact that both terms most often appear in singular form reinforces their problematic nature and the difficulty of drawing distinctions between them. But despite his reservations McHale, like Hassan, implicitly perpetuates the sense of break or rupture that has had such a lasting impact on the collective view surrounding modernism and postmodernism. Hassan and McHale have long been recognized as two of the foremost historians of postmodernism, which lends an inherent legitimacy to the many distinctions they draw.

In pointing out these problematics, I want to be careful not to engage in a straw-man argument myself against postmodern criticism. Theories of the postmodern are of course numerous and widely varied. McHale, for example, quips: "There is John Barth's postmodernism, the literature of replenishment; Charles Newman's postmodernism, the literature of an inflationary economy; Jean-François Lyotard's postmodernism, a general condition of knowledge in the contemporary informational regime; Ihab Hassan's postmodernism, a stage on the road to spiritual unification of humankind; and so on. There is even Frank Kermode's construction of postmodernism, which in effect constructs it right out of existence" (4). The Hassan and McHale examples are, accordingly, not meant as cherry-picking, but are used because they meaningfully represent a prevailing trend among postmodern critics to construct a diminutive conception of modernism that puts the innovation of postmodernism into greater relief. Because postmodernism relies on modernism as its very raison d'être, it seems that critics have felt compelled to view it not merely as a successor but as a sort of conqueror that has boldly gone where modernists were too afraid to go, or were incapable of going.

But if we accept this view, then modernism inevitably begins to look like merely a nascent form of postmodernism that has not yet reached its full potential. If we instead allow modernism to speak for itself, then we realize that it in fact already speaks the language of postmodernism (both its literature and its theory). This fact undermines the construction of a postmodern divide and suggests that the distinctions made by Hassan and others function at best as arguments by degree. Sure, we might find more instances of metonymy, more widespread preoccupation with the role of the signifier, or a willingness to accept or even produce incoherence to a larger degree in artistic creation after World War II, but the fact that one sees these same tendencies operating in significant ways in pre–World War II fiction implies hereditary lines of continuity between modernism and postmodernism (again in the realm of both literature and theory) rather than any radical break. Fortunately, as a result of Nicholls's and more recent efforts, the landscape of modernist studies has considerably diversified and is more expansive in our present moment than it was a quarter century or even fifteen years ago.[2] In fact, the term *modernist studies* itself only recently gained widespread recognition with the establishment in 1999 of the Modernist Studies Association, now the flagship organization in the field. While modernist studies has had to battle for relevance in the past several decades, its rebranding has been essential to its resurgence, and Nicholls's pluralization of the long-standing term *modernism* encapsulates the essence of this rebranding.[3] The shift to a broader conception of modernisms, modernist studies, and, most recently, new modernist studies and global modernisms suggests a field that has become far more inclusive, diverse, and robust.

Nonetheless, some critics suggest that this new inclusivity has had its limits. Ironically, given its importance in shaping postmodernism, according to Stephen Ross, "theory has been marginalized in the new modernist studies" (*Modernism and Theory* 1). Ross, whose 2009 collection *Modernism and Theory* seeks to act as a corrective to this problem, explains that theory "is seen as an outdated instrument whose usefulness has been superseded by a return to the archive and historicism" (1). This is not to say that theory-based work is not being done in modernist studies, but the underlying current in the field has been broadly New Historical in character for several decades now. While archival work, in particular, has been instrumental in helping us reassess modernism's scope and context, Ross makes a convincing case that the character of modernist writing itself calls for a deeply theoretical approach:

> Phenomenology, existentialism, third-wave feminism, queer studies, postcolonial theory, Lacanian psychoanalysis, structuralist Marxism and neo- or post-Marxism, structuralism and post-structuralism do not merely parallel the development of modernism, but partake of it. Theory continues modernism's concerns, aesthetics, and critical energies. The same cannot be said of any other literary movement: the affinities between modernism and theory are wide, deep, and pervasive—and they demand exploration. There is a massive amount of work to be done here, extending the boundaries of modernism even further, and enhancing our understanding of the unique affinity between modernism and theory. If we are truly to understand either of them, modernism and theory simply must be thought together. (2)

This, in essence, is what the present volume intends to do. It takes up Ross's call to arms and, I hope, will play some small part in mapping out a new direction for the role of theory in the new modernist studies.[4] In doing so, I have been careful to avoid the shopworn practice of merely applying theory to literature and instead I try to uncover the theoretical registers of the literature itself. I try to avoid, in other words, simply "reintegrating theory into modernist studies in a purely instrumental fashion" (*Modernism and Theory* 15)—an approach that Ross rejects—but rather show how theoretically informed close readings of modernist texts may provide us with new ways of framing modernism's prescient representations of subjectivity. In particular, I am committed to showing how "modernist writing thinks theoretically and theory writes modernistically" because, as Ross explains, "they are not simply interestingly coincidental phenomena, but mutually sustaining aspects of the same project" (2). In other words, if we are to truly appreciate the intellectual contributions of modernist literature, we *must* recognize this fact. What the readings in this book reveal is that the considerations of subjectivity found in modernist fiction and postmodern theory are one and the same, merely two facets of the same project.

In order to give a brief sense of what this modernism/theory nexus looks like in practice, let us name a few illustrative examples. For instance, Susan Stanford Friedman's introduction to *Joyce: The Return of the Repressed* (1993) comes to mind. In introducing this collection of essays that approach the work of James Joyce by way of poststructuralism, Friedman writes that "at their best, readings of Joyce as the prototypical poststructuralist engage theory in a mutual dialogue with literature that avoids what Shoshana Felman calls the 'subordination' of the literary text to the higher authority of theory and fosters new insights into both theory and text produced by their juxtaposition and interpenetration. At their weakest, such readings remain caught in a hermeneutic circle: Joyce becomes the ideal terrain upon which to prove the theories that his texts themselves anticipate" (3).[5] With this counsel in mind, I aim to "consider literary narrative as a place where theory takes place" (135), as Judith Butler remarks in *Bodies That Matter* (1993). Indeed, my methodology is modeled after Butler's, particularly her chapter "Passing, Queering: Nella Larsen's Psychoanalytic Challenge," which reads Larsen's *Passing* (1929) as "a theorization of desire, displacement and jealous rage that has significant implications for rewriting psychoanalytic theory in ways that explicitly come to

pecially unique is that she does not simply analyze the novel through
a particular theoretical lens, as most theoretically informed literary
criticism does. Rather, she describes her task as illuminating a meaning—namely, a particular view of subjectivity—that is already contained within the literary text that she is interpreting. In other words,
Butler is not creating *new* theory so much as she is shining a light on
what Larsen has already done in literary form. While the more common approach is to use preexisting theory to frame a reading of a literary text, Butler acts more as a vessel that channels and gives new voice
to the theorizing that Larsen has performed. In the readings of individual modernist texts that follow, I use a similar approach in showing
how the theoretical work purportedly done by postmodern critics has
already been done by the modernist authors we will consider.

Permutations of the Post/Modern Subject

These perambulations naturally bring us to the question, What, precisely, is the "postmodern subject" named in the subtitle of this book?
Although postmodern theory and, in turn, postmodern conceptions of
subjectivity are certainly informed by postcolonialism, gender studies,
queer theory, and other disciples that prevailed in the last quarter of
the twentieth century and up to the present, this book takes the view
that the postmodern subject was fundamentally shaped by three in-
tersecting theoretical strains: Marxism (for the sake of clarity I prefer to use the term *Marxism* throughout, though it should be assumed
in reference to postmodern theory that this would include strains of
neo-, post-, and other Marxisms as well), psychoanalysis, and poststructuralism. Taken together, these intellectual traditions and their
offshoots have been seminal in unifying the psychological, political/
economic, and linguistic dimensions of subjectivity. This delineation
is not meant to minimize the contributions of feminism, postcolonial
and ethnic studies, disability studies, queer theory, or other fields in
advancing postmodern theories of subjectivity, but each of these fields
intersects to varying and sometimes substantial degrees with the more
broad-based formulations of Marxism, psychoanalysis, and poststructuralism. Other important fields of thought will accordingly factor into
the chapters that follow, but we will maintain an underlying focus on

this theoretical triad as generative of the "postmodern subject" of the book's title.

As I have alluded to above, my goal in utilizing both primary theoretical sources from the realm of postmodern theory and those critics who approach works of literature from a postmodern perspective is not to use postmodern theory to analyze works of modernist fiction, but rather to call attention to the ways in which we can observe the critical practices of postmodern theory as already operative in the modernist novel. I argue that the representation of subjectivity in what we might call "deconstructive fictions," or modernist novels that articulate a "subject-in-process,"[6] prefigures the intersection of Marxism, psychoanalysis, and poststructuralism that prevails in so much postmodern theory. I follow Astradur Eysteinsson in his suggestion that if we approach modernism from this perspective, "it would be possible. . . . to see modernism in its totality as a deconstructive practice in the Derridean sense. Thus, we could read texts such as *Ulysses* (not to mention *Finnegans Wake*), *The Waves*, *The Sound and the Fury,* and *Das Schloß* with an emphasis on how they undermine the human desire for stable centers of representation by constantly displacing signifiers, frustrating immediate 'presence' of meaning, decentering the subject or whatever constitutes a production of convention-bound reference, and dispersing it in the linguistic field" (48). The present book sets out to show, among other things, that deconstructive practices (both in the Derridean sense and in the sense of deconstructing prior notions of subjectivity) are in fact pervasive in modernist fiction. The novels covered in the chapters that follow, which offer just a small selection of examples from the modernist canon that could very well be supplemented by the texts that Eysteinsson names and many more, deliberately undermine traditional concepts of subjective stability. Like many of the postmodern fiction writers who are often recognized as more radical than their modernist predecessors in this respect—Borges, Pynchon, Calvino, or any number of others—the authors discussed here do not yearn to recover some lost sense of order, as is often said of modernist writers, but rather revel in the disorder of subjective experience.

This parallel between conceptions of subjectivity produced by modernist fiction and those produced by postmodern theory is not surprising, given that the theoretical triad of Marxism, psychoanalysis, and poststructuralism also corresponds to the three central preoccupations of modernist art: modernization, industrialization, and the broadening hegemony of global capitalism; the birth of psychoanalysis and new explorations of the human mind in psychology and related fields; and the questioning of conventional assumptions about language and narrative. The seminal intellectual figures in each of these realms—Karl Marx, Sigmund Freud, and Ferdinand de Saussure—were active shortly before and during the modernist period, and the influence of their work and that of their successors on modernist writers has been well documented. These figures, along with their intellectual companions and descendants, inspired modernist writers to explore unprecedented new ways of representing the human experience. This is not an unknown fact, of course, and yet we have nonetheless failed to appreciate the scope of modernism's prescience in anticipating the confluence of these fields in the realm of postmodern theory.

Broadly speaking, there are a number of ways in which these three intellectual strains overlapped throughout the course of the twentieth century, but their most substantial points of contact occur in theories of the subject. And while twentieth-century theories of the subject themselves have been varied, this book takes the perspective that in one way or another they orbit around the work of Jacques Lacan. Lacan was, first of all, an intellectual descendent of Hegel, one of the most important philosophers of the previous century. Although Lacan was medically trained as a psychoanalyst, his work—particularly his "Mirror Stage" essay, which was first presented in 1936 and remains his most widely recognized contribution to psychoanalysis—was influenced by his attending Alexandre Kojève's seminars on *The Phenomenology of Spirit*. He was a fierce defender of Freud when many had begun to abandon his work, although his take on Freud may be considered revisionary. In the 1950s and 1960s Lacan's own work took on a decidedly structuralist character, as the incorporation of Saussurian linguistic concepts into his work led him to famously remark that the unconscious is structured like a language. His famous seminars, which ran from the 1950s through the mid-1970s, were attended by the likes of Michel Foucault, Gilles Deleuze, Luce Irigaray, Jean Hyppolite, and Julia Kristeva. He also formed a close alliance with Louis Althusser, who managed a faculty position for him at the École Normale

Supérieure, "an amazing feat given the hostility to psychoanalysis of the French Communist Party and much of the French academic world at that time" (Kirshner 219). It is not an understatement to say that Lacan's work sent shock waves through the French intellectual scene, which in the second half of the twentieth century was ground zero for producing novel theories of subjectivity that were then widely adopted throughout Europe and eventually North America. While Freud was the founding father of psychoanalysis, it was Lacan who most profoundly (re)shaped the field as it moved toward the new millennium.

To all this we can add the additional influence of Dadaism and surrealism, which were major components of the modernist movement in Europe. Lacan maintained close relationships with a number of major modernist figures early in his life, a fact that surprisingly is rarely mentioned in historical accounts of the modernist period. This is a striking omission given that, as Thomas Brockelman has put it, "of the fact that Lacan was a modernist it would seem that there can be no doubt" (208). Although Lacan did not begin making notable contributions to the field of psychoanalysis until the late 1930s, at the tail end of modernism's heyday, biographical sources show that he was in fact engaged with modernist art and artists as early as the mid- to late 1910s. His definitive biographer, Élisabeth Roudinesco,[7] and other sources suggest that Lacan's connection to modernism was not merely biographical, but that his formative years were steeped in modernist art and thought in ways that undoubtedly influenced the character and direction of his work. As John Rajchman remarks in "Lacan and the Ethics of Modernity, "In la modernité, one's 'duty' is rather to create oneself as work of art, or as singular artifice. It is within this culture of singularities, his culture of exceptions, that Lacan will formulate the ethical question of the savoir-faire with the unconscious. His theory of the subject supplies a vocabulary with which we can describe how modernist art and writing replaced morality in our culture and established a kind of ethical and amorous bond among us" (53).

Lacan and his work are an embodiment of an intellectual and artistic lineage that stretches back to Hegel, runs through Freud and modernism, and then branches out into the work of Michel Foucault, Louis Althusser, Julia Kristeva, Judith Butler, Slavoj Žižek, Luce Irigaray, Éric Laurent, Renata Salecl, Jacques Derrida, Alain Badiou, and others.

Even those who have refuted his work have nevertheless had to address it. All of this book's central concerns—modernism, postmodernism, Marxism, psychoanalysis, poststructuralism, subjectivity—have been touched by Lacan in one way or another. And despite critical theory's waning influence since the turn of the century, the popularity of the work of Slavoj Žižek and others who have not only carried on the Lacanian tradition but also tapped into elements of the Marxist and poststructuralist intellectual histories testifies to the continuing relevance of the issues taken up here. Two recent works, Samo Tomšič's *The Capitalist Unconscious: Marx and Lacan* (2015) and Todd McGowan's *Capitalism and Desire: The Psychic Cost of Free Markets* (2016), are notable testaments that suggest there is still much to be said on this topic.

With that being said, the present volume is meant to be suggestive rather than exhaustive. Several of the important postmodern figures mentioned above are not mentioned again in the pages that follow. Nor do I cover the many authors whose novels also anticipate postmodern conceptions of subjectivity, like Jean Rhys, Djuna Barnes, Marcel Proust, Nella Larsen, or William Faulkner. For that matter, readers may wonder why only fiction is considered and not poetry, drama, or even film and the visual arts. Certainly one can find many examples in other arenas that would be appropriate in this study as well. Briefly, there are a few reasons for this: First, I have chosen depth over breadth. Of course, many modernist authors and artists were interested in issues of subjectivity, and many more than are represented here write about or otherwise represent subjectivity in ways that also anticipate postmodern theory, but I am more interested in exploring *how* particular authors write about subjectivity than in creating a catalog of all the authors who do. Second, I have sought to construct a narrative that takes us from the turn of the twentieth century through the beginning of World War II and gives a sense for how thoughts on subjectivity evolve *within* the modernist period as well. The process of selecting authors and works to include has been an organic rather than a prescriptive one. And the third reason, to which I will return in chapter 1, is that the novel genre is uniquely positioned to capture the varieties of human experience in a way that other forms are not and thus has a singular ability to actually produce theoretical ideas.

I begin by showing in chapter 1 how modernist fiction understands the subject as ideologically situated, arguing that Joseph Conrad's *Nostromo* (1904) enacts a self-reflexive mode of ideology critique that overhauls the contemporaneous Marxist notion of ideology as false consciousness and the prevailing Jamesian portrait of human psychology, thereby anticipating late twentieth-century conceptions of ideology critique that emerge from the Althusserian tradition, most notably that advanced by Slavoj Žižek in his influential essay "The Spectre of Ideology" (1994). With reference to Althusser's "Ideology and Ideological State Apparatuses" (1970) and Judith Butler's reconsideration of his essay in *The Psychic Life of Power* (1997), I first show how the characters in *Nostromo* are ideologically constituted as subjects through processes of interpellation that reproduce their submission to existing power structures. I then show how Conrad's spectral narrativity (which I bring into focus through Jacques Derrida's *Specters of Marx*) and imagery—which operate at a textual level but also penetrate the world of the novel—subtly reveal that the Costaguanan people participate in their own subjugation through the perpetuation of imperialist ideology thinly veiled as religious parable. I maintain that the novel lays bare (à la Žižek) the ways in which ideological processes themselves contain the keys to their own critique. As Conrad's fiction embodies the transition from Victorian to modernist—signaling, among other things, a major cultural shift in attitudes toward identity—it offers an ideal starting point for our narrative history of subjectivity in modernist fiction. The principles of ideology critique explored in the first chapter also lay the groundwork for the theoretical praxis of later chapters, which sift through the tautological propositions of late twentieth-century theorists and critics that have obscured our understanding of modernist subjectivity.

Chapter 2 builds upon the notion of modernist subjectivity as ideologically situated and engages Conrad with two of modernism's most formidable figures, James Joyce and Virginia Woolf. This chapter conceptualizes Conrad, Joyce, and Woolf as writers who analogously depict human subjectivity as a self-driven ideological illusion that masks an essential void of subjectivity. I explore in the life and writings of Conrad, Joyce, and Woolf the intersectionality of three fundamental intellectual disciplines: science, religion, and art. As all three authors are religious skeptics living in an age of rapid scientific advancement, their fiction oscillates between scientific and religious worldviews, each making claims to totalizing knowledge that either denies the void (in the case of science, which involves processes of psychological foreclosure) or fills the void with God (in the case of religion, which psychologically displaces the void). I go on to show that the movement from the religious belief that each author (as well as many of each author's main characters) is born into entails a residual guilt that must be expiated in some way by that which displaces the religious belief. In light of these authors' hesitancy to fully embrace the totalizing claims of science, I conclude by arguing that each ultimately locates redemption in the process of artistic creation, which organizes itself around the void and offers the most satisfying and psychologically beneficial way of confronting the void of subjectivity and accepting oneself as fundamentally unstable and incoherent. Conrad, Joyce, and Woolf are held up as exemplars of the modernist fiction writer in that they see themselves not as organizers of chaos but as representationalists (in the psycho-philosophical sense) who render the incoherence of subjective experience in the modern world.

While the first two chapters establish that subjectivity in the modernist novel is conceptualized not as an ontological fixity but as an ideological (and thus linguistic) construction, which suggests the notion of subjectivity as "in process," chapter 3 shows how this process operates in relation to the psychoanalytic dimension of (racial) identity in *The Great Gatsby,* one of the most widely read novels in American universities and yet one whose treatment of subjectivity has been largely neglected by critics. *Gatsby*'s articulation of subjectivity shatters the understanding of the Freudian ego that was popular in its time and reveals an unexplored angle that intersects with later psychoanalytic ideas centered around Lacan's "fundamental fantasy." I argue that Gatsby's object of desire (*objet a*), Daisy, is the maternal figure in a (self-) destructive adult repetition of an Oedipal drama that is complicated by her metaphorical associations with the American landscape and her husband Tom's patriarchal and nativist views. I claim that the novel's symbolic structure is haunted by a latent desire to reconstitute Gatsby's ambiguous socially projected racial makeup as only figuratively white. In doing so, I show how the novel is ahead of its time in its treatment of the subjective dimensions of race.

With a particular focus on three modernist novels set in Los Angeles—Nathanael West's *The Day of the Locust* (1939), Aldous Huxley's *After Many a Summer Dies the Swan* (1939), and F. Scott Fitzgerald's *The Love of the Last Tycoon* (1941)—chapter 4 argues that while Los Angeles has been widely viewed as a quintessentially postmodern city (by Baudrillard, Soja, Jameson, and others), it ought to serve as a major critical fault line in (re)conceptualizing the postmodern divide. Los Angeles in each of these novels comprises a pastiche of architectural styles stacked one on top of another in a fashion at once decentered/decentering and alienated/alienating. This visual incoherence, in turn, penetrates its psychologically unstable inhabitants. Upon closer examination, we find that West, Huxley, and Fitzgerald pivot away from the more popular psychological advances of the time, like B. F. Skinner's behaviorist theories, and anticipate the intersection of subjectivity and space in the "spatial turn" of the late twentieth century that centers around the work of Henri Lefebvre, Michel Foucault, David Harvey, and others. Los Angeles has long held powerful symbolic value as the western endpoint where the frontier is finally pushed up against the Pacific Ocean. The city, and to an extent the state of California as a whole, has been viewed as the "end of the road," and accordingly each novel in this chapter shows it as producing profound anxiety and disillusionment; its subjects are pushed to the psychic edge toward irreparable rupture. As in later *post*modern novels like Thomas Pynchon's *The Crying of Lot 49* (1966), these largely overlooked modernist exemplars demonstrate the deep understanding of prewar novelists surrounding the complex relationship between place and identity. In this chapter I show not only that these writers already recognized changing physical landscapes emerging out of the time-space compression of rapidly expanding global capitalism (à la Harvey, Soja, etc.) but that their acute perception in connecting this phenomenon to the looming crisis of subjectivity ought to encourage us to reconsider the conventional notion that such observations did not emerge until the late twentieth century.

Chapter 5 focuses on Samuel Beckett's first published novel, *Murphy* (1938). Although it is chronologically out of step with the otherwise linear progression of the book, *Murphy* pushes the boundaries of modernist subjectivity to their absolute limit. Furthermore, Beckett, whose literary career stretched from the interwar period to the 1980s and whose radical experimentation profoundly (re)shaped the face of modern literature, embodies the persistence of modernism's critical energy into the latter half of the twentieth century. Like Lacan, *Murphy* affirms the notion that language inevitably casts us into the process of desire. Beckett and Lacan both maintain that it is impossible to conceive of subjectivity outside the context of desire; and because we are always already implicated in the social realm, we are therefore implicated in the desire of others. Unlike Conrad's Martin Decoud, who desperately gropes for his sense of self in the absence of others, the titular Murphy attempts to extricate himself from all human contact, renounce his bodily desires, and thereby deliberately negate his own subjectivity. But with a brilliantly crafted dramatic irony, this chapter argues, Beckett continually undermines Murphy's endeavor and reaffirms Althusser's assertion that we are all implicated as subjects, willingly or not. Chapter 5's reading of *Murphy* thus brings our project full circle, from the Conradian lamentation that ideology ensnares us as subjects to Beckett's revelry in the ironic Hegelian/Lacanian notion that our conception of self is inextricably bound to our desire for the other's desire.

I conclude by juxtaposing Conrad's famous description of history as a knitting machine to Thomas Pynchon's troping of Remedios Varo's painting *Bordando el Manto Terrestre* in his postmodern classic *The Crying of Lot 49*. I use these examples as a springboard for showing how Pynchon's treatment of ontology, which is widely seen as prototypically postmodern, is in fact anticipated in Conrad and the other authors treated in this work. I use this example to illustrate my broader rejection of the common notion of postmodern art and theory as more evolved forms of a primitive modernism, insisting that we legitimately recognize the role of modernism in constructing and defining subjectivity in the twentieth century.

The trajectory of this project as it moves from early to late modernism—1904 to 1941, based upon the publication dates of the novels it takes up—traces the development of modernist attitudes toward subjectivity. The subject is considered in relation to ideology, art, race, and spatiality, until finally Samuel Beckett begins to imagine a subjectivity that transcends corporeality altogether, only to undermine this possibility by reminding us that through language we have always already been interpellated as subjects and are left with no other option but to confront our ontological limitations head on. Taken together, the novels that make up this study reflect the complexity and multiformity of modernist fiction's concern with subjectivity while at the same time employing common narrative modalities that ultimately deconstruct it. What we finally end up with is a version of modernist fiction that looks much different than the one described by Hassan, McHale, and many other postmodern critics. The authors covered in the pages that follow make no attempt to envision new coherent versions of subjectivity or recover a challenged or lost transcendental ego. They not only depict and confront the fragmented self but maintain an intentional open-endedness that explicitly rejects any sense of closure. In doing so, they produce theorizations of subjectivity that profoundly shaped the intellectual trajectory of the twentieth century to an extent that, for all their acclaim, still has not been fully appreciated.

Chapter 1
THE INTERPELLATED SUBJECT
Specters of Ideology in Joseph Conrad's *Nostromo*

Haunting belongs to the structure of every hegemony.
—JACQUES DERRIDA, *Specters of Marx*

There are two central reasons why Joseph Conrad's sprawling novel *Nostromo* (1904) is an ideal starting point for our exploration of modernism and subjectivity. The first is chronological. While there is widespread debate about when modernism begins, there is general consensus that the technological, cultural, and artistic changes occurring around the turn of the twentieth century mark a decisive shift in the zeitgeist that justifies the drawing of an epochal distinction. As Conrad's first serious attempts at writing began in the early 1890s, his writing career coincides with the dawn of modernism. Although his first two novels—*Almayer's Folly* (1895) and *An Outcast of the Islands* (1896)—were largely reflective of his footing in Victorian realism and the adventure fiction of Haggard, Kipling, and Stevenson, by the time his writing began to fully mature in the subsequent *Nigger of the "Narcissus"* (1897), *Heart of Darkness* (1899), and *Lord Jim* (1900) it was prototypically modernist in its form, style, and themes. On account of this dual footing in the old and the new, Conrad is widely viewed as a transitional figure who exemplifies that period when modernist innovation eclipsed the more conservative literary traditions of the nineteenth century. His modern(ist) sensibility becomes especially evident in the penetrating depth of psychological exploration that we find in the novels of his so-called major phase, which spanned the years 1897–1911. His writing during this phase unmistakably shows that modernism's revolutionary insights with respect to subjectivity were present from its nascency. The second reason is that while Conrad's other major-phase novels contain many of the same themes—the tension between the individual and society; the baseness of colonialism and imperial capitalism; the struggle to locate "truth," or objectively narrate history; the instability of identity—it is in *Nostromo* that he most effectively incorporates all of these themes and unveils the ideological dimensions of subjectivity in a way that presciently anticipates theories of the subject coming out of the late twentieth-century (neo- and post-) Marxist, psychoanalytic, and poststructuralist theoretical traditions with which this book is concerned.

The key to understanding how the ideological dimensions of subjectivity operate in the novel can be found in its opening pages, which unfold like a panning shot across Sulaco, a coastal town in the imaginary South American republic of Costaguana that is insulated from the sea by a vast and tranquil gulf (the Golfo Plácido). The short first chapter is devoted almost exclusively to describing the geography of the town and its key topographical features, with one notable exception: the recounting of a local parable about "two wandering sailors—Americanos, perhaps, but gringos of some sort for certain" (6)—who disappear along with a servant and a stolen donkey while searching for a fabled gold treasure on the craggy peninsula of Azuera, which overlooks the Golfo Plácido. The mythopoeic implications of the parable are evident in the enduring legend that "the two gringos, spectral and alive, are believed to be dwelling to this day amongst the rocks, under the fatal spell of their success. Their souls cannot tear themselves away from their bodies mounting guard over the discovered treasure. They are now rich and hungry and thirsty—a strange theory of tenacious gringo ghosts suffering in their starved and parched flesh of defiant heretics, where a Christian would have renounced and been released" (6). Many critics have remarked upon the parable's symbolic overtones—the critical reaction is perhaps best illustrated by Eloise Hay Knapp's observation that "the superstition provides an allegorical framework for the obsession with the silver that gradually takes possession of the novel's two central gringos, Gould and Nostromo" (84)—but I insist that there is something more at work here, a more far-reaching set of reasons why this parable anticipates and then continually haunts the remainder of the novel.[1]

These reasons are connected to the spectral imagery that appears in the Azuera parable and features prominently throughout Conrad's fiction.[2] But while other critics have focused predominantly on the aesthetic and symbolic dimensions of Conrad's spectral imagery,[3] his spectral engagement runs much deeper than has been previously acknowledged. In *Nostromo*, spectrality functions synchronously across symbolic, narrativistic, and ideological registers. These spectral engagements produce a self-contained form of ideology critique that operates simultaneously within and outside the world of the novel, thereby outstripping contemporary notions of ideology as "false consciousness" (à la Marx) and anticipating the later formulations of Louis Althusser and post-Marxist theorists like Judith Butler, Fredric Jameson, and Slavoj Žižek. *Nostromo* exemplifies modernist fiction's capacity to anticipate theoretical insight and, furthermore, reinforces the indispensable value of ideology critique at a time when the rise of authoritarian populism across the globe has made it all the more imperative that we explore new modes of thinking about how oppressive power dynamics are legitimized through processes of ideological mystification. The eminent critic J. Hillis Miller has proclaimed that "somewhat paradoxically, one of the best ways to understand what is happening now in our time of globalization is to read this old novel by Conrad" (173). I would agree with his assessment and contend that *Nostromo* epitomizes the singular ability of the novel form to open up a space for a meaningful critique of *how* ideology functions across both theoretical and psychological registers.

Spectrality, Ideological Engagements, and Mystification

Spectral imagery has been prevalent in critiques of capitalism and ideology, dating back to the memorable opening line of Marx and Engels's *Communist Manifesto* (1848): "A spectre is haunting Europe—the spectre of communism" (78). In the *Manifesto, Capital* (1867–94), and elsewhere, Marx frequently refers to ghosts, hauntings, and other mystical images in order to explain the often elusive and shadowy ways in which everyday objects become fetishized and to evocatively describe the figurative bloodletting effected by capitalist forces. The specter also proves to be a fitting image for the workings of ideology, which can often seem so mysterious and haunting; demonic possession serves as an apt metaphor for the ways in which our actions can be manipulated by ideological mechanisms that we may not even recognize. Of course, Marx actually saw religion as a possession of sorts, famously writing that "religion is the sigh of the oppressed creature, the sentiment of a heartless world, and the soul of soulless conditions. It is the *opium* of the people" (Marx, "Contribution to the Critique" 54). Indeed, Marx proclaims that "the criticism of religion is the premise of all criticism" (53), which makes the significance of religion in his worldview quite clear. His critique of religion also plays a central role in Jacques Derrida's only major engagement with Marxist thought, *Specters of Marx* (1994), in which he remarks upon "the absolute privilege that Marx always grants to religion, to ideology as religion, mysticism, or theology, in his analysis of ideology in general" (185). As Derrida says elsewhere, "Religion . . . was never one ideology among others for Marx" (51); in other words, *all* ideology functions as religion.

This concept will be particularly important in this chapter for two reasons. First, Conrad's well-documented religious skepticism suggests that he too sensed a fundamental connection between religion and ideology. Second, this religion/ideology nexus informs other important theoretical formulations that will help us understand what Conrad is up to in *Nostromo,* particularly Judith Butler's *The Psychic Life of Power* (1997). In her chapter on Althusser, she wonders why "the mention of conscience in Althusser's 'Ideology and Ideological State Apparatuses' has received little critical attention, even though the term, taken together with the example of religious authority to illustrate the force of ideology, suggests that the theory of ideology is supported by a complicated set of theological metaphors" (109). She goes on to argue that "although Althusser explicitly introduces 'the Church' merely as an *example* of ideological interpellation, it appears that ideology in his terms cannot be thought except through the metaphorics of religious authority" (109). As we will see, the function of ideology in *Nostromo* also intersects with religion, in both direct and indirect ways. As in Marx, we find a confluence of both theological and mystical imagery, particularly in relation to the characters' various ideological commitments.

More specifically, Butler's remarks help us appreciate how Conrad also uses "religious authority to illustrate the force of ideology" via the Azuera parable, which maligns the gringos as "heretics" who would have been spared their spectral slavery had they (like Christians) renounced their earthly treasure. The effect is that the poor (who would seem to be most of Costaguana's population) associate "by an obscure instinct of consolation the ideas of evil and wealth" (5), which serves to reinforce the hegemony of the ruling class by virtue of the fact that the poor's perception of wealth as "evil" arrests their desire to pursue it themselves. By linking the aspiration to accrue wealth with sin, the parable serves as a haunting reminder for the lower classes of the dangers inherent in attempting (or even desiring) to transcend their social class. The Azuera parable propagates what Stephen Ross calls a "slave morality," which "keeps the people of Sulaco satisfied in their poverty while the material interests get rich" (*Conrad and Empire* 132). The Azuera parable is instrumental in showing how what Althusser calls the "Ideological State Apparatus" works in service of the ruling class by covertly warning the lower classes not to challenge the social order lest they fall victim—as do the treasure-hunting gringos—to "the fatal spell of their success" (6). It is essential that we recognize, then, that while religious ideology in the novel might initially appear at odds with the "material interests" with which the characters of the ruling class are primarily concerned, the two are in fact continuous. As Althusser reminds us, "What unifies their [i.e., the various Institutional State Apparatuses: religious, educational, private, political, cultural, etc.] diversity is precisely this functioning, insofar as the ideology by which they function is always in fact unified, despite its diversity and its contradictions, *beneath the ruling ideology,* which is the ideology of 'the ruling class'" (146). In one way or another, all the characters in *Nostromo* find themselves serving the material interests of the ruling class, either consciously or unconsciously.

As the title character, Nostromo is the lynchpin not only of the plot but of the novel's exploration of how ideology intersects with subject formation. The title of the novel, according to Benita Parry, "functions as a metonym for an ethos that, by consecrating the private ownership of property, legitimises the concept of the person as possession" (102–3). This is certainly true, and Nostromo ("our man") turns out to be the greatest possession of all. It is thus via Nostromo that this warning against challenging the social order comes full circle when he "appears in his full dimensions as a vision of the Imperial subject who becomes aware of the arbitrariness of ideological/value systems, yet is unable to break free from them and is emphatically punished for attempting to transgress them" (Ross, *Conrad and Empire* 149). *Nostromo* explicitly acknowledges his symbolic kinship with the Azuera specters on several occasions, most notably when the new lighthouse is built 150 yards from the silver he has buried: "He could never shake off the treasure. His audacity, greater than that of other men, had welded that vein of silver into his life. And the feeling of fearful and ardent subjection, the feeling of his slavery—so irremediable and profound that often, in his thoughts, he compared himself to the legendary Gringos, neither dead nor alive, bound down to their conquest of unlawful wealth on Azuera—weighed heavily on the independent Captain Fidanza" (377). One of the things that makes Nostromo's actions in the novel particularly compelling is his awareness, which proves limited but is nonetheless notable, of the ideological mechanisms that are influencing his actions. In the above passage, he imagines himself as "bound down," a metaphor for the way in which the "material interests" of the ruling class have ensnared him.

Nostromo's movement among competing ideological registers brings us into contact with recent conceptions of ideology, like those advanced by the Slovenian philosopher Slavoj Žižek, beginning with his first major work, *The Sublime Object of Ideology* (1989). In particular, Nostromo's (limited) awareness of how his actions are influenced by competing ideological commitments intersects with Žižek's account of Peter Sloterdijk's thesis that "ideology's dominant mode of functioning is cynical, which renders impossible—or, more precisely, vain—the classic critical-ideological procedure." "The cynical subject," Žižek goes on to explain, "is quite aware of the distance between the ideological mask and the social reality, but he none the less still insists upon the mask. The formula, as proposed by Sloterdijk, would then be: 'they know very well what they are doing, but still, they are doing it'" (29). In other words, while it may seem paradoxical that Nostromo recognizes his kinship with the Azuera specters and yet proceeds with his theft of the silver anyway, Žižek (via Sloterdijk) reminds us that this is in fact one of the key ways that ideology functions. Viewed in this context, *Nostromo* reads as a prototype of the cynical subject and an exemplar of Conrad's provident depiction of ideology.

But we might bring into relief yet another layer of Conrad's use of the parable as a framing device by turning to another of Žižek's works, published the year after *Specters of Marx*:[4] his essay "The Spectre of Ideology,"[5] which introduces his edited collection *Mapping Ideology* (1994). In that essay, Žižek responds to the popular contention that if there is no way to step "outside" ideology—as many postmodern critics have maintained—then perhaps the very notion of ideology has outlived its usefulness within the discourse of political resistance. In response to such criticism, Žižek insists that "we must none the less maintain the tension that keeps the *critique* of ideology alive" by presupposing that "it is possible to assume a place that enables us to maintain a distance from it" (17). Anyone familiar with the discourse surrounding ideology will know that this is a problematic proposition, for if we are to achieve this goal, we must first recognize and overcome the paradoxical fact that "*the stepping out of (what we experience as) ideology is the very form of our enslavement to it*" (6, emphasis in original). There is an always present danger, in other words, that our response to what we perceive to be ideological mystifications will be equally informed (and therefore problematized) by other forms or manifestations of ideology. This, Žižek maintains, is the central challenge to the relevance of ideology critique.

We can get a sense for how this challenge is framed in *Nostromo* by turning to an example that Žižek draws from Renata Salecl's *The Spoils of Freedom* (1994). In order to show how ideological mystification is perpetuated in times of political conflict, Salecl juxtaposes media coverage of the Bosnian War with that of the Gulf War: "Instead of providing information on social, political or religious trends and antagonisms in Iraq, the media ultimately reduced the conflict to a quarrel with Saddam Hussein, Evil Personified, the outlaw who excluded himself from the civilized international community. Even more than the destruction of Iraq's military forces, the true aim was presented as psychological, as the humiliation of Saddam who had to 'lose face'" (13). This represents what we might call the reductive approach, which occupies one end of the spectrum of ideological mystification. In this example, rather than exploring the complexity of historical, social, and political circumstances surrounding a particular conflict, the media metonymically reduces it to a representative constitutive element in order for it to be more easily criticized or vilified. The ideological seductiveness of this scenario is all the more evident considering that we now realize that this depiction of Saddam (who was ubiquitously and

tellingly referred to by first name alone) as "Evil Personified" maintained profound symbolic force at least until his eventual capture and
execution in 2006. Salecl goes on to explain that

> in the case of the Bosnian war, however, notwithstanding iso-
> lated cases demonizing the Serbian president Milosevic, the
> predominant attitude reflects that of the quasi-anthropological
> observer. The media outdo one another in giving us lessons on
> the ethnic and religious background of the conflict; traumas
> hundreds of years old are being replayed and acted out, as if, in
> order to understand the roots of the conflict, one has to know
> not only the history of Yugoslavia but the entire history of the
> Balkans from medieval times. Or as a journalist says: "The his-
> tory of all the southern Slavs in the Balkans is a tangled tragedy
> of mass rape and barbaric slaughter, the product of the kind of
> ethnic hatred that perhaps only people who are closely related
> to each other could nurture so well for so long." In the Bos-
> nian conflict, it is therefore not possible simply to take sides,
> to name evil, to assign blame, because we are dealing with "ir-
> reconcilable warring tribes." One can only patiently try to grasp
> the background of this savage spectacle, so alien to our civilized
> system of values . . .
>
> Such an approach involves an ideological mystification even
> more cunning than the demonization of Saddam Hussein. (13,
> ellipsis in original)

In this instance, rather than the conflict being personified through a
representative and symbolically overdetermined figure, the complexities of the circumstances are used as an excuse to become disengaged
altogether for fear that commitment to any particular position will fail
to take into account some other important factor(s). We can use Salecl's example, which serves as a useful outline of how ideology affects
the analysis of social and political antagonism, to show how the tendency to gravitate toward one or another of these extremes problematizes the attempt to critique ideology in *Nostromo*, both for its characters and for its readers.

On the one hand, the novel's semi-omniscient narrator[6] gives readers some sense of the complexity of Costaguanan history. We might describe the narrator, following Salecl, as "a quasi-anthropological observer" whose continual digressions add increasingly intricate layers of context to the more particular story with which he or she is primarily concerned, namely the Revolution and the efforts of the Gould Concession to save the silver of the San Tomé mine. But many of the novel's pivotal events are not actually described, leaving gaps that are, in the words of Fredric Jameson, "present/absent in the most classic Derridean fashion" (*Political Unconscious* 270).[7] Conrad resists master narratives, instead exploring the actions of conflicted individual characters in the face of overwhelming social, political, economic, and other obstacles. The narrative organization of the novel reflects the complexity of Costaguana's history and politics, ultimately suggesting that any attempt to objectively record history or establish historical causality is a fool's errand. For those within the world of the novel and without, then, there is a problem akin to the one Salecl describes above in attempting to make any coherent sense out of circumstances with such long and puzzling histories. Instead, the novel's many narrative gaps leave our understanding of Costaguanan history and politics inevitably incomplete.

On the other hand, in keeping with Salecl's example we find the opposite tendency at work within the world of the novel by way of the local journalists, who make no apparent attempt to inform the public about the political tensions at hand or investigate their context, but rather engage in exaggerated and highly personal attacks against the political opponents of the parties they represent. Martin Decoud, for instance, is enlisted by the Blancos to combat what the narrator describes as "the lies disseminated by the press," specifically "the atrocious calumnies, the appeals to the people calling upon them to rise with their knives in their hands and put an end once for all to the Blancos, to these Gothic remnants, to these sinister mummies, these impotent paralíticos, who plotted with foreigners for the surrender of the lands and the slavery of the people" (116). Although he views politics as a farce, Decoud publishes personal attacks on Montero for the Blanco-backed *Porvenir* and, in doing so, implicitly condones character attacks over meaningful political engagement. Paradoxically, then, while readers struggle to comprehend the abundant historical and political context given by a narrator who fails to portray the central events around which that context has emerged, the opposite form of ideological mystification is perpetuated within the world of the novel by the Costaguanan media, with the result that the view of political conflict in the country as an unending and unstoppable farce ossifies in the collective social consciousness. The media thus constitutes yet another layer of ideological mystification.

But the work of ideological mystification operates on another level as well, one that again recalls the specters of the Azuera parable, as the Costaguanan people's views of their political leaders are transmogrified into religious myths that reinforce prescribed moral guidelines. This is evident in the propaganda of the regime: the Blancos are depicted not simply as political opponents but as spectral remnants of an antiquated and sinister imperial ideology. And this same type of demonization occurs on the other end of the political spectrum as well. The central mythologized figure in liberal Costaguanan history is Guzmán Bento: "It was the same Guzmán Bento who, becoming later on Perpetual President, famed for his ruthless and cruel tyranny, reached his apotheosis in the popular legend of a sanguinary land-haunting spectre whose body had been carried off by the devil in person from the brick mausoleum in the nave of the Church of Assumption in Sta. Marta" (37). Ironically, the perpetuation of these myths, particularly by the lower classes, actually reinforces political paralysis, as the lower-class citizens of Costaguana—those who are least insulated from the adverse effects of its political instability and ongoing violence—tend to extricate themselves from their country's social and political complexities. Ultimately, such fanciful denigrations of Bento and other political figures facilitate their integration into the preexisting religious/ideological structure that underlies the world of the novel.

Furthermore, in keeping with Žižek's adage "they know very well what they are doing, but still, they are doing it," even those characters who are seemingly aware of these ideological constructs and their damaging effects are nonetheless complicit in their propagation, often for self-serving reasons. We have already seen how Nostromo displays at least some awareness of ideology's hold over him. But his level of awareness is eclipsed by that of Emilia Gould, who is especially attentive to the workings of such ideologies: "In all these households she

could hear stories of political outrage; friends, relatives, ruined, imprisoned, killed in the battles of senseless civil wars, barbarously executed
in ferocious proscriptions, as though the government of the country
had been a struggle of lust between bands of absurd devils let loose
upon the land with sabres and uniforms and grandiloquent phrases.
And on all the lips she found a weary desire for peace, the dread of of-
ficialdom with its nightmareish [sic] parody of administration without
law, without security, and without justice" (66). Given that the Gould
Concession is an inextricable part of Costaguana's political landscape,
Mrs. Gould must know that her husband plays at least some role in the
suffering of which she has heard. And she is similarly troubled later
by how Sulaco's inhabitants accept brutal violence as an inevitability:
"That it should be accepted with no indignant comment by people of
intelligence, refinement, and character as something inherent in the
nature of things was one of the symptoms of degradation that had the
power to exasperate her almost to the verge of despair" (82). The spectral imagery ("bands of absurd devils," etc.) used to describe her sentiments suggests that it is, in part at least, the prevailing local religious
ideology that has instilled the notion that the country's class distinctions are "inherent in the nature of things."

Ironically, though, given that Emilia is so attuned to this attitude
among the Costaguanan people, their resulting "weary desire for
peace" sets the stage for the Gould Concession and its singular concern
with "material interests" to install a dictator in Ribiera whose loyalty to
Western economic and political influence trumps his concern for the
well-being of his people. As the matriarch of the Gould Concession,
Emilia is complicit in the ideological structure that ensures the capitulation of the lower classes to the ruling ideology, however seemingly
disturbed she may be by their plight. The Gould Concession, which
is concerned purely with profit, provides the country with a sense of
peace and stability that masks the struggle and conflict that actually
constitute its social reality. It is not until the Gould Concession has in-
delibly entrenched itself that people begin to realize "that the Ribierist
reforms meant simply the taking away of the land from the people"
(141). By this time, there is little recourse from the stranglehold of the
Ribierist regime and the Gould Concession other than submission to a
new "band of absurd devils."

The muddling and masking of class struggle by the juxtaposed chaos of warring political factions and stability of the Gould Concession once again anticipates Žižek, whose equation of class struggle with the Lacanian real frames his main argument in "The Spectre of Ideology." In order to show how Conrad anticipates Žižek, let us first review what Lacan means by the real. The real, for Lacan, is distinct from what we generally call "reality." It is one register of his triadic structure of the psyche, alongside the imaginary and the symbolic. Our entrance into the symbolic realm of language, Lacan explains, irreversibly severs us from the real, which we might describe as the realm of pure materiality. As Lacan continually reminds us, though his descriptions of the three registers evolve throughout his career, it is impossible for us to access the real. We are able to come close only in rare moments, namely, traumatic ones, when our essential materiality is most evident to us—in the flight from death, for example. In order to understand Lacan's structure of the psyche, it is essential to distinguish between the real and what we experience as "reality" because Lacan tells us that this experiential interface with the world around us in fact belongs to the realm of the imaginary. Because our interaction with the world is mediated through language (which, according to Lacan, forms the structure of our unconscious mind), we are only ever able to access a subjective reality that is sealed off from the real.

Žižek's conceptualization of the "spectre of ideology" hinges upon his unique reading of the Lacanian real not as something that lies *behind* the imaginary like a palimpsest but as something that is woven into its very fabric. "To put it simply," he explains, "reality is never directly 'itself,' it presents itself only via its incomplete-failed symbolization, and spectral apparitions emerge in this very gap that forever separates reality from the real, and on account of which reality has the character of a (symbolic) fiction: the spectre gives body to that which escapes (the symbolically structured) reality" (21). In other words, we might think of the specter, as Žižek describes it, as a fleeting ghostly apparition of the inaccessible real. If what we know or experience as "reality" is to become apparent to us (since the real itself cannot), "something has to be foreclosed from it" (21). Thus, *what the spectre conceals is not reality but its 'primordially repressed,' the irrepresentable X on whose 'repression' reality itself is founded*" (21, emphasis in original).

As we can see, unlike in earlier (neo-)Marxist formulations, for Žižek ideology is not simply "illusion"; rather, it is continuous with the realm of the symbolic and an indelible facet of our lived experience.

Because the Lacanian process of signification (in which meaning is structured around a central absence) is so important for Žižek's conception of ideology, it will be useful here to outline two seminal readings of ideology in *Nostromo* that traffic in a similar language, although neither would be considered Lacanian. The first comes from Terry Eagleton's *Criticism and Ideology* (1976). Eagleton claims that the plot, or action, of each of Conrad's novels revolves around a central absence. "It is precisely in these absent centres," he argues, "which 'hollow' rather than scatter and fragment the organic forms of Conrad's fiction, that the relations of that fiction to its ideological context is [sic] laid bare" (138–39). The result, for Eagleton, is that Conrad's narrative forms do not "express" an ideology, but rather produce ideological contradictions. This production, as he explains it, is ironically deconstructive in character: "The tale or yarn 'foregrounds' action as solid and unproblematic; it assumes the unimpeachable realities of history, character, the objective world. Yet these assumptions are simultaneously thrown into radical doubt by the penumbra of spectral meanings which surround the narrative, crossing and blurring its contours. If the narrative is reduced to a yarn, those crucial meanings dissolve; if the meanings are directly probed, it is the narrative which evaporates" (139).

What adds to the complexity of Conrad's narrativity, as many critics have pointed out, is his appropriation of the adventure story, which is generally formulaic. But one hallmark of Conrad's fiction is his tendency to subvert the classic adventure story with a thematic complexity that belies its formulaic simplicity. In the face of the contradictions produced, for Eagleton Conrad's fiction insists that "faith, work and duty must not be allowed to yield to scepticism if the supreme fiction of social order is to be sustained. It is for this reason that Conrad the pessimist insists that the artist's task is not to convey moral nihilism, but to cherish undying hope. Yet that hope can never be anything other than ambiguous" (139). This last sentence is emblematic of Eagleton's critique of Conrad, whom he sees as unwilling or unable to resolve the ideological contradictions that his fiction produces. Eagleton himself has been criticized, and rightly so in my estimation—he perhaps takes too literally a letter he cites from Conrad to Edward Garnett in which he writes "that my fate is to be descriptive, and descriptive only" (qtd. in Eagleton 139)—for undervaluing the sophistication of Conrad's depiction of ideology. Eagleton believes that Conrad's failure to narrate the central events of his novels produces a "corrosive negation" (139) that is never resolved and is flawed as a result.

Like Eagleton, Jameson is interested in the novel's decenteredness but instead focuses on the displacement of "actual" history by so-called strategies of containment. Jameson reads *Nostromo* as "a dialectical intensification and transformation of the narrative apparatus of *Lord Jim*" (*Political Unconscious* 269) and views it as "a demonstration of structural transformations, and the way in which analogous materials are utterly metamorphosed when they are wrenched from the realm and categories of the individual subject to the new perspective of those of collective destiny" (269). Jameson hones in on what he calls "ideological interference," which he describes as "threefold and layered," involving Conrad's adoption of the "classic 'Anglo' picture of a Latin 'race,' lazy, shiftless, and the like, to which political order and economic progress must be 'brought' from the outside" (270); his own political attitudes, which are presupposed by readers and "rhetorically reinforced by ethical and melodramatic markers (the Blancos are good, the Monteristas evil)" (270); and the text's relegation of *ressentiment* toward the central event in the novel—the revolution—to "the frame or border of the text proper" (271). This picture of ideology in the novel lays the groundwork for his observation, mentioned above, that "this central event is therefore present/absent in the most classic Derridean fashion, present only in its initial absence, absent when it is supposed to be most intensely present" (270). For Jameson, in other words, the "real" historical events of the novel are effaced, and the corresponding blank space is filled by narrative. He builds upon Edward Said's contention in *Beginnings* that "instead of mimetically authoring a new world, *Nostromo* turns back to its beginning as a novel, to the fictional, illusory assumption of reality: in thus overturning the confident edifice that novels normally construct *Nostromo* reveals itself to be no more than a *record* of novelistic self-reflection" (137). In short, what Eagleton takes to be a flaw, Jameson takes to be one of Conrad's great accomplishments. His "high evaluation of *Nostromo*," according to Terry Collits, "links the grandeur of the novel's narrative design with its author's authoritative knowledge" (6). And so "Jameson sees the novel's refusal of closure as key to its method" (6).

I argue that the spectral meanings in *Nostromo* do not "surround the narrative," as Eagleton maintains, but fill the "absent centres" and gaps that he and Jameson describe. We might view such absent centers and gaps, then—namely, the revolution—as symptoms of the gaps between the real and reality. The ideological mystifications explored above conceal the deeper class struggle out of which the perpetual political revolutions of Costaguana have arisen. This phenomenon is in keeping with Žižek's assertion that it is precisely the real of class struggle that must be repressed in order for experiential reality to emerge: "The consequent thinking-out of this concept compels us to admit that there is no class struggle 'in reality': 'class struggle' designates the very antagonism that prevents the objective (social) reality from constituting itself as a self-enclosed whole. . . . The ultimate paradox of the notion of 'class struggle' is that society is 'held together' by the very antagonism, splitting, that forever prevents its closure in a harmonious, transparent, rational Whole—by the very impediment that undermines every rational totalization" ("Spectre of Ideology" 21–22). This paradox raises a number of ironies, namely, the fact that "peace" actually emerges out of struggle, in the sense that a state of peace signals the winning out of one particular side of an oppositional faction; the apparent condition of peace hides the actual antagonism that closes the social reality. Consequently, if the citizens of Costaguana were to have their "weary desire for peace" fulfilled, that "peace" would exist not in the absence of struggle but as a consequence of it.[8]

The implication of Žižek's reading of class struggle, finally, "is that the very constitution of social reality involves the 'primordial repression' of an antagonism, so that the ultimate support of the critique of ideology—the extra-ideological point of reference that authorizes us to denounce the content of our immediate experience as 'ideological'—is not 'reality' but the 'repressed' real of antagonism" (25). And it is in the Azuera parable that we find the "'repressed' real of antagonism" in *Nostromo*. The parable ultimately effaces the underlying struggle that creates the social reality of the country; it functions as a "symbolic fiction" that exemplifies "the primordial repression" of the antagonism of class struggle. To take the point further, there is a form of doubling whereby the specter as thematic device emerges in this symbolically overdetermined parable, which in turn itself functions as the very Žižekian "specter of ideology" that offers a glimpse of how "reality" emerges within the world of the novel. The first chapter of the novel sets the stage for later moments that show the parable's ideological resonance, as the complexities of political conflict and class struggle are continually effaced. When, for example, a churchgoer asks Father Román in what direction Europe is situated, he cautions that "ignorant sinners like you of the San Tomé mine should think earnestly of everlasting punishment instead of inquiring into the magnitude of the earth, with its countries and populations altogether beyond your understanding" (78). Harking back to the legend of Azuera, the religious dogma perpetuated by the likes of Father Román teaches followers to accept their position in the social hierarchy and make no attempt to involve themselves in thinking beyond their own faith—a faith that keeps them ensnared within the ideological trap of imperialist interests.

But Conrad's critique is not aimed merely at religious dogma; as discussed above, all ideology functions like religion. Accordingly, the members of the Costaguanan ruling class, who are not as overt as the lower classes in their religious devotion, instead worship what is referred to throughout the novel as "material interests." The Azuera parable is emblematic of the wider spectral phenomena that haunt all the novel's characters, as the importance of "action" among the capitalist class functions as the foil to faith. The driving force of material interests in the novel is the San Tomé mine, which itself carries a haunted/haunting history: "Mr. Gould, senior, did not desire the perpetual possession of that desolate locality; in fact, the mere vision of it arising before his mind in the still watches of the night had the power to exasperate him into hours of hot and agitated insomnia. . . . He also began to dream of vampires" (42–43). Wise enough to understand that the mine will become the battleground for Costaguana's perpetual and inevitable political quarrels, Gould writes to his son "with words of horror at the apparently eternal character of that curse. For the Concession had been granted to him and his descendants forever" (44). It would seem that Gould senior, with his Hamlet-esque spectral hold over his son, understands the ideological mechanisms of Costaguana quite well, but

the son's desire to overcome his father's failings leave him blind to the
"reality" of his situation. As he grows older, he comes to believe that
"with advancing wisdom, he [has] managed to clear the plain truth of
the business from the fantastic intrusions of the Old Man of the Sea,
vampires, and ghouls, which had lent to his father's correspondence
the flavour of a gruesome Arabian Night's tale" (44–45). In fact, however, "by the time he was twenty Charles Gould had, in his turn, fallen
under the spell of the San Tomé mine. But it was another form of en-
chantment, more suitable to his youth, into whose magic formula there
entered hope, vigour, and self-confidence, instead of weary indignation
and despair" (45). Charles does not overcome his father's obsession but
merely displaces it with his own, as his inability to adequately appreciate the mine's corrupting influence leads him to believe that he can
succeed where his father failed.

What Charles fails to recognize is that the "absurd moral disaster"
(50) the mine becomes is not a chance occurrence but an inevitable
consequence of the absurdity that is the modus operandi of Costaguanan politics. Naively thinking that proper management of the mine
will establish peace in the province, he hopes to atone for his father's
failure. According to his twisted Ayn Randian brand of ideology, he
believes that his own financial gain will bring peace to the people of
Sulaco, when in fact, as Žižek has shown, peace is a symptom of, not
an antidote to, class struggle. Charles's misrecognition is brought into
further relief by the novel's narrator, who deconstructs his ideological
commitments and shows how the mediation of our interaction with
the world through the realm of the symbolic ultimately constitutes a
"flattering illusion":

> It hurt Charles Gould to feel that never more, by no effort of
> will, would he be able to think of his father in the same way he
> used to think of him when the poor man was alive. His breath-
> ing image was no longer in his power. This consideration,
> closely affecting his own identity, filled his breast with a mourn-
> ful and angry desire for action. In this his instinct was unerring.
> Action is consolatory. It is the enemy of thought and the friend
> of flattering illusions. Only in the conduct of our action can we
> find the sense of mastery over the fates. (50)

Although Charles may feel a "sense of mastery over the fates," it becomes clear to readers that there is nothing supernatural or fatalistic about the success of the San Tomé mine, which is assured by the powerful influence of global capitalist interests and the ideological myths that perpetuate the passivity of those who would oppose it. As we zoom out and survey the various ideological commitments in the novel, we see that while the religious devotees are rendered passive by the deceptive comfort of faith, those representing the imperial enterprise are driven by an equally mystifying ideology of action. The novel shows how the ruling-class ideology maintains the status quo and touches everyone within its reach; ideology functions as a hegemonic force that ensures that all dissent is in one way or another subsumed into the service of maintaining the existing power dynamics.

The most tragic dissenter is Martin Decoud, who takes a critical and even ironic view of Costaguana's ideological landscape but is nonetheless complicit in its function. Unlike the many characters in the novel who appear unaware of the extent to which their actions are driven by their ideological commitments, Decoud is strikingly conscious of his own personal illusions. In this sense he comes much closer to an actual realization of how ideology acts upon him and others than Nostromo, who is less introspective. But Decoud's death ultimately becomes another cautionary tale against buying into the "sustaining illusion" of "action" that deceives us into believing that we are our own free agents: "After three days of waiting for the sight of some human face, Decoud caught himself entertaining a doubt of his own individuality. It had merged into the world of cloud and water, of natural forces and forms of nature. In our activity alone do we find the sustaining illusion of an independent existence as against the whole scheme of things of which we form a helpless part. Decoud lost all belief in the reality of his action past and to come" (357). Decoud is undoubtedly far less a materialist than Charles Gould, and yet "action" similarly comes to constitute his subjective reality. The "desire for action" that we find in Charles collapses inward on Decoud, so that action itself becomes a proxy for desire. And if we approach this scene from the perspective of "the 'repressed' real of antagonism" that Žižek describes, we may also read *action* as a code word for "material interests" and, in turn, for the antagonism of class struggle itself. We might say that only in our relationship to material interests, or within the world of class struggle, do we find "the sustaining illusion of an independent existence." In the absence of action/desire, Decoud is irreversibly traumatized by his glimpse of the real and can no longer endure his existential suffering. Ultimately both Decoud and Nostromo become ensnared in the ideological interests of those they serve. In the case of Nostromo, the false "revelation" that his own interests do not reflect those of the people to whom he has been enslaved shows merely the reinforcement of his own sustaining illusion when viewed within the novel's broader ideological landscape. Conrad brilliantly demonstrates how various forms of either "faith" or "action" serve to fill the gap of the real for each individual subject. It is in these moments of false revelation that Conrad most skillfully deconstructs Marxist notions of ideology as false consciousness and highlights the interpenetration of ideology and subjectivity, ultimately exposing the ways in which political and class conflict act upon the individual psyche.

Fully teasing out this inextricable link between the personal and the political is especially important because, as Stephen Ross explains, there has been "a tendency among politically concerned critics like Said, Watt, Albert J. Guerard, Claire Rosenfield, and Alan Friedman to minimize the importance of reading Nostromo as a subject in order to arrive at an adequate understanding of the novel's political critique" (*Conrad and Empire* 115).[9] On the contrary, I would contend that one *must* explore the intricacies of the novel's individual subjects in order to fully appreciate its political critique. Ross's contention "that the key to reading *Nostromo* lies in recognizing that, for all that the majesty of its scale seems to diminish the importance of individual experience, it remains a focused vision of the human experience of modernity" (115) is thus an important reminder that *Nostromo* does much more than explore large-scale issues like history and politics. It does that too, but alongside the granular level of individual experience. Ross later argues that "*Nostromo*'s wild oscillations from sweeping panorama to focused interiority . . . show the fundamental continuity between the subjective and the ideological in a highly compressed yet widely relevant critique of Empire's emergent order" (148), highlighting the ways in which political affairs of global consequence are always cut through with the day-to-day proceedings of individual subjects. Unlike most earlier Conrad critics, Ross is attuned to the fact that it is precisely Conrad's amalgamation of the psychodramas of individual subjects and the inevitable march of imperial capitalism that make *Nostromo* so inscrutable yet so compelling. As we have seen, in order to truly appreciate the novel's interpretive potential, one must view these seemingly antipodal elements as inextricably linked.

While we find this intersection in a number of characters throughout the novel, it is seen most powerfully in Nostromo. His "slave morality" in the early part of the novel is particularly striking, as his loyal service to the O.S.N. Company interpellates him as an imperial subject. And so the "construction and performance of 'Nostromo' [a corruption of the Italian *nostro uomo,* or "our man"] as his persona indicates a radical displacement of identity that replays on an exaggerated scale the drama of fissuring and loss that Lacan says characterizes the infant's first situation in the symbolic order. In his public manifestation, 'Nostromo' becomes little more than a nodal point in that biopolitical order, a signifier that signifies other signifiers—that is, he is a function of the operation of signification in its ideological configuration" (134). Because Nostromo's ego is entirely constructed around the persona he has created in service of others (that is, he believes that he is "really" their man), once the competing ideologies of those who "possess" him are stripped away, we find, as with Decoud, a yawning void (or an absent center) at his core.

Misrecognition and the Displaced Subject

The (self-)destructions of Nostromo and Decoud underscore the importance of intersubjectivity in self-formation. Nidesh Lawtoo's work on this topic in Conrad has been especially valuable, as he offers a novel way of examining what he calls "the phantom of the ego." "Above all," Lawtoo writes, "the modernist unconscious is not located in a solipsistic model of the psyche interrogated in isolation, but emerges from intersubjective forms of lived, affective communications experienced in daily social situations" (15). Lawtoo maintains that in Conrad and other modernist writers "the ego is formed *by* the other, *through* the other, in a relation of unconscious communication *with* the other" (18) and that as a result what we find in place of the ego is, in fact, a phantom of the ego that exists only in an intersubjective mimetic relationship to an other. According to Lawtoo, Conrad "relegates the modern moral subject to the sphere of crowd psychology and the mimetic unconscious it entails. For Conrad, as for Nietzsche before him, we live in the *Jahrhundert der Mass:* the phantom has taken possession of the ego and, as he severely adds, 'few men realize it'" (93).

This is certainly an apt way of describing Decoud, who does not appear to fully appreciate his reliance on an other until he is faced with prolonged solitude. And it is an apt way of describing Nostromo as well. Consider the scene in which he washes up and awakens exhausted on the mainland after successfully concealing the silver that all others believe to be missing: "With the lost air of a man just born into the world . . . he threw back his head, flung his arms open, and stretched himself with a slow twist of the waist and a leisurely growling yawn of white teeth, as natural and free from evil in the moment of waking as a magnificent and unconscious beast" (295). Initially, Nostromo would seem to experience a sort of epiphany here, and it might seem that his subsequent decision to renounce those who have possessed him as "our man" and instead serve only his own needs would constitute his finally stepping outside ideology.[10] But as we have seen, such a notion of ideology lapses back into what Žižek calls the "representationalist problematic," an outdated Marxist conception of ideology as an "illusion" that displaces "actual" reality. Instead, we are compelled to view Nostromo's "revelation" as a false one that leads him not "outside" ideology but back into it. As Stephen Ross explains, when "he determines to replace the fantasy structure of 'Nostromo' with the materialist fantasy structure of Empire," Conrad "lays bare the interdependence of subjective *méconnaissance* and ideological misrecognition, exposing the workings of ideology as an imaginary construction whose only defining feature is its own reproduction in further imaginary constructions" (*Conrad and Empire* 142). What is finally laid bare in Nostromo, in the words of Lawtoo, is the "phantom of the ego" that is exposed when the competing ideological layers that constitute his subject position are peeled away and reveal not an essential self but a void.

And it is precisely this "psychic dispossession" (Lawtoo's term) that renders the Conradian subject innately vulnerable to the "spell" of ideology. From the "fatal spell" that besets the gringo ghosts of Azuera to Teresa Viola, who "was under the spell of that reputation the Capataz de Cargadores had made for himself" (16), to Charles Gould "under the spell of the San Tomé mine" (45), to Nostromo falling under "the accursed spell of the treasure" (387) in his tragic repetition of the Azuera parable, Conrad's spectral engagements suggest the inevitability of our psychic subjugation to power. Let us then turn again to Butler, who confronts the problem that "the story by which subjection is told is, inevitably, circular, presupposing the very subject for which it seeks to give an account" (11). This circularity is explained by Butler's insistence that "if, following Foucault, we understand power as *forming* the subject as well, as providing the very condition of its existence and the trajectory of its desire, then power is not simply what we oppose but also, in a strong sense, what we depend on for our existence and what we harbor and preserve in the beings that we are" (2). In other words, our psychic subjugation to power is not only inevitable but fundamental to our subject formation. "In this view," Butler goes on to explain, "neither submission nor mastery is *performed by a subject*; the lived simultaneity of submission as mastery, and mastery as submission, is the condition of possibility for the emergence of the subject" (117). Conrad clearly anticipates Butler on this point, as Nostromo's conception of self is ironically predicated upon his submission to the power structure that sustains him.

As we look back, we can understand how it first appears that because none of the characters in *Nostromo* escape the corrupting influence of imperial ideology (whether political, emotional, spiritual, etc.), the novel may seem not only deeply pessimistic but in line with the very idea of ideology that Žižek criticizes. In fact, however, a closer reading shows how the novel's spectral engagement with ideology maintains the possibility of meaningful critique—and such critique is vital to our understanding of the intersectionality of the political and the individual in Conrad, but also in modernism more generally. If one of the tasks of ideology critique must be "to designate the elements within an existing social order which—in the guise of 'fiction,' that is, of 'Utopian' narratives of possible but failed alternative histories—point towards the system's antagonistic character, and thus 'estrange' us to the self-evidence of its established identity" (Žižek, "Spectre of Ideology" 7), then Nostromo is essential to our critique of ideology because his life itself is held up as *the* defining "utopian narrative" for the people of Costaguana.

Widely considered to be "incorruptible," politically indifferent, and absolutely loyal, Nostromo represents an alternative history within the world of the novel, the possibility of an infinitely trustworthy and nonpartisan heroic figure who would bring peace and stability to the country. This enduring false narrative makes it all the more important that his "epiphany" is a false one, because, rather than escaping the spell of ideology that has been cast upon him by those who have used him to perpetuate their own material interests, he simply adopts a clichéd ideology of "rebellion" that further expedites his downfall and eventually leads to his death. And we cannot overstate the importance of the fact that the novel does not end with Nostromo's death, but rather folds it back into the utopian myth that is perpetuated by Captain Mitchell and others: "Dr. Monygham, pulling round in the police-galley, heard the name pass over his head. It was another of Nostromo's successes, the greatest, the most enviable, the most sinister of all. In that true cry of love and grief that seemed to ring aloud from Punta Mala to Azuera and away to the bright line of the horizon, overhung by a big white cloud shining like a mass of solid silver, the genius of the magnificent Capataz de Cargadores dominated the dark Gulf containing his conquests of treasure and love" (405). The novel's final paragraph suggests that Nostromo's legacy, the utopian narrative that has been built up around him, will live beyond him and, by implication, continue to estrange its adherents from the social antagonism that it has obscured. If, as Benita Parry maintains, "in the end Nostromo survives his abject capitulation to live on in the minds and hearts of Costaguana's poor as exemplar of their aspirations" (127), then the parable of the gringo specters is brought back around full circle to Nostromo in the novel's final pages, and the (fictive) parable of his life that fails to account for his theft of the silver will continue to ensure the capitulation of all inhabitants of Costaguana to the ruling ideology that haunts them.[11]

However, while Nostromo's legacy is a utopian misrecognition of his *actual* life, and thus reads as tragedy, it importantly "point[s] toward the system's antagonistic character" in the way that Žižek describes. Which begs the question, How can ideology be critiqued here if only the utopian version of Nostromo survives and the *real* story is lost? In response, we must not forget that the narrator's occasional (though rare) use of first-person pronouns indicates that he or she exists within the world of the novel, indicating that, in fact, the *real* history of Nostromo endures after all. That we can continually return to the legend of the gringos on Punta Mala in the opening chapter for the first foreshadowing of Nostromo's later actions demonstrates Conrad's strategy of placing his readers "above" the action through the perspective of the semi-omniscient narrator, which allows us a privileged view of Costaguana's ideological landscape, while still remaining "inside" it via a narrator who exists within the world of the novel—and thus avoiding the postmodern problem that Žižek seeks to overcome.[12] While Nostromo appears incorruptible in the eyes of those who rely upon his help and loyalty, from the beginning of the novel he in fact "estranges" those who come into contact with him from the reality of "the system's antagonistic character." Nostromo straddles the fault line of social antagonism in the novel; in him we find embodied the tensions that underlie every social and political interaction.

It is easy to see, then, why so many critics have read the novel as deeply pessimistic. On the contrary, however, the Azuera parable not only authorizes readers of *Nostromo* to engage in a meaningful critique of ideology but suggests that the characters within the world of the novel could potentially do the same, by creating "a place that enables [them] to maintain a distance from [ideology]" (Žižek, "Spectre of Ideology" 17), even if it is not possible to actually step outside it. Conrad not only shows us the ideological dimensions of subject formation in remarkably prescient ways that anticipate theoretical formulations that come about decades later but also provides a model of how the ideological mechanisms that interpellate us *as* subjects can be meaningfully critiqued.

These achievements belong to Conrad, but they also belong to the novel form, which, as I have said, is uniquely positioned to capture such elaborate systems of political and individual thought. In his essay on Dickens and Conrad, Robert Caserio makes the claim that both authors share "a pride of art that employs the novel form to criticize other intellectual endeavors—indeed to put most modes of nonnovelistic reflection to shame" (339). Conrad's pride of art comes from his ability to so deftly exploit the novel form by amalgamating strains of thought from historical, sociological, anthropological, philosophical, theological, artistic, and other perspectives. No other artistic form can accommodate such an undertaking. Caserio goes on to write that "the novel as Conrad practices the form challenges the authority of history, sociology, philosophy, and science. This kind of novel in effect claims its authority to be superior to theirs and its portrayal of life to be more precise than direct observation and documentary evidence, more acute than logical analysis or philosophical speculation" (339). While this is true of Conrad's fiction generally, the novel that most embodies this ability is *Nostromo,* and it is thus the quintessential early modernist novel that sets the stage for the readings that follow.

Chapter 2

THE VOID OF SUBJECTIVITY

Sublimation and the Artistic Process in
Conrad, Joyce, and Woolf

All religions, arts and sciences are branches of the same tree. All these aspirations are directed toward ennobling man's life, lifting it from the sphere of
mere physical existence and leading the individual toward freedom.
—ALBERT EINSTEIN, *Out of My Later Years*

Joseph Conrad, James Joyce, and Virginia Woolf may not, upon first
glance, appear to have much in common. Aside from each playing a
major role in shaping the novel form—and particularly the modernist novel—they are otherwise quite different writers. Born of Polish
radical, working-class Irish, and upper-class English parents, respectively, they also have few biographical similarities.[1] Stylistically speaking, Joyce and Woolf were pioneers of stream of consciousness and
free indirect discourse, while Conrad's prose was far less experimental
and grounded in more conventional Victorian narrative modes, including the classic adventure novel, about which much has been written.[2]
There are, however, two interrelated aspects of their lives and writings
that are quite significant: their skepticism toward the prevailing institutions of their time and their unwavering belief in the superior abil-
ities of art and the artist in shaping culture and society. Taken at face
value, these perhaps do not appear to be especially unique characteristics among great artists, but what makes them notable are the analogous ways these writers use their artistic craft as a means of resolving
personal tensions that developed out of their skepticism toward science and religion, two of the prevailing institutions of the early twentieth century. This chapter shows how both their personal and fictive
responses to these doubts anticipate Lacan's account of the three dominant forms of sublimation—religion, scientific discourse, and art—

which represent competing ways of approaching what he called the void at the heart of subjectivity.

Lacan's conception of the void is intimately tied to language. As the biological fact of human existence precedes language, the acquisition of language thus introduces the possibility of constitutive absence, which Lacan called the "void." In the most elemental sense, the void is the absent center around which subjectivity is constructed, the unbridgeable gap that separates our desire from the sense of completeness for which we are always longing. As such, the void cannot be filled, although we nonetheless spend our lives attempting to fill it and restore a sense of lost psychic unity—a psychic unity that existed only as a fantasy. Because religion and science represent the prevailing belief systems that individuals and societies have used to explain human existence, in order to make any sense of that existence one tends to put faith in one or the other. But for those who find both suspect, the existential implications can be terrifying.

In order to give some sense of how doubt intersects the void, we might consider Jean-Michel Rabaté's assertion that "doubt offers a key not only to obsessional neuroses, and its usual connection with religion, as Freud repeatedly stated in *The Future of an Illusion,* but, because of the great 'suspension' it affords, to the essence of Life" (xxv). Rabaté, whose *Joyce upon the Void: The Genesis of Doubt* (1991) is especially useful in framing this chapter's argument, points out that "life is founded upon the void in Stephen's post-Freudian view of 'mystical paternity,' just as the world is founded upon the void in Bloom's post-Einsteinian universe" (xxv). In what follows, we will expand upon Rabaté's characterization of Joyce and show how doubt and the void intersect in similar ways in Conrad and Woolf as well.

Before we delve into the religion-science-art nexus that informs this chapter, it will be useful to review how Lacan relates it to the void.[3] This involves, first of all, establishing what Lacan means by *sublimation,* as his use of the term differs from Freud's. For Freud, sublimation is a defense mechanism that channels unhealthy, threatening, or potentially painful desire into an activity that is socially acceptable. This is how we have typically come to use the term *sublimation* in popular discourse. For Lacan, however, sublimation is related to the unbearable symbolic loss of the mother, a loss that produces "the Thing," or the void around which our drives revolve. Lacan alternately calls the Thing *das Ding* and *la chose* throughout his seminar of 1959–60. He uses the concept, which he adapts from Freud, to describe an imagined lost object (i.e., an object that can never be represented)[4] that would fill the void, but forever eludes the subject (later in his life, Lacan revises his focus—as he so often did—from *das Ding* more toward *objet a*, a physical object, person, or attribute that stands in for a psychic loss associated with the void). Lacan describes the thing as "the beyond-of-the-signified" (*Ethics of Psychoanalysis* 54), an unknowable *x* in the vein of Kant's "thing-in-itself" that resides in the realm of the real. He explains elsewhere in the same seminar that "this thing will always be represented by emptiness, precisely because it cannot be represented by anything else—or more exactly, because it can only be represented by something else. But in every form of sublimation, emptiness is determinative. . . . All art is characterized by a certain mode of organization around this emptiness" (129–30). This is precisely why he turns to the example of the vase, a nod to the jug in Heidegger's essay "*Das Ding*," to allegorize the process of artistic creation. Lacan maintains that the process of sublimation involves the process through which objects of desire are situated in relation to this loss, and thus in the process of sublimation "the object is elevated to the dignity of the Thing" (112). Lacan in turn sees, as processes of sublimation, religion as an attempt to fill the void, science as an attempt to reject the void, and art as an attempt to create something around the void. The image of the vase is significant because it is organized around an emptiness that represents the Thing. Paradoxically, though, Lacan also points out that the vase *creates* the emptiness, showing how "the fashioning of the signifier and the introduction of a gap or a hole in the real is identical" (121).

Because "the fashioning of the signifier" involves our entry into the realm of the symbolic, we must also understand Lacan's symbolic order, which comprises the symbolic, the imaginary, and the real. According to Lacan, we are always already implicated in the realm of the symbolic from the moment of birth. The symbolic, which is the realm of language and signification, precedes us and has already made determinations for us—our name, our gender, and so on—prior to our arrival. Our existence in the symbolic inevitably detaches us from the real, which is located beyond the symbolic and resists signification.

Jacques-Alain Miller describes the real as "the ineliminable residue of all articulation, the foreclosed element, which may be approached, but never grasped: the umbilical cord of the symbolic" (280). In other words, because our very conception of self is a symbolic construction, we can never transcend the world of signification into the realm of the real. We are thus prisoners, in a sense, to what Lacan calls the imaginary, our relationship to "reality" (meaning reality as we conventionally know it, which is distinct from the real) as it is mediated through the realm of the symbolic. We might recall here Louis Althusser's description of ideology as "a 'representation' of the imaginary relationship of individuals to their real conditions of existence" (162) in illustrating how the Lacanian real is made perpetually elusive by our inability to transcend the realm of the symbolic. Thus, while for Freud the ego is the essential force that holds the subject together in a coherent whole, for Lacan the subject is radically decentered and exists only in symbolic opposition to the void. The void is closely aligned with the real precisely because the real is unknowable. Desire, which for Lacan is the driving force of subjectivity, is a perpetual attempt to fill this void, which opens when we enter the realm of the symbolic.

Because this desire to fill the void risks becoming pathological, Lacan identifies the three primary forms of sublimation named above, through which subjects engage the void: religion, which he aligns with neurosis; science, which he aligns with paranoia; and art, which he aligns with hysteria. In her book *Theology after Postmodernity* (2013), which offers an especially fitting example because it recalls Stephen Daedalus's exploration of Aquinas in *Portrait*, Tina Beattie gives a description of Lacan's secular theoretical paradigm that is particularly apt in this context: "Thomas builds the edifice of the human around the goodness and mystery of God at the heart of creation, but Lacan asks what happens to the human when there is no God and when creation itself is a product of language encircled around a void (the Lacanian real)" (15–16). I emphasize the intersection of God and void in Lacan because religious skepticism is essential to the argument that I wish to make about Conrad, Joyce, and Woolf, whom I characterize as writers who adopt comparable ways of depicting human subjectivity as a self-perpetuated ideological illusion that masks an essential void of subjectivity.

Below I will outline the skeptical attitudes to be found in the biographies and fiction of each writer and then explore three particularly illustrative and complementary examples of the void in the work of each: the scene of Decoud's existential terror alone on the Great Isobel Island, which was discussed briefly in the previous chapter; the "Proteus" episode of *Ulysses,* in which Stephen wanders alone along Sandymount Beach; and the "Time Passes" section of *To the Lighthouse,* when the world of the novel is plunged into darkness in the absence of human presence and definition. I conclude my discussion of each author by addressing the role of art and redemption, showing finally how each elevates the role of art as the ideal response to the void.

The Great Void and Conrad's Search for Truth

Conrad's skepticism has been the topic of a great deal of scholarly work.[5] This is not surprising given that he made no secret of his skeptical disposition and could even be said to have used it as a bludgeon at times. Consider the following illustrative example from a letter to John Galsworthy: "You want more scepticism at the very foundation of your work. Scepticism, the tonic of the minds, the tonic of life, the agent of truth,—the way of art and salvation" (2:359). For Conrad, skepticism was not an exclusively negative mental state, although it did at times manifest itself in what some critics have called a solipsistic or even nihilistic worldview.[6] Without a doubt such views appear frequently in Conrad's fiction. To name just one example that we saw in the previous chapter, certainly "it is Decoud's skepticism that destroys him; he has nothing to sustain him because he believes in nothing" (Peters 124). But skepticism at times carries a markedly positive value for Conrad too, as suggested in his letter to John Galsworthy. If we take Conrad at his word, the implication is that it is skepticism, rather than certainty, that leads us to the truth. Consider the case of Charles Gould, whose absolute certainty that he can avoid the fate of his father and transform the nation of Costaguana is in fact his greatest vulnerability, or the deeply skeptical tone of Marlow in *Lord Jim:* "They wanted facts. Facts! They demanded facts from him, as if facts could explain anything!" (22). Ultimately, according to John Peters, "Conrad must walk a thin line" between skepticism and truth: "On the one hand, skepticism can lead to some knowledge of the truth, but on the other, it can also lead to the abyss of despair. Conrad's balancing act between the two is the ability to recognize the nature of human existence but at the same time possess a means to shelter one's self from such potentially withering knowledge" (125). An excellent example of this tension is to be found throughout *Lord Jim,* as Marlow despairingly searches for some notion of truth, both the truth of what happened to Jim and the true nature of Jim's character. Marlow says at one point: "I cannot say I had ever seen him distinctly—not even to this day, after I had my last view of him; but it seemed to me that the less I understood the more I was bound to him in the name of that doubt which is the inseparable part of our knowledge. I did not know so much more about myself" (134). In Conrad's formulation, doubt is not something that is overcome on the way to knowledge but an "inseparable part" of knowledge itself.

With that in mind, let us further explore how Conrad's conceptions of knowledge and truth intersect with his views on art. A 1913 letter to Warrington Dawson is particularly illuminating on this topic and is thus worth quoting at some length:

> As to the Eternity of Art—I don't suppose it is more or less eternal than the earth itself. I can't believe in the eternity of art any more than in the eternity of pain or eternity of love (subjects of art, those) whose emotions art (and of all arts music) brings home to our breasts. Art for me *is* an end in itself. Conclusions are not for it. And it is superior to science, in so far that it calls in us with authority to behold! to feel! whereas science at best can only tell us—it seems so! And thats [sic] all it can do. It talks to us of the Laws of Nature. But thats [sic] only one of its little jokes. It has never discovered anything of the sort. It has made out with much worry and blundering certain sequences of facts beginning in the dark and leading god knows where. And it has built various theories to fit the form of activity it has perceived. But even the theory of evolution has got a great big hole in it, right at the very root. And it is amusing to see the scientists walk round it with circumspection for the last sixty years, while pretending all the time that it isn't there.
>
> You don't suppose that I am fool enough to deny the *fact* of evolution. All I say is that the "truth of life" is not in it wherever

else it might lay; and that "truth of life" is too vague an expression to link art's achievement to. For me the artists [sic] salvation is in fidelity, in remorseless fidelity to the *truth of his own sensations*. Hors de là, point de salut. (*Collected Letters* 5:237–38, emphases in the original)

This letter contains just one example of Conrad's very particular notion of truth: he is skeptical of the type of absolute truth claimed by science and instead prefers the truth of one's own sensations. In other words, truth for Conrad is something that is fleeting and momentary, not absolute or permanent. His skepticism toward the power of science is one of the many ways in which Conrad departs from many of his fellow Victorians, whose faith in science to cure the ills of society had reached new highs toward the end of the nineteenth century. Truth, for Conrad, is more like an impression, hence the impressionistic style that he adopts in his fiction. His ambivalence toward religion is more subtle here, and will be made more explicit below, but we can nonetheless point to some suggestive linguistic and metaphorical choices in this example that give some sense of how Conrad situates the role of art in relation to religion as well. For instance, he questions the eternity not only of art but also of pain and love. But the Bible tells us that God's love is eternal, that Christ's pain is eternal. And in the context of Victorian religiosity, even the very notion of a "remorseless fidelity to the *truth of [one's] own sensations*" betrays the classical devotion to serving God above all things. Unlike the true religious believer, Conrad does not believe in the idea of transcendental truth.

But for Conrad's most important exposition on art in relation to science and religion we must turn to his often cited preface to *The Nigger of the "Narcissus,"* which is generally considered to be the most emblematic representation of his artistic credo.[7] Like the letter to Warrington, it is worth quoting at length:

A work that aspires, however humbly, to the condition of art should carry its justification in every line. And art itself may be defined as a single-minded attempt to render the highest kind of justice to the visible universe, by bringing to light the truth, manifold and one, underlying its every aspect. It is an attempt to find in its forms, in its colors, in its light, in its shadows, in the aspects of matter and in the facts of life what of each is fundamental, what is enduring and essential—their one illuminating and convincing quality—the very truth of their existence. The artist, then, like the thinker or the scientist, seeks the truth and makes his appeal. Impressed by the aspect of the world the thinker plunges into ideas, the scientist into facts—whence, presently, emerging they make their appeal to those qualities of our being that fit us best for the hazardous enterprise of living. They speak authoritatively to our common-sense, to our intelligence, to our desire of peace or to our desire of unrest; not seldom to our prejudices, sometimes to our fears, often to our egoism—but always to our credulity. And their words are heard with reverence, for their concern is with weighty matters: with the cultivation of our minds and the proper care of our bodies, with the attainment of our ambitions, with the perfection of the means and the glorification of our precious aims.

It is otherwise with the artist. (11–12)

Conrad's definition of art as "a single-minded attempt to render the highest kind of justice to the visible universe" is telling in itself of how much esteem he grants to the artist. He also juxtaposes the role of the artist to that of the scientist, or thinker (one can infer philosopher here). His distinction suggests that perhaps we trust the latter too much, that in fact thinkers often appeal to our egoism and our prejudices. Although Conrad sees the artist, the scientist, and the thinker as essentially pursuing the same ends, he suggests that the artist is most successful in achieving what he regards as truth. And while the religious overtones are again somewhat subtle, we can fairly extrapolate that to seek "the very truth" of the existence of the facts of life is a pursuit in the vein of that undertaken by the religious believer. The notions of art as "render[ing] the highest kind of justice to the visible universe" and "bringing light to the truth" carry very strong religious overtones as well. The latter connection between truth and light is steeped in the kind of language that we find throughout the Judeo-Christian Bible, as in Ephesians 5:13–14, "everything exposed by the light becomes visible; for everything that becomes visible is light," or when Christ says in John 8:31–32, "If you continue in my word, you are truly my disciples; and you will know the truth, and the truth will make you free" (*New Oxford Annotated Bible*). Biblical dogma holds that the truth can only become manifest through light and that only the truth can lead to redemption. These connections between light and truth are especially compelling in relation to Conrad's fiction, which often employs light/dark imagery. Marlow's reflection upon his pursuit of Kurtz from *Heart of Darkness* offers just one notable example: "It seemed somehow to throw a kind of light on everything about me—and into my thoughts. It was sombre enough, too—and pitiful—not extraordinary in any way—not very clear either. No, not very clear. And yet it seemed to throw a kind of light" (107). Taken together, these various example suggest that in Conrad's formulation the artist, like Christ, carries the light, and the light brings the truth. But while Christ's truth is eternal, Conrad's is the momentary truth of a sensual impression rendered by the artist.

Thus while religious imagery is quite common in Conrad's work, as John Lester shows in his 1988 study *Conrad and Religion,* in fact its importance is more symbolic than practical. "Conrad's use of a religious lexis in his writings indicates the spiritual nature of society's malaise," Lester explains. "The inadequacies of established beliefs had left a gap in man's existence which he endeavored to fill with his own concerns" (168). Interestingly, Lester's description evokes precisely the Lacanian framework used in this chapter. He seems to describe, albeit unintentionally, the void of subjectivity, which must be sublimated via religion, science, art, or other means. Lester documents a number of Conrad's deprecatory statements about religion, including two letters to his editor and friend Edward Garnett. In the first Conrad writes, "It's strange how I always, from the age of fourteen, disliked the Christian religion, its doctrines, ceremonies and festivals" (*Letters from Conrad* 188), and in the second, "Christianity—is distasteful to me. I am not blind to its services but the absurd oriental fable from which it starts irritates me. Great, improving, softening, compassionate it may be but it has lent itself with amazing facility to cruel distortion and is the only religion which, with its impossible standards, has brought an infinity of anguish to innumerable souls—on this earth" (265). Indeed, while Conrad utilizes religious imagery quite frequently in his work, ultimately his use of it would seem to be related not so much to any actual religious belief but to his reverence for the artistic process. In yet another letter to Edward Garnett, before we lay the subject to rest, Conrad wryly referred to the art of literature as a "persecuted faith" (194), perhaps best illustrating how he favored religious imagery in spite of his own ambivalence.[8]

We thus find in his conflicted relationship with religion one example of how Conrad often felt as though there was something queer about him that did not quite suit the European society in which he found himself. It is not surprising, then, that one of the major themes across his fiction is the tension between the individual and his or her social conditions. In countless situations throughout Conrad's novels, this tension produces moments of crisis in the individual subject. We see this even in his early work, for example, in the sailors from *The Nigger of the "Narcissus,"* who are conflicted between their humanitarian impulses and their professional duties, and in Kurtz of *Heart of Darkness,* whose identity is hollowed out when detached from the traditional British values around which his sense of self has cohered. We could certainly look to the latter example as an instance of the void, as the imagery of darkness, the novel's "Hollow Men" epigraph, and Kurtz's unquenched search for some undefined something that ends in "The horror! The horror!" are evocative in themselves. But we will focus on the passage from *Nostromo* that anticipates Decoud's suicide:

> After three days of waiting for the sight of some human face, Decoud caught himself entertaining a doubt of his own individuality. It had merged into the world of cloud and water, of natural forces and forms of nature. In our activity alone do we find the sustaining illusion of an independent existence as against the whole scheme of things of which we form a helpless part. Decoud lost all belief in the reality of his action past and to come. . . . The solitude appeared like a great void, and the silence of the gulf like a tense, thin cord to which he hung suspended by both hands, without fear, without surprise, without any sort of emotion whatever. Only towards the evening, in the comparative relief of coolness, he began to wish that this cord would snap. He imagined it snapping with a report as of a pistol—a sharp, full crack. And that would be the end of him. (357)

That Conrad uses the word *void* is obviously coincidental; nonetheless, it shows just how closely his conception of subjectivity mirrors Lacan's. To take the comparison a step further, we might think of the "thin cord" by which Decoud hangs as the umbilical cord described by Miller above, which maintains the connection between the symbolic and the real. The image of the cord then returns in the scene of Decoud's suicide, after he has shot himself in the chest and rolls over the side of his small raft: "The stiffness of the fingers relaxed, and the lover of Antonia Avellanos rolled overboard without having heard the cord of silence snap aloud in the solitude of the placid gulf, whose glittering surface remained untroubled by the fall of his body" (359). It is fitting that Decoud's body eventually falls into the water, which then goes on as if nothing had happened, emphasizing just how insignificant our individual subjective existences are despite the conceptions we hold of our own place in the world.

In the previous chapter I examined this passage in the context of "action" as a "sustaining illusion" around which one's sense of self is built. What Decoud confronts in this moment is the "great void" that lies at the heart of the sustaining illusion that constitutes his subjective self. Aside from Conrad's prescient use of the word *void*, what makes this episode such a striking anticipation of Lacan is how Decoud's realization that his personality is a fantasy occurs when he is confronted with the absence of those sustaining illusions that appear in the form of objects and people who act as tethers to our internal selves.[9] To take the implications a step further, we might think about the natural world that Conrad describes as the Lacanian real, or that which escapes representation. It is fitting that Conrad's language mentions Decoud's loss of "all belief in the reality of his action," because for Lacan the distinction between the real and what we call reality is essential, in that reality is essentially an illusion. This passage functions as a primary example of Conrad's metaphysics, which recall Jonathan Rée's statement above that "twentieth-century approaches to subjectivity are dominated by the anxiety not to be Descartes." Conrad veers away from "cogito, ergo sum" toward a conception of self that arrives via Marx and Hegel in a decidedly Lacanian territory. What makes this scene further compelling is Decoud's rationalist Enlightenment thinking: he recalls Lacan's description of science as denying the existence of the void, which leaves him ill-equipped to manage the existential drama that faces him. The only option for Decoud, unable to cope with the void that confronts him, is suicide.

The description of Decoud's suicide is exceedingly bleak, and Conrad's fiction is generally seen as quite gloomy. But as I attempted to show in the previous chapter, I believe there is something surprisingly hopeful in Conrad as well. As we turn to the idea of redemption, I would like to look once more at the preface to *The Nigger of the "Narcissus"* and again call attention to Conrad's notion of truth:

> To arrest, for the space of a breath, the hands busy about the work of the earth, and compel men entranced by the sight of distant goals to glance for a moment at the surrounding vision of form and colour, of sunshine and shadows; to make them pause for a look, for a sigh, for a smile—such is the aim, difficult and evanescent, and reserved only for a very small few to achieve. But sometimes, by the deserving and the fortunate, even that task is accomplished. And when it is accomplished— behold!—all the truth of life is there: a moment of vision, a sigh, a smile—and the return to an eternal rest. (16)

For all that Conrad himself has said about the artistic process, there are not many artists in his fiction who might serve as living examples of his credo. He did not give us a Stephen Daedalus or a Lily Briscoe. But if we suppose that for Conrad truth lies in a moment of artistic purity, one in which even "a moment of vision, a sigh, a smile" can take on outsized proportions in the work of art, then I suggest that we take Charles Marlow as Conrad's prototypical artist. After all, as a storyteller Marlow traffics in the art of crafting narratives and interpreting the events and people with whom he becomes involved. The following passage from *Heart of Darkness* gives a sense of Conrad's characterization of Marlow: "The yarns of seamen have a direct simplicity, the whole meaning of which lies within the shell of a cracked nut. But Marlow was not typical (if his propensity to spin yarns be excepted), and to him the meaning of an episode was not inside like a kernel but outside, enveloping the tale which brought it out only as a glow brings out a haze, in the likeness of one of these misty halos that sometimes are made visible by the spectral illumination of moonshine" (105). There are undeniable similarities between this description and Conrad's preface to *The Nigger of the "Narcissus"* in terms of both imagery and intent. And of course there is the fact that critics have long viewed Marlow as a proxy for Conrad, a vessel through which Conrad can insert many of his own thoughts and reflections. And Marlow, like Conrad, frequently turns, as in the passage above, to the imagery of light and darkness. He does this, as well, in another passage from *Heart of Darkness,* one that brings us back to the problem of "truth" and raises the difficulty of ever escaping our own subjective experience:

> He [Kurtz] was just a word to me. I did not see the man in the name any more than you do. Do you see him? Do you see the story? Do you see anything? It seems to me I am trying to tell you a dream—making a vain attempt, because no relation of a dream can convey the dream-sensation, that commingling of absurdity, surprise, and bewilderment in a tremor of struggling revolt, that notion of being captured by the incredible which is of the very essence of dreams. . . .
> He was silent for a while.
> . . . No, it is impossible to convey the life-sensation of any given epoch of one's existence—that which makes its truth, its meaning—its subtle and penetrating essence. It is impossible. We live, as we dream—alone. . . . (129–30, ellipses in original)

Marlow struggles with describing Jim as well, saying of him that "he was like a figure set up on a pedestal, to represent in his persistent youth the power, and perhaps the virtues, of races that never grow old, that have emerged from the gloom. I don't know why he should always have appeared to me symbolic. Perhaps this is the real cause of my interest in his fate" (159). In both *Heart of Darkness* and *Lord Jim,* Marlow appears to understand that absolute truth is in fact an illusion and does his best to give readers a glimpse of some fleeting moment of truth.

The paradigmatic example of Marlow's struggle occurs at the end of *Heart of Darkness,* when he lies to Kurtz's intended, telling her that Kurtz's last word had been her name, when in fact he had uttered "The horror! The horror!" This brings us back, again, to the notion of "truth" and what it means to be "truthful." Marlow's lie is, paradoxically, an act of artistic creation and an act of redemption. Marlow feels a sense of guilt for his participation in the imperializing force whose brutality has allowed Kurtz to emerge. His lie is, then, an act of redemption both for himself and for Kurtz. While Kurtz perhaps confronts the void in the end, in his final words, as the teller of the tale, the artist, Marlow transforms what Kurtz had become in order that he might continue to fulfill the symbolic function necessary for his widow's psychic well-being. His lie is obviously not a religious act, and in skewing the "truth" it is not a scientific one. But if one accepts the idea that the best we can do is create fleeting moments of truth, then the "truth" that Marlow crafts for Kurtz's intended can in fact be seen not simply as a dishonest act but as an act of compassion that sustains a glimmer of hope in the face of so much darkness.

Joyce's Portrait of Doubt and the Resurrection of the Artist

Like Conrad, Joyce also renounced the Catholic Church, but he nonetheless frequently turned to religious themes and imagery in his fiction. The extent and timing of Joyce's split with the Catholic Church continues to be a topic of debate among critics, but at the very least his ambivalence toward the church, and toward organized religion more generally, is undeniable. Many critics, however, are willing to go much further. Geert Lernout, for instance, argues unequivocally that "James Joyce was an unbeliever from the start of his life as a writer, that he never returned to the faith of his fathers and that his work can only be read properly if that important fact is taken into account" (*Help My Unbelief* 2). Such an attitude is borne out in a 1904 letter from Joyce to his wife, Nora, about his abandonment of the Catholic Church: "Six years ago I left the Catholic Church, hating it most fervently. I found it impossible for me to remain in it on account of the impulses of my nature. I made secret war upon it when I was a student and declined to accept the positions it offered me. By doing this I made myself a beggar but I retained my pride. Now I make open war upon it by what I write and say and do" (*Letters* 2:48). But despite Joyce's own bold proclamation, other critics like Roy Gottfried are more tempered in their assessment. In *Joyce's Misbelief* (2008), Gottfried depicts Joyce not as a *dis*believer but as a *mis*believer, who maintained an intellectual connection with the church but transformed its imagery and ideology for his own ends.[10] This characterization is substantiated by Joyce's definitive biographer, Richard Ellmann, who writes of Joyce's time at Belvedere College in the early 1980s and of how body and mind clashed amid the influence of his readings and experiences:

> As he said in A Portrait, his soul threw off the cerements that covered it and spurned the grave of boyhood. His graveclothes included, by one of those curious transvaluations of Christian images that Joyce was to delight in, his allegiance to the Church; and his resurrection, for which Christ's was so useful a descriptive metaphor, was as an artist rather than as a risen god. His sins became serious, and his sense of sin, "that sense of separation and loss," brought him to consciousness, from which vantage point he sloughed off all but the vestiges of Christian guilt. (42)

With this brief background in mind, my goal is not to make any definitive argument about Joyce's religious belief other than to emphasize above all his undeniable skepticism. More to the point, though, I suggest that we use Ellmann as a springboard for identifying Joyce's rejection of the notion of religious redemption in favor of artistic redemption. These respective notions of redemption are important in Joyce, as the language of the latter is often couched in the language of the former. Although his split with the Catholic Church is well known and he often expressed an aversion toward religion, we nonetheless should not view his animosity in purely negative terms. As was the case with Conrad, despite his ambivalence toward religion itself, religious imagery plays an important role in Joyce's fiction. This stems from the fact that doubt, not only about religion but as a more general approach to life, was elemental for Joyce. Jean-Michel Rabaté explains that "doubt always retained a functional value for Joyce (who was as thrifty for his fiction as he was spendthrift in real life), and eventually provided him with his major faith: has faith in himself, which alone could underpin his faith in the real world" (xii). This faith in himself that Rabaté identifies equates (particularly in his fiction) to faith in the artistic pursuit. Like Conrad, Joyce was an absolute believer in the transformative power of art. We should also add that Joyce's early philosophical influences likely played a vital role in his skepticism as well. In particular, he was influenced by Berkeley and Hume as a young man, both of whom, according to Rabaté, "can be said to work in the right descent from the radical phenomenalism of the early Greek sceptics, even if they start from Locke's theory of perception. What Joyce took from them confirmed his sense that language was the key to any approach to reality" (xv). It is not surprising, then, that Joyce anticipates Lacan's insights about the relationship between subjectivity and language.

Joyce's thoughts about science, on the other hand, were markedly more positive, particularly in the latter part of his career. As Jeffrey Drouin has shown in *James Joyce, Science, and Modernist Print Culture* (2015), which uses documentary evidence to show how Joyce was engaged with and inspired by the popular science periodicals of his day, Joyce in fact utilized many scientific references in his fiction, especially to Albert Einstein, whose theory of relativity was widely known and inspirational to many modernist writers.[11] The subtitle of Drouin's book, *"The Einstein of English Fiction,"* references a quote by the then head of the BBC, Harold Nicolson, who described Joyce in those words in a broadcast pamphlet urging readers to abandon light popular reading in favor of authors like Joyce, who were more meaningfully engaging the spirit of the day. Although Nicolson's moniker likely has as much to do with the fact that Joyce, like Einstein, sought to understand the intersection of space, time, and consciousness, it nonetheless provides a useful way to think about Joyce, particularly as *Ulysses* and, to a greater degree, *Finnegans Wake* are rife with scientific references. Biographical evidence suggests that by the end of his life Joyce had certainly become quite interested in the topic of science.

This apparent interest is complicated, however, by other biographical evidence. Avrom Fleishman, for instance, points out that the pursuit of scientific meaning "has been discouraged by Joyce's own passing barbs at science and scientists [he cites as an example Joyce's critical reference to Frederick Soddy in *Finnegans Wake*], by his apparent adherence to the anti-scientific maxims of Tolstoy and other anti-rationalists, and by the scanty evidence of his studies of the subject after his early distaste for the classical 'natural philosophy' offered by his Jesuit schoolmasters" (378). Ultimately, the biographical and fictive evidence does not lead to any definitive determination about Joyce's feelings toward science, but I do think it is notable that Joyce's interest in science peaked later in his life and centered on principles that seemed to cast uncertainty upon what previously had been thought to be scientific truths. Indeed, uncertainty is a driving force for Joyce, and his depiction of knowledge was often ironic, as Allen Thiher points out:

> The joyous celebration of knowledge means that parody is Joyce's natural rhetorical mode. This parody is highly ambivalent. Parody is often affirmative, but Joyce indulges in such parodic exuberance that one finally wonders if the knowledge of everything really has much importance. . . . In Joyce, everything can be the object of knowledge, and there is no more reason, it seems, to grant greater importance to the principle of the conservation of energy than, say, to the somewhat shabby contents of Bloom's memory—though Bloom's memory may well call forth the principle of the conservation of energy, and that principle may in turn explain some aspects of his memory. (172–73)

Thiher thus concludes that "after surveying much of the criticism on Joyce and science, one may be tempted to agree with Grace Eckley that the central parable about space and time in *Finnegans Wake* is about the failure of science; or at least it queries if whatever science cannot explain might not be better turned into art" (198). I would agree with Thiher and, in fact, apply this perspective to Joyce's more general attitude toward science, stressing above all that while Joyce certainly cultivated an interest in scientific concepts and included them in his work, he nonetheless remained skeptical of the notion that the institution of science, like the institution of religion, could help us adequately understand the human experience—for that, art remained paramount in Joyce's estimation.

Stephen Daedalus is equipped with the mind of the artist. He accepts or even embraces the void, and he confronts the void with artistic creation that builds around it. "Proteus" offers an apt illustration of Joyce's universe—and an invitation for thinking about how that universe resembles Conrad's. Let us begin by observing the first paragraph of the episode:

Ineluctable modality of the visible. At least that if no more, thought through my eyes. Signatures of all things I am here to read, seaspawn and seawrack, the nearing tide, that rusty boot. Snotgreen, bluesilver, rust: coloured signs. Limits of the diaphane. But he adds: in bodies. Then he was aware of them bodies before of them coloured. How? By knocking his sconce against them, sure. Go easy. Bald he was and a millionaire, *maestro di color che sanno.* Limit of the diaphane in. Why in? Diaphane, adiaphane. If you can put your five fingers through it, it is a gate, if not a door. Shut your eyes and see. (37)

The passage is Stephen's stream-of-consciousness reflection upon Aristotle's essay "On Sense and Sensible Objects," which describes seeing as "the superior sense." Significantly for Stephen, sight does not allow him to see the true nature of the objects he observes, but rather "signatures of all things I am here to read." As in Conrad, there is an intimate connection between truth and sensory experience. The essential question is, How is thought translated from the sensory experience of sight to the neural experience of cognition? Because the process of sight is so complex and because elements of the seeing process like light and color (both Aristotle and Berkeley foreground the importance of color in the process of seeing) can be experienced so differently by different viewers, Stephen wonders how accurate sight is in constructing a truthful sense of reality. Berkeley, evoking Plato's famous allegory of the cave, contends that sense perception is inherently unreliable because we can never ultimately distinguish between external reality and the internal "reality" that is constructed by our thoughts. Thus, as in Conrad, there is a recognition in the vein of Lacan that the objects we see are processed through language and thus inaccessible as objects in themselves. "Reality," in other words, must be read. Thus, as we observed above, we remain forever trapped in the realm of the symbolic. What Stephen encounters on his walk, in other words, is not so much truthful perceptions of Sandymount Strand and its surroundings but momentary impressions of what his senses are processing.

The final sentence of the paragraph, which although representing Stephen's thoughts could also be read as a directive to the reader, suggests a questioning of whether the external world exists, since that world effectively vanishes at the closing of one's eyes. The answer is given later on the same page: "See now. There all the time without you: and ever shall be" (37). This shows a particular aspect of Joyce's attitude that is very important to understanding his perspective. Like Einstein, Joyce is interested in the relationship between time and space, which is reflected in the movement of Stephen's feet as he walks: The *nacheinander* (one in front of the other) is associated with the audible and linear, and thus the passage of time; the *nebeneinander* (side by side) is associated with the visual, and thus the spatial relationship of objects to one another. Thomas Jackson Rice, in making his case for viewing Joyce as a "realist," maintains that Joyce "accept[ed] the existence of a concrete, aboriginal real that exists independently of the subjective individual's act of observation" (7). In addition to resembling Einstein here, Joyce actually also resembles Lacan and his ultimate rejection of relativism as it relates to the real—that is, that which lies outside of human subjectivity.

Of course, one might argue that there is little comfort in the notion that the world exists outside of us, particularly if we are not present to sense it. Ultimately, one is invited to consider that the senses tether us to the external world. Without them, we would exist in a void. And it is thus the senses alone that obscure the void at the center of our being. As Lacan shows us, this void is present from birth. And thus Stephen reflects upon his own birth: "One of her sisterhood lugged me squealing into life. Creation from nothing" (37). The act of creation, whether in the form of birth or of art, emerges not from the divine but from the void. This is also important because for Lacan the void is linked with the mother, and thus with the other. The mother is a lost object for which the subject attempts to compensate by seeking out other little objects (*objets a*) that act as substitutes; this accounts for the subject's desire and his or her identification with the other. Accordingly, Stephen is attuned to the other, as exemplified in his consideration for the man who has recently drowned near Maiden's Rock: "I want his life still to be his, mine to be mine. A drowning man. His human eyes scream to me out of horror of his death" (46). We see here Stephen conflicted by his own subjectivity. He recognizes the man as "other" and yet still feels the urge to identify with him. This recalls Decoud's inability to conceptualize his own subjectivity in the absence of an "other." We recognize our separation from others, in other words, but still rely upon their mirroring recognition. Throughout "Proteus" we find in Stephen's ruminations on both others and himself a fixation upon and curiosity about the importance of absence, which thus brings us back to the importance of sight as a functional reminder of our subjective reality.

I would thus like to conclude this discussion of Joyce by returning to Conrad and his preface to *The Nigger of the "Narcissus,"* which elevates sight above the other senses: "My task which I am trying to achieve is, by the power of the written word to make you hear, to make you feel—it is, before all, to make you *see*. That—and no more, and it is everything. If I succeed, you shall find there according to your desserts: encouragement, consolation, fear, charm—all you demand—and, perhaps, also that glimpse of truth for which you have forgotten to ask" (14). This brings us back around, first of all, to Conrad's notion of truth—and here it is sight that best offers the truth (Conrad's notion of sight is obviously overdetermined here beyond the literal sense). It also aligns Conrad with Joyce's "ineluctable modality of the visible," which recalls Aristotle's suggestion that sight, unlike sound, cannot be modified by its corresponding sensory organ. In Joyce, furthermore, Don Gifford and Robert Seidman give us the reference for "coloured signs" as "the Irish educator, philosopher, and Church of Ireland bishop of Cloyne George Berkeley (1685–1753), [who] argued in *An Essay Towards a New Theory of Vision* (Dublin, 1709) that we do not 'see' objects as such; rather, we see only colored signs and then take these to be objects" (44–45). And this brings us back, also, to the opening of "Proteus," which we looked at above, particularly the line "Shut your eyes and see." Both Stephen and Conrad are punning on what it means to actually "see." That is, each explores the operation of literal sight in relation to the other senses, but each is also concerned with a "sight" that is possible with eyes shut, a sight that must be aligned with meaning and subjectivity on some deeper, darker level that functions in opposition to the void. And to bring the meaning full circle with Joyce's secular use of transformative religious imagery, we might recall John 9:25, in which a blind man who has been cured by Jesus remarks, "One thing I do know, that though I was blind, now I see" (*New Oxford Annotated Bible*).

Both Joyce and Stephen turn away from their Catholic faith, but neither fully escapes the guilt that lingers after his departure, and it thus inevitably factors into their artistic pursuits, although it is manifested symbolically rather than literally. This is certainly evident, to name one last example, in the famous penultimate paragraph of *Portrait*: "*26 April:* Mother is putting my new secondhand clothes in order. She prays now, she says, that I may learn in my own life and away from home and friends what the heart is and what it feels. Amen. So be it. Welcome, O life! I go to encounter for the millionth time the reality of experience and to forge in the smithy of my soul the uncreated conscience of my race" (275–76). Stephen's "Amen" indicates his achievement of psychological closure, as he has finally reconciled his lack of religious faith with his faith in his ability as an artist to redeem not only himself but his entire race (the Irish). Out of the void, even in the absence of God, the artist may be redeemed.

Time, Vision, and the Artist in Virginia Woolf

Like Conrad and Joyce, Woolf harbored persistent doubts about some of the prevailing institutions and ideas of her day. She was an avowed atheist, for example, and spoke of carrying an "anti-religious bias" (Knight 28).[12] Biographical materials do show, however, that her thoughts about religion and spirituality evolved throughout her life. She became especially interested in mysticism, particularly in the latter stages of her life. She was averse to it at first, having notably criticized E. M. Forster in 1922 as "mystic, silly" (*Letters* 2:204). According to Julie Kane, however, by at least 1928 Woolf had begun to harbor more favorable views of mysticism. Kane argues that Woolf was influenced by the Theosophical Movement, which she describes as "filling the spiritual void left in the wake of Darwinism with non-Christian, non-deistic, humanistic, yet 'religious' teachings" (329). If we take the years 1922–28 as representative of a general timeline of Woolf's spiritual evolution, then *To the Lighthouse* (1927) is published at a pivotal moment.

Although Woolf maintained an interest in science throughout her life, as with religion we find in Woolf an underlying skepticism about its power to help us comprehend the true depths of human experience. That said, we do know quite a bit about Woolf's interest in science, thanks to some incisive scholarship on the subject.[13] There are suggestions that Woolf, like Joyce, was interested in the work of Albert

Einstein, as were many after his theory of relativity turned him into an international celebrity, but it is unclear whether Einstein or any other scientific principles influenced her work directly. Certainly the notion of time being relative can be found throughout Woolf's work, including in *To the Lighthouse,* as Woolf adopts the Proustian method of drawing out certain descriptions (like time passing slowly at the Ramsays' cottage), while giving others only momentary mentions (as when Mrs. Ramsay is killed within the space of a bracket). But several critics have pointed out that such examples are not particularly accurate representations of Einstein's theories, suggesting that Woolf did not necessarily engage with his work in a deep way but was more interested in what it had evoked in the popular imagination.

We should add that while Woolf's interest in the sciences is undeniable, her life and writing also indicate that she did not view science as a singular explanation of life and its mysteries. Paul Tolliver Brown notes that while "Woolf's exploration of the fuzzy boundaries between subjects and objects coincides with the quantum physical understanding of a holistic universe," she "also seems fascinated with the notion of group consciousness" (42–43), which is not in line with mainstream scientific thought but more closely aligns with her interest in mysticism. In short, what we find in Woolf, as in Conrad and Joyce, is an undeniable connection with religion and science, but one that plays an ambivalent role in her life and work and that is overshadowed by her unquestionable belief in the transcendent possibility of art, which for Woolf was in itself mystical in character. Although there are episodes in *To the Lighthouse* that approach mystical transcendence, the most significant instances are interwoven with the artistic process.

But before we attend to the mystical quality of artistic creation in Woolf, we must first locate the void that art is meant to fill. The void in Woolf, as in Joyce, is connected to absence and presence as they intersect with subjectivity. Consider the following passage near the beginning of *To the Lighthouse,* in which Lily Briscoe reflects upon Mr. Ramsay's philosophical work: "Whenever she 'thought of his work' she always saw clearly before her a large kitchen table. It was Andrew's doing. She asked him what his father's books were about. 'Subject and object and the nature of reality,' Andrew had said. And when she said Heavens, she had no notion what that meant. 'Think of a kitchen table then,' he told her, 'when you're not there'" (23). Like Stephen, Mr. Ramsay reflects upon notions of presence and absence in relation to subjective perception. The idea, however, is more obscure for Lily than for Stephen, as her sensibilities are more purely artistic. In both cases, though, the character is symbolically aligned with the idea of absence that implies the void, and each author suggests artistic creation as the exemplary response to that void. There has been much discussion of Woolf's treatment of the subject's connection to the external world, with some critics seeing Woolf deliberately engaging in her own brand of philosophical inquiry and others arguing that she sought to reject philosophical inquiry altogether.[14] As with Joyce's relationship to religion (and Woolf's, for that matter), what is clear above all is her ambivalence. Her treatment of Mr. Ramsay is, if not censorious, certainly caricatural. Like Conrad she appears, in *To the Lighthouse* at least, to be skeptical about philosophy's attempt to truly capture the complexities of human subjectivity. Like Conrad, the Woolf of *To the Lighthouse* suggests that this is a task best suited to art.

I mentioned above that for Woolf artistic creation is connected to her developing interest in mysticism. In particular, critics have seized on Woolf's statements about and depictions of ecstasy. James Naremore writes of Woolf's desire to explore new modes of representing subjectivity and stream of consciousness in ways distinct from those employed by Joyce and Dorothy Richardson. According to Naremore, she was skeptical of their particular brand of stream of consciousness, which was "'centered in a self.' It is a claustrophobic technique which, for better or worse, imprisons the reader inside a character. It is egotistic, just as all the villains in Mrs. Woolf's fiction are egotists; it never 'embraces or creates what is outside itself and beyond'" (123). Instead, Naremore argues, "it is likely that Virginia Woolf regarded the aesthetic act, whether in the form of a party or a painting, as a means of apprehending an ever-present order which is concealed from us by our everyday lives. Thus her characters 'create' so that they might 'embrace'" (123). Such a characterization would be equally suitable for Stephen Daedalus. But we should take a moment to further examine Naremore's portrait of Woolf's fiction, as it offers some more useful insight into Woolf's treatment of subjectivity, particularly as it relates to her attempt to connect the interior life of her characters with the external world. The model for this mode, according to Naremore, is Proust, but he argues that Woolf takes the method further:

> The Proustian novel shows the personality being liberated from time and space, but Mrs. Woolf takes us to the point where the personality itself becomes dissolved in communion with what is "outside . . . and beyond." In these moods, the character often has a sense of contact with "reality." But "reality" here is something apart from the social order of experience, removed from the dialectic of active personal relationships, and perhaps even inaccessible by means of language. Such intimations of "reality" are not solipsistic; the characters often say that what they feel is no different from what everyone could feel, and they are shown experiencing these moments in concert. But the experience is always brief, and it is inevitably followed by some sharp and unpleasant intrusion from what Rachel [Rachel Vinrace, the heroine in Woolf's 1915 novel *The Voyage Out*] calls the "superficial" world—like an auto backfire or a doorbell—or by a vast and peaceful darkness. (131)

Naremore does not mention Lacan—he quotes the likes of R. D. Laing's *The Divided Self* (1955) instead—but his characterization of "reality" in Woolf invites a comparison to Lacan's concept of the real. If we adopt Lacanian terminology, it is actually the real that Naremore is describing as "something apart from the social order of experience, removed from the dialectic of active personal relationships, and perhaps even inaccessible by means of language." It is in line with this reading, also, that the characters' moments of contact are brief and fleeting. But while these moments of contact with the real are terrifying in Conrad (recall Decoud), for Woolf's characters they are moments of ecstasy, as the characters sense a connection with something elemental and primal beyond (or perhaps behind) the realm of the symbolic—this being the real, or the void.

The tension between the ecstasy of order and the terror of the void builds in the early part of the novel, as the Ramsay family and their companions come together for a dinner gathering. As the evening approaches, Mrs. Ramsay is at first distraught by the failure of Paul and

Minta, along with her children Andrew and Nancy, to return from their walk, which has left her feeling "alone in the presence of her old antagonist, life" (79). Mrs. Ramsay is worried about the return of her children and their companions not only because she is concerned for their well-being but because she, like Clarissa Dalloway, thinks of herself as someone who brings people together. Thus, even after the party has returned and everyone has been seated for dinner, she laments that "nothing seemed to have merged. They all sat separate. And the whole of the effort of merging and flowing and creating rested on her" (83). The subsequent dinner scene is predominated by various characters' reflections upon order and unity.

At first Mrs. Ramsay's desire for unity goes unfulfilled: the dinner feels chaotic and contentious. Particularly disconnected and disenchanted is Mr. Bankes, who reflects that the dinner "was not worth it for him. Looking at his hand he thought that if he had been alone dinner would have been almost over now; he would have been free to work. Yes, he thought, it is a terrible waste of time" (88). He goes on to complain about "how trifling it all is, how boring it all is . . . compared with the other thing—work" (89), and we are eventually told that "the truth was that he did not enjoy family life. It was in this sort of state that one asked oneself, What does one live for? Why, one asked oneself, does one take all these pains for the human race to go on? Is it so very desirable? Are we attractive as a species? Not so very, he thought" (89). As we saw in the earlier exchange between Mr. Bankes and Lily, his mind is focused entirely on science, leaving him with a blind spot for appreciating the feelings of connection experienced in human relationships. Unlike Lily and Mrs. Ramsay, Mr. Bankes is unable to locate any sense of order or meaning within the space of social interaction. And we see the same happen with Charles Tansley, for whom "nothing had shaped itself at all. It was all in scraps and fragments" (90). Like Mr. Bankes, Tansley is led by his sterile intellectual perspective on life to turn inward: "He felt extremely, even physically, uncomfortable. He wanted somebody to give him a chance of asserting himself" (90).

Eventually, though, a feeling of unity does begin to form. Mrs. Ramsay first begins to feel a sense of connection with Augustus Carmichael when both fixate on the plate of fruit at the center of the table. Although "that was his way of looking, different from hers," nonetheless "looking together united them" (97). But the deeper sense of connection forms as the narrator reflects upon the contrast between the interior of the Ramsays' house and the world outside: "Now all the candles were lit up, and the faces on both sides of the table were brought nearer by the candlelight, and composed, as they had not been in the twilight, into a party round a table, for the night was now shut off by panes of glass, which, far from giving any accurate view of the outside world, rippled it so strangely that here, inside the room, seemed to be order and dry land; there, outside, a reflection in which things wavered and vanished, waterily" (97). The unification of the various characters during the dinner scene is aestheticized and juxtaposed to the wildness of the natural world outside. It is in the next paragraph that we are told of how "some change at once went through them all, as if this had really happened, and they were all conscious of making a party together in a hollow, on an island; had their common cause against that fluidity out there" (97). Although it is clear from the description that no particular character actually observes this aesthetic effect, let alone reflects or comments upon its symbolism, the narrative blending of the image with the scene taking place adds to the ethereal quality that pervades the novel. It also serves to remind us of Lily's painting, which is always in the back of her mind and is accordingly always looming just under the surface of the text. On several occasions throughout the night Lily thinks of how "she would move the tree rather more to the middle" (102) when she next has the opportunity to work on her painting.

The dinner scene is thus crucial in that it brings together Lily's painting and the novel's broader aesthetic and connects them with both Mrs. Ramsay's and Lily's desire for unity. As the partygoers establish a rhythm in their interactions Mrs. Ramsay finally experiences her own moment of rapture:

> Nothing need be said; nothing could be said. There it was, all round them. It partook, she felt, carefully helping Mr. Bankes to a specially tender piece, of eternity; as she had already felt about something different once before that afternoon; there is a coherence of things, a stability; something, she meant, is immune from change, and shines out (she glanced at the window with its ripple of reflected lights) in the face of the flowing, the fleeting,

the spectral, like a ruby; so that again tonight she had the feeling she had had once today, already, of peace, of rest. Of such
moments, she thought, the thing is made that endures. (105)

The operative words in the passage—*eternity, coherence, stability*—suggest the transcendental nature of human connection, along with human thought and emotion. "The thing . . . that endures," one presumes,
is memory, which lives inside the human mind. But we might also
imagine that "thing" to be Lily's painting, which captures a moment
as a memory but endures (or has the capability of enduring) beyond
the lives of the individual characters. Indeed, the section ends along
with the party, which leaves Mrs. Ramsay feeling somber: "With her
foot on the threshold she waited a moment longer in a scene which
was vanishing even as she looked, and then, as she moved and took
Minta's arm and left the room, it changed, it shaped itself differently;
it had become, she knew, giving one last look at it over her shoulder,
already the past" (111). While Mrs. Ramsay, like Clarissa Dalloway, is
ultimately successful in bringing people together, that moment of unity
is inevitably fleeting.

And like Clarissa Dalloway, although she is often dismissed by the
other characters, Mrs. Ramsay is in fact a deep thinker who on several occasions ponders the nature of existence. And given her rosy demeanor, she is surprisingly cynical in her thoughts, although she ultimately tries to persuade herself to remain positive. After she puts her
youngest child to bed in the opening scene of the novel, she laments
that "they were happier now than they would ever be again" (59) and
reflects that "oddly enough, she must admit that she felt this thing
that she called life terrible, hostile, and quick to pounce on you if you
gave it a chance" (59–60). But just as she reaches this thought she
veers back: "And then she said to herself, brandishing her sword at
life, Nonsense. They will be perfectly happy" (60). In the next section
she remarks on the relief she feels when her children have gone to bed
because "now she need not think about anybody. She could be herself,
by herself" (62). Although she cherishes this feeling of solitude, these
moments when she is not in the process of giving herself to others, she
nonetheless recognizes that "beneath it is all dark, it is all spreading, it
is unfathomably deep" (62). After she acknowledges, finally, that "this

core of darkness could go anywhere, for no one saw it" (62), her reverie
is finally broken by the stroke of the Lighthouse.

Woolf's characters in *To the Lighthouse* walk perilously along the
edge of the void. Each character's sense of self is continually met with
the threat of annihilation, which is embodied by the middle ("Time
Passes") section of the novel. Consider the following passage near the
beginning of the section, in which the world (synecdochally represented by the Ramsays' summer house) is plunged into an unsettling
darkness in the absence of any human figure that would give it shape
or definition:

> So with the lamps all put out, the moon sunk, and a thin rain
> drumming on the roof a downpouring of immense darkness be-
> gan. Nothing, it seemed, could survive the flood, the profusion
> of darkness which, creeping in at keyholes and crevices, stole
> round window blinds, came into bedrooms, swallowed up here
> a jug and basin, there a bowl of red and yellow dahlias, there the
> sharp edges and firm bulk of a chest of drawers. Not only was
> furniture confounded; there was scarcely anything left of body
> or mind by which one could say, "This is he" or "This is she."
> Sometimes a hand was raised as if to clutch something or ward
> off something, or somebody groaned, or somebody laughed
> aloud as if sharing a joke with nothingness. (125–26)

Just as Decoud melds into the natural environment in the absence of
any human companion, the absence of human figures in "Time Passes"
leaves no one, or no(thing), to make meaning of the material world. It
is as though a void opens up and swallows all light, all sound, and all
humanity—and, by extension, all language that would give definition
to these objects that now exist purely in the realm of the real. According to James Mellard, "In 'Time Passes' Woolf, indeed, insists on that
nether, dark, hidden side of the subject, the veiled origin of subjectivity, of consciousness" (*Using Lacan, Reading Fiction* 161). The humanity
of the first part of the novel is swallowed in the second, only to re-
emerge in the third in the figure of the Lighthouse, the object of desire
around which the subjectivity of each character revolves.

The Lighthouse, with its clear phallic symbolism, lies at the center of an Oedipal drama that pervades the novel. The opening scene sets this drama in motion when Mrs. Ramsay's suggestion that James might accompany the family on a trip to the Lighthouse "if it's fine tomorrow" (3) is rejected by Mr. Ramsay's insistence that "it won't be fine" (4). Woolf is explicit about James's Oedipal rage, as his response to Mr. Ramsay's symbolic "no" demonstrates: "Had there been an axe handy, or a poker, any weapon that would have gashed a hole in his father's breast and killed him, there and then, James would have seized it" (4). This opening scene is particularly noteworthy if we pass through Freud's account of the Oedipus complex to Lacan's concept of the Name-of-the-Father. In the original French, Lacan puns on *le nom du père,* which is also the father's "no" (*le "non" du père*). Read in this context, the scene takes on the double meaning of illustrating the way in which Mr. Ramsay intercepts James's desire for his mother's love (this is true of all of his children, in fact, as the narrator goes on to explain that "such were the extremes of emotion that Mr. Ramsay excited in his children's breasts by his mere presence" [4]) and also showing how Mr. Ramsay fulfills the broader role of the "symbolic father," who is identified with the figure of the law. This figure is crucial, according to Lacan, because it situates the subject within the realm of the symbolic and is thus integral to the subject's identity formation. The Lighthouse functions as an object of desire for James (what Lacan calls *objet a*); in other words, it is important not for what it embodies in itself but because James views going to the Lighthouse as a rite of passage. Mr. Ramsay's intervention is critical not only in relation to James's Oedipal desire for his mother's love but for the deeper desire that constitutes his subjectivity.

Mr. Ramsay also contrasts with James—and with Mrs. Ramsay and Lily Briscoe as well—because he expresses no discernible outwardly projected desire; he is pure ego. Consider the twofold source of his authority: it is physically manifested in his paternity and psychologically manifested in his imperious intellect. And he is not merely an authority but an authoritarian, as his belief in his own infallibility leaves no room for dissent:

> What he said was true. It was always true. He was incapable of untruth; never tampered with a fact; never altered a disagreeable word to suit the pleasure or convenience of any mortal be-

ing; least of all from his own children, who, sprung from his loins, should be aware from childhood that life is difficult; facts uncompromising; and the passage to that fabled land where our brightest hopes are extinguished, our frail barks founder in darkness (here Mr. Ramsay would straighten his back and narrow his little blue eyes upon the horizon), one that needs, above all, courage, truth, and the power to endure. (4)

Woolf's masterful use of free indirect discourse is especially suggestive in passages like this one, in which the use of third-person pronouns implies an objective point of view, but the perspective is clearly Mr. Ramsay's. It is only in the context of Mr. Ramsay's unbridled narcissism that he is "incapable of untruth." Although the novel is told almost entirely from the perspective of its characters, there is an underlying and persistent challenge to the impartial authority of "truth" and "facts." In this sense, Woolf's skepticism lines up with Conrad's; each of the novel's characters pursues some version of "truth," but those versions are distinct and are judged differently by the novel's overriding point of view.

Woolf also mirrors Conrad in supplanting scientific notions of "truth" with more abstract forms of knowledge and wisdom that resonate with emotional and artistic sensibilities rather than purely intellectual ones. While the former in Woolf's fiction tend to collapse upon themselves into gratuitous self-involvement, the latter involve engaging with the human community. Thus what disturbs Mrs. Ramsay most about her husband is his failure to look beyond his own ego: "To pursue truth with such astonishing lack of consideration for other people's feelings, to rend the thin veils of civilisation so wantonly, so brutally, was to her so horrible an outrage of human decency" (32). Mrs. Ramsay does not emerge as the ultimate heroine of the novel, but her compassion for others is in large part what makes her "ten thousand times better in every way than he [Mr. Ramsay] was" (4). Although this observation is addended by the parenthetical "(James thought)," it is obvious that the assessment extends beyond James to the authorial/ ethereal voice of the novel as well.

As Makiko Minow-Pinkney explains in *Virginia Woolf and the Problem of the Subject* (1987), Mr. and Mrs. Ramsay act not only as oppositional forces within the world of the novel but as symbolic oppositions representing the literary against the philosophical: "Mrs. Ramsay outdoes her spouse in both directions, and this is appropriate, since she represents fictionality or literature against his philosophy. Literature is more material than philosophical discourse, because it offers a sensuous 'body' while the latter aspires to the grey universality of the concept. Yet it outdoes philosophy on the latter ground too. The very concentration of the literary text allows it to concentrate a wealth and play of ideal meaning far above philosophy's stricter joining of single signifieds to unambiguous signifiers" (96). Although Mr. Ramsay is a philosopher and not a scientist, we can justly broaden the opposition to the intellectual versus the imaginative. This is not to say that there is no imaginative capacity in intellectual pursuits and no intellectual capacity in imaginative pursuits; rather, Woolf's skepticism encompasses all systems of thought (whether philosophical, scientific, or theological) that claim ownership of "truth."

Ultimately, Woolf's critique is not leveled at philosophers or scientists per se, but at those who (mis)use "facts" and "truth" as cudgels in service of their own self-interest. But while the compassionate and deferential Mrs. Ramsay thus outshines her husband in this respect, her willing submission to men as the dominant force in society prevents her from escaping the novel's judgment: "Indeed, she has the whole of the other sex under her protection; for reasons she could not explain, for their chivalry and valour, for the fact that they negotiated treaties, ruled India, controlled finance; finally for an attitude toward herself which no woman could fail to find agreeable, something trustful, child-like, reverential" (6). Even allowing for the generally more conservative views of Mrs. Ramsay's time regarding gender, one is disturbed that she seems to admire the very worst in men: their paternalistic, infantilizing treatment of women; their stranglehold on political power; their subjugation of colonized people.

Mrs. Ramsay's inability, or unwillingness, to move out from under her husband's shadow opens the door for Lily Briscoe to emerge as the true heroine of the novel and the one who most successfully embodies the imaginative values that distinguish her from the novel's other characters. From her first introduction, Lily stands in striking contrast not only to Mr. Ramsay but to Mrs. Ramsay as well, who "could not take her painting very seriously" (17): "The jacmanna was bright violet; the wall staring white. She would not have considered it honest to tamper with the bright violet and the staring white, since she saw them like that, fashionable though it was, since Mr. Paunceforte's visit, to see everything pale, elegant, semitransparent. Then beneath the colour there was the shape. She could see it all so clearly, so commandingly, when she looked: it was when she took her brush in hand that the whole thing changed" (18–19). Unlike Mr. Ramsay, Lily is committed to the authenticity of her own senses rather than a fixed notion of objective truth. And Woolf uses a very telling word in describing Lily's relationship with her senses: *honesty*. Like Conrad, Woolf (via Lily) suggests that fidelity to one's own senses—and hence one's individual notion of "truth"—is more powerful and more genuine than fidelity to so-called objective truth. Thus it is fitting that, as Julia Briggs explains in *Virginia Woolf: An Inner Life*, "the early pages of the novel locate Lily firmly outside the more traditional schools of painting, in particular the high Victorians (painters who made their own colours, according to Mrs Ramsay), and the English impressionists typified by Mr Paunceforte, who worked in 'green and grey,' with lemon-coloured sailing boats, and pink women on the beach'" (180–81). In other words, the suggestion is that Lily is a postimpressionist, obviously inspired by Woolf and her husband's involvement with postimpressionist art and artists. Mrs. Ramsay does not appear to be in tune with the new trends in painting, as is evident in her walk with Tansley when she catches a glimpse of the Lighthouse: "That was the view, she said, stopping, growing greyer-eyed, that her husband loved" (13). And then: "She paused a moment. But now, she said, artists had come here" (13). She appears bothered here on two levels: first, that the artists crowd one's view of the Lighthouse; second, that their (impressionist) representations of the Lighthouse somehow diminish it. "Since Mr. Paunceforte had been there, three years before," the passage goes on, "all the pictures were like that, she said, green and grey, with lemon-coloured sailing-boats, and pink women on the beach" (13). Although Mrs. Ramsay is more progressive than her husband, she is certainly not as progressive as Lily in her artistic sensibilities or in her appreciation for the artistic pursuit. Lily is deathly serious about her painting, even in the face of tremendous struggle to translate her vision onto the page: "Such she often felt herself—struggling against terrific odds to maintain her courage; to say: 'But this is what I see; this is what I see,' and so to clasp some miserable remnant of her vision to her breast, which a thousand forces did their best to pluck for her" (19). We are thus given a glimpse even very early on in the novel of how uniquely independent Lily is in relation to the novel's other characters.

The juxtaposition of science and art in the novel is especially evident when Mr. Bankes and Lily first discuss her painting. He is fascinated by Lily's decision to represent James sitting in Mrs. Ramsay's lap with a "triangular purple shape" (52): "Mother and child then—objects of universal veneration, and in this case the mother was famous for her beauty—might be reduced, he pondered, to a purple shadow without irreverence" (52). Like many people during this time, Mr. Bankes is trying to comprehend a postimpressionist form of art that is radically different from the more conventional forms of representation with which he would have been familiar, like the painting of cherry blossoms that hangs in his drawing room. But Mr. Bankes's aesthetic habit is not the only reason that he has difficulty comprehending Lily's method, for we are also told that "he took it [Lily's painting] scientifically in complete good faith" and that he undertakes a "scientific examination of her canvas" (53). Despite his open mind, Mr. Bankes's ability to fully appreciate what Lily is after is limited by his assumption that art can be understood from a scientific perspective. This prospect is undermined by the narrator's remark that "she could not show him what she wished to make of it, could not see it even herself without a brush in her hand" (53). In other words (for Lily, at least), there is nothing resembling the scientific method involved in her artistic process; in fact, she does not know herself what she is trying to achieve until she performs the act of painting itself.

Interestingly, though, the subject of Lily's painting does propel Mr. Bankes into "a rapture—for by what other name could one call it?" (47):

> It was love, she thought, pretending to move her canvas, distilled and filtered; love that never attempted to clutch its object; but, like the love which mathematicians bear their symbols, or poets their phrases, was meant to be spread over the world and become part of the human gain. So it was indeed. The world by all means should have shared it, could Mr. Bankes have said

why that woman pleased him so; why the sight of her reading a fairy tale to her boy had upon him precisely the same effect as the solution of a scientific problem, so that he rested in contemplation of it, and felt, as he felt when he had proved something absolute about the digestive system of plants, that barbarity was tamed, the reign of chaos subdued. (47)

Mr. Bankes's rapture is described in essentially the same artistic language that is used to describe Lily's relationship to her painting, but unlike Lily, Mr. Bankes is not able to comprehend his experience on an aesthetic level, nor does he have the ability to transpose it into an artistic endeavor that would "spread [it] over the world." Instead, he is only able to compare his experience to "the solution of a scientific problem." Thus, although late in the novel Lily does remark that "thanks to his scientific mind he understood [her philosophy toward painting]—a proof of disinterested intelligence which had pleased her and comforted her enormously" (176), Woolf nonetheless insists that Mr. Bankes can never truly comprehend the significance of Lily's vision.

This juxtaposition of the ways Lily and Mr. Bankes react to the same scene is a perfect illustration of why the artist eclipses the scientist in capturing the depth and profundity of the human condition. Unlike the scientist, who seeks to classify, the artist (Lily) undertakes her painting with only some general notion of what she wants to achieve: "It was a question, she remembered, how to connect this mass on the right hand with that on the left. She might do it by bringing the line of the branch across so; or break the vacancy in the foreground by an object (James perhaps) so. But the danger was that by doing that the unity of the whole might be broken" (53). For Lily, the ultimate goal is "unity," and all other concerns—aesthetic and otherwise—are subsumed into this singular pursuit. In that sense, the scientist and the artist do share a similar desire for creating order out of chaos, but they go about it in much different ways. This is sharply illustrated in the final sentence of the novel: "I have had my vision" (209). Lily's concluding remark embodies the elusiveness and ambiguity of the artistic process, which is much different than the scientific approach that Mr. Bankes takes toward understanding her painting. And it is different than what Mrs. Ramsay possesses as well, in spite of her thoughtfulness and depth of emotion. Lily imagines Mrs. Ramsay's intuitiveness about others as "tablets bearing sacred inscriptions" (51) that are locked away within her. But Lily does not aspire to be like Mrs. Ramsay, because "it was not knowledge but unity that she desired, not inscriptions on tablets, nothing that could be written in any language known to men, but intimacy itself, which is knowledge" (51). It is for this reason that the knowledge possessed by Mr. Ramsay, Mr. Bankes, and Charles Tansley can never reach the level of Lily's art.

In Charles Tansley's case, we find not a scientific mind but an atheistic one. In fact, he is first introduced as "the atheist Tansley" (5), which suggests that his atheism is his defining feature in the eyes of the novel's other characters. And we are quickly told, as well, that the children in particular do not much like him: "It was not his face; it was not his manners. It was his point of view. When they talked about something interesting, people, music, history, anything, even said it was a fine evening so why not sit out of doors, then what they complained of about Charles Tansley was that until he had turned the whole thing round and made it somehow reflect himself and disparage themselves he was not satisfied" (8). The novel implies a connection between Tansley's atheism and his egotism, as though the lack of belief in God leaves one susceptible to an oppositional tendency to obsess over oneself. Although the novel does not advocate for religious belief, it suggests that everyone believes in something and that what one believes is grounded in one's belief, or disbelief, in God. Indeed, even when Tansley realizes that he harbors an attraction to Mrs. Ramsay, his emotions are again couched in the language of self-involvement, as it is twice repeated that "for the first time in his life Charles Tansley felt an extraordinary pride" (14). Unlike Lily, however, Tansley has no object (other than Mrs. Ramsay) on which to project his desire. Confronted with the void, Tansley can only retreat into narcissism and bitterness.

Lily alone successfully navigates the existential challenges that the novel raises and goes on to "forge. . . . the uncreated conscience of [her] race" (*Portrait* 276). There is, of course, no referent in Woolf comparable to Joyce's concern with Irish independence, but there is nonetheless more to Woolf's depiction of the artistic process than a mere argument about art. There is, first of all, a transcendentally humanist conception of art. But there is also a deeply involved critique of traditional gender roles.[15] Lily is therefore concerned not only with her art but with the advancement of the female sex. Her art stands as a testament both to the power of women and to the power of art to confront the void of subjectivity via artistic, humanistic, and political awareness. It is, after all, the artistic act that produces the novel's greatest insight and awakening. It is thus on a number of fronts that Woolf anticipates the psychoanalytic insights of the late twentieth century.

We can see, finally, that the artistic act for Lily is many things, and above all mystical. To get a sense of the breadth of Lily's journey, let us consider the following juxtaposition of the first paragraph of the final section of the novel, "The Lighthouse," with the final paragraph of that section and of the novel:

> What does it mean then, what can it all mean? Lily Briscoe asked herself, wondering whether, since she had been left alone, it behooved her to go to the kitchen to fetch another cup of coffee or wait here. What does it mean?—a catchword that was, caught up from some book, fitting her thought loosely, for she could not, this first morning with the Ramsays, contract her feelings, could only make a phrase resound to cover the blankness of her mind until these vapours had shrunk. For really, what did she feel, come back after all these years and Mrs. Ramsay dead? Nothing, nothing—nothing that she could express at all. (145)

Taken by itself, this opening paragraph does not suggest the potential for a profound insight or awakening. On the contrary, Lily seems as far as can be from any epiphany on either an artistic or a personal level. But, in fact, it is precisely Lily's initial failure as an artist that helps illuminate the looming of the void in the novel. In her failure, Lily recognizes that any notion of wholeness or completeness is fleeting, rather than a given state of subjective stability.[16] This also emphasizes why the mystical moment of ecstasy is so important for Woolf. That is, she recognizes that because of the void, one will never achieve a permanent state of subjective wholeness but can only manage fleeting moments of ecstasy that bring one into contact with such a state—and for Woolf, like Conrad and Joyce, the act of artistic creation is the best means to achieve such moments. Thus, *To the Lighthouse* fittingly ends not with Lily achieving a permanent state of transformative psychic well-being but rather with a moment of ecstasy when she finally realizes her artistic vision:

> Quickly, as if she were recalled by something over there, she turned to her canvas. There it was—her picture. Yes, with all its greens and blues, its lines running up and across, its attempt at something. It would be hung in the attics, she thought; it would be destroyed. But what did that matter? she asked herself, taking up her brush again. She looked at the steps; they were empty; she looked at her canvas; it was blurred. With a sudden intensity, as if she saw it clear for a second, she drew a line there, in the centre. It was done; it was finished. Yes, she thought, laying down her brush in extreme fatigue, I have had my vision. (208–9)

The moment of revelation begins with the adverb *quickly,* which emphasizes that Lily's epiphany is ephemeral and risks evading her if she does not act upon it immediately. It is also striking how she recognizes that the picture is not likely to have a significant life beyond her. It will "be hung in the attics," or even "destroyed." But her recognition that the permanence of the painting is immaterial intersects with her recognition that the revelatory power of artistic creation lies not in the lasting impact of the creation but in the mystical moment when the artistic vison is realized. This final paragraph is thus particularly striking for how Lily openly recognizes and accepts the transitory nature of her "vision"; that is, her moment of revelatory artistic creation is significant in and of itself. It also shows, in the vein of Conrad and Joyce, the interrelationship between artistic creation and subjective well-being. The ecstatic consciousness of the artist grows out of the moment of creation itself, rather than the reaction of an audience, and thus achieves a sublime personal relevance that exceeds that offered by either science or religion.

Chapter 3

THE SUBJECT IN PROCESS
Repetition, Race, and Desire in *The Great Gatsby*

Although his fiction might not suggest many similarities at first glance, F. Scott Fitzgerald was a great admirer of both Conrad and Joyce. In a short entry entitled "10 Best Books I Have Read," in the April 24, 1923, edition of the *Jersey City Evening Journal*, he listed *A Portrait of the Artist as a Young Man*, writing, "Because James Joyce is to be the most profound literary influence in the next fifty years," and *Nostromo*, "The great novel of the past fifty years, as *Ulysses* is the great novel of the future" (86). He later wrote, in a public letter to the *Chicago Daily Tribune* on May 19, 1923, "I'd rather have written Conrad's *Nostromo* than any other novel" ("Confessions" 87). He spoke of his admiration for Conrad on a number of occasions, once remarking to John Galsworthy, for example, "You are one of the three living writers that I admire most in the world: you and Joseph Conrad and Anatole France!" (Mizener 132). He even attempted a sort of bizarre tribute, as related in Arthur Mizener's *The Far Side of Paradise* (1951), which describes how Fitzgerald and his friend Ring Lardner devised "a typical Fitzgerald scheme" in order to meet Conrad during his much-publicized visit to America in 1923. "They would go to the Doubledays [where Conrad was staying] and perform a dance on the lawn," Mizener explains. "Their notion was that this dance would make Conrad see he was dealing with men who knew how to turn an amusing, yet delicate and sincere, compliment and that from there everything would be clear sailing. But before Conrad could be properly charmed they found themselves thrown off the Doubleday estate for creating a drunken disturbance" (158). Alas, despite Fitzgerald's best efforts, the two writers would never meet.

Fitzgerald did, however, meet Joyce. Sylvia Beach, owner of the famous Shakespeare and Company bookstore on the Left Bank in Paris, relates the following anecdote: "Scott worshiped James Joyce, but was afraid to approach him, so Adrienne [Monnier] cooked a nice dinner and invited the Joyces, the Fitzgeralds, and André Chamson and his wife, Lucie. Scott drew a picture in my copy of *The Great Gatsby* of the guests—with Joyce seated at the table wearing a halo, Scott kneeling beside him" (116). In another of his eccentric, intoxicated moments (like his performance on the lawn outside Conrad's room) Fitzgerald apparently threatened to jump out of a fourth-floor window, allegedly leading Joyce to remark, "That young man must be mad" (116). And Herbert Gorman claims that at another of Beach's dinner parties Fitzgerald asked Joyce, "How does it feel to be a great genius, Sir?" and remarked, "I am so excited at seeing you, Sir, that I could weep" (116). The interaction, which apparently followed the threatened self-defenestration incident, made Joyce quite uncomfortable. Ironically, Fitzgerald also criticized what he called the "Joyce cult," a phrase he used to describe authors who he felt were derivative. To be fair, we certainly could not call Fitzgerald's writing derivative of Joyce's—although there is some evidence that he may have found inspiration for *This Side of Paradise* (1920) from *A Portrait of the Artist as a Young Man*.[1]

When it comes to Conrad, on the other hand, Fitzgerald's borrowing is far more obvious. We see this most clearly in the fact that *The Great Gatsby* is essentially a retelling of *Heart of Darkness*, set in urban New York City rather than the wilderness of Africa.[2] Both narratives are recounted retrospectively by narrators who are personally involved in the stories being told; both narrators journey to an unfamiliar setting and become fixated on a mysterious and charismatic figure; both have their illusions shattered but nonetheless come to paint their subjects in an undeservedly positive light; and each book ends with the narrator sustaining the illusions of the subject's loved ones in order to shield them from their moral failings. Thematically speaking, both novels also explore obsessive desire and psychological disintegration. And at least two critics have suggested that "the title *The Great Gatsby* is a deliberate allusion to a passage in . . . *Lord Jim* (1899) in which a businessman with a thick Swiss German accent tells the narrator Charles Marlow that Jim is 'of great gabasidy' [capacity]" (Martell and Vernon 57).

But Conrad's influence goes well beyond these examples. In his book *Our Conrad: Constituting American Modernity* (2010), Peter Lancelot Mallios suggests that we might go so far as to "reconsider the 'lost generation' in terms of the 'Conrad generation'" (222). Mallios is particularly interested in how American expatriate writers turned to Conrad as a model for envisioning new understandings of nationhood and national identity. He argues that "what Fitzgerald ultimately discovered [from Conrad] was a means of 'undiscovering' his country: of approaching nationhood as not an objective fact but an imaginative social construct, and anatomizing the various imaginative techniques and material interferences through which U.S. nationalist imaginings advanced and receded in the 1920s" (235). Mallios shows how Fitzgerald's understanding of nationhood plays out in his fiction, particularly in how Nostromo and Gatsby suggest ethnic otherness and blur national boundaries. But whereas Conrad explores individual subjectivities within a fictional nation as it succumbs to the influence of Anglo-American capitalism, in *Gatsby* the capitalist dream has been fully realized and the social antagonism has been almost entirely effaced by the rampant ideology of both personal and national "success." Certainly we would view *Gatsby* much differently had it been published after the stock market crash of 1929, but much of what makes *Gatsby* great is its prescient understanding of the antagonisms that lurk beneath the prevailing ideology and its deeply Conradian rendering of the individual subjects who are torn asunder by them. And we should add that Fitzgerald's interest in the intersectionality of national and personal identity is reminiscent not just of Conrad but of Joyce as well. In this respect we can begin to see how the three hold similar views about how the individual is shaped by his or her notions of nationality.

Race was the elephant in the room in Fitzgerald studies for decades, but since around the mid-1990s it has been a hot-button issue. A smattering of critics as early as the late sixties and early seventies began exploring Fitzgerald's personal racial politics, but it was the likes of Richard Lehan's *"The Great Gatsby": The Limits of Wonder* (1990), Jeffrey Louis Decker's "Gatsby's Pristine Dream: The Diminishment of the Self-Made Man in the Tribal Twenties" (1994), and Walter Benn Michaels's *Our America: Nativism, Modernism, and Pluralism* (1995) that set the stage for a thriving discourse on race in Fitzgerald's fiction, and especially *The Great Gatsby*. A major catalyst for these seminal readings was the rise of New Historicism, which led to a reexamination of the nativist ideology that proliferated following World War I. "The social climate of the early 1920's," says Decker, "specifically as it is expressed in increasingly racialized forms of nativism, creates the conditions under which Fitzgerald's narrator imagines Gatsby as a figure for America" (56). In sharpening our perception of the social, cultural, and historical conditions that *Gatsby* grows out of, New Historical influence sowed the seed for the recent outcrop of critical attention to the novel's treatment of race. This new cycle of criticism, with noteworthy contributions including Meredith Goldsmith's "White Skin, White Mask: Passing, Posing, and Performing in *The Great Gatsby*" (2003), Benjamin Schreier's "Desire's Second Act: 'Race' and *The Great Gatsby*'s Cynical Americanism" (2007), and Greg Forter's chapter on *Gatsby* in *Gender, Race, and Mourning in American Modernism* (2011), has situated the novel's racial politics in relation to prevailing contemporary critical approaches, including performance studies, queer studies, and narratology, helping to establish what is now a well-defined body of scholarship.

This chapter follows the lineage outlined above by considering *race* as a highly contested and politically charged term, with a particular focus on its role in the process of psychoanalytic development. A slew of critical studies over the past twenty or so years drawing inspiration from Frantz Fanon's engagement with Lacanian psychoanalysis have added a compelling and valuable dimension to the study of race and have considerably expanded the influence and visibility of the field.[3] Although *Gatsby* is well suited to psychoanalytic interpretations, surprisingly few critics have treated it meaningfully from this perspective. Of those who have, which would include A. B. Paulson, John Hilgart, Barbara Will, Richard Godden, and James Mellard, none have considered such interpretations alongside the issue of race.

The broad goal of this chapter is to show how *The Great Gatsby* anticipates both Lacanian understandings of subject formation and the psychoanalytic dimensions of racial identity. As a foundational principle, I adopt Kalpana Seshadri-Crooks's assertion that "Lacan's theory of subject constitution provides us with cognitive landmarks or positions by which to bring the subject of race into representation" (2). With that in mind, we might argue that a psychoanalytic reading of race in

Gatsby involves identifying the major "cognitive landmarks" in the life of the title character. These are primarily manifested in adult repetitions of childhood—and teenage—fixations. In order to make sense of these landmarks, we should begin by contextualizing Gatsby's desire in relation to Lacan's "fundamental fantasy." A reading of the novel that places Gatsby as the barred subject—the void of subjectivity—and situates him in relation to Daisy as *l'objet petit a* allows us to see Daisy not just as mere commodity fetish but rather as an object manifestation of Gatsby's primal lack, the signifying phallus. While commodity fetish is one facet of Daisy's symbolic overdetermination, the novel, through Nick, tells us quite clearly what Gatsby is *really* after: "He talked a lot about the past and I gathered that he wanted to recover something, *some idea of himself perhaps, that had gone into loving Daisy*" (117, emphasis mine). Although Nick's suggestion is frequently cited, critics tend to revert to the standard interpretation of Daisy as just another item in Gatsby's list of "things." But we ought to take Nick's proposition more seriously and pay closer attention to the construction and function of Gatsby's desire in the text.

Benjamin Schreier has made the valuable observation that *Gatsby* "enacts a deeply problematical drama of identification whereby the representational capacity of identity—ultimately *American* identity—is an object alternatively of desire and skepticism" and that the novel "ultimately lacks faith in the symbolic orders on which stable conceptions of identity rely" (155). Yet a more concentrated (re)contextualization of Lacan's symbolic order relative to race helps us bring the novel's psychodynamics into sharper focus. If we look beyond—or, perhaps more accurately, through—Daisy as commodity fetish, she may be viewed as an object manifestation of Gatsby's desire to return to the realm of the pre-symbolic, prior to the figurative castration of the Oedipal drama. Her maternal role, which is crystallized through the association of the green light at the end of her dock with the "fresh, green breast of the new world" on the final page of the novel, suggests her metaphorical role in the text as America itself. And as "Gatsby is 'borne back ceaselessly' into a Nordic past as recollected within the climate of the Tribal Twenties, when conceptions of whiteness both narrow and become a sign not of skin color but of national identity" (Decker 53), we might argue that she ultimately represents Gatsby's desire to reconstitute his

ambiguous—suggestively Jewish—racial identity in line with a fantasized Nordic American past. Adopting Walter Benn Michaels's broader
claim about Jewish identity helps us further contextualize this process:
"The point, then, of identifying as a Jew the 'stranger' who wants to
marry into your family is to identify as American the family he wants
to marry into, which is to say, to transform American identity from the
sort of thing that could be acquired (through naturalization) into the
sort of thing that had to be inherited (from one's parents). Insofar as
the family becomes the site of national identity, nationality becomes an
effect of racial identity" (8). Put in this broader context, we can read
Gatsby's renouncing of his biological family as a denial of his racially
adulterated lineage and his desire to marry Daisy as an attempt to create a family that would regenerate his socially projected ancestry as
figuratively white. This reading offers us a unique way of reconciling
the symbolic duality of Gatsby's autopoietic process and America's fantasized (and racially whitewashed) mythopoeic past.

Situating Gatsby's Desire

Just after the midway point in the novel, Nick recounts what must inevitably be considered an unverifiable account of Gatsby's adolescence:
"His parents were shiftless and unsuccessful farm people—his imagination had never really accepted them as his parents at all. The truth
was that Jay Gatsby, of West Egg, Long Island, sprang from his Pla-
tonic conception of himself. He was a son of God—a phrase which, if
it means anything, means just that—and he must be about His Father's
Business, the service of a vast, vulgar and meretricious beauty. So he
invented just the sort of Jay Gatsby that a seventeen year old boy would
be likely to invent, and to this conception he was faithful to the end"
(104). Outside of the general unreliability of both our title character
and narrator, Nick's admission that "he told it to me at a time of confusion, when I had reached the point of believing everything and nothing
about him" (107) leads us to further question the story's veracity. But
what is particularly interesting about Gatsby's account is that it holds
equal interpretive value whether it is true or not. Either his parents
actually were "shiftless and unsuccessful farm people" whom he never
really accepted or else he fabricated the account and, in doing so, refuses to accept whoever they *really* were. Nevertheless, the suggestion

that his parents either were or may have been farm people has substantial though multiple and perhaps competing implications. On the one hand, this lineage may symbolically tie Gatsby to America's earliest settlers, implying a hereditary stake in the nation's history and emphasizing his essential "Americanness." On the other, an association with itinerant immigrant farmers may imply a family lineage that could potentially be perceived as nonwhite. Gatsby's account reflects the ambiguity into which he is continually cast (and casts himself) throughout the novel, and ultimately we do not come to understand his history with any more certainty. Instead, we are confronted with the essential polysemy of the novel, which, as critics have observed, arises out of the many narrative and textual contradictions that cleave fissures in the meaning of the text.[4] But however we characterize or interpret Gatsby's family history, what matters is that he renounces it and in doing so symbolically extricates himself from the Oedipal drama and sets the stage for "an adult repetition of a childhood phenomenon"—a phrase that James Mellard uses in his essay "Oedipus against Narcissus" (55) to describe Fitzgerald's 1922 short story "Winter Dreams."

In his reading of "Winter Dreams," part of what has come to be called the "Gatsby cluster" of short stories that prefigure the novel, Mellard argues that this tale of ill-fated romance "illustrates how we may read the dialectic of desire not only in the context of oedipal authority—the Lacanian Law of the Symbolic Father—but also in that of the abjected mother residing in the semiotic *chora* Julia Kristeva posits as prior to the patriarchal order ultimately repressing it" (51). In the story, a young boy named Dexter Green, who aspires to transcend his humble upbringing and join the ranks of the upper class, falls in love with a wealthy girl named Judy Jones. Much like Gatsby, he covets her as a symbol of the wealth and status that he hopes to acquire. The narrator tells us at one point that "he wanted not association with glittering things and glittering people—he wanted the glittering things themselves" (220–21). Like *Gatsby*, the story speaks through the language of commodities, as material possessions are tantamount to social stature. Matthew J. Bruccoli describes the story as "the strongest of the Gatsby-cluster stories," explaining that "like the novel, it examines a boy whose ambitions become identified with a selfish rich girl. Indeed, Fitzgerald removed Dexter Green's response to Judy Jones's home from the magazine text and wrote it into the novel as Jay Gatsby's response to Daisy Fay's home" (introduction to "Winter Dreams" 217). By reading Dexter's desire through Lacan's account of the Oedipal plot, Mellard chronicles the eventuation of Dexter's Oedipal resolution. Like Daisy, "from the beginning Judy wears a halo of desirability because of her metonymic association with a place—and eventually, a subject—of wealth and power" (Mellard, "Oedipus against Narcissus" 58). Through the metonymy of Dexter's desire, Judy ultimately represents the symbolic phallus that Dexter lacks on account of the figurative castration of the Oedipal drama. "As a symbol of the phallus," Mellard says of Judy, "she represents something beyond desire" (66), and "as the symbol of that which the subject wants but cannot have, she invokes castration in the prohibitions of the law of the father" (67).

The Oedipal drama unfolds almost identically in *Gatsby*. The crucial difference is that while at the story's end "Dexter has truly become the postoedipal subject, has resigned himself to loss, loss not of grief or of Judy but of that which every oedipalized subject loses— the phallus" (74), Gatsby instead charges on toward the painful *jouissance*[5] that resides in possession of Daisy and is eventually punished for his transgression of the law of the Name-of-the-Father. Like Dexter's, Gatsby's desired object (Daisy) is merely one manifestation in a deeper signifying chain. And as Mellard explains, "Since the object is never attainable, both Gatsby and Dexter approach it (as do most subjects) from the side, for, in the beginning, they focus not on the woman as such, but on the accouterments of wealth with which they associate the woman and in which they display their right to her, the one who symbolizes their fantasies" (54–55).

For Gatsby, this association is formed the first time he visits Daisy's house, which Nick tells us "had amazed him—he had never been in such a beautiful house before. But what gave it an air of breathless intensity was that Daisy lived there—it was as casual a thing to her as his tent out at camp was to him. There was a ripe mystery about it" (155). Gatsby realizes, however, that as "a penniless young man without a past" (156) he will not be able to marry Daisy. As Walter Benn Michaels argues, "The real problem is that he is 'without a past' and to get Daisy he must get a past. Thus Jimmy Gatz's efforts to improve himself, which begin in the Franklin-like scheduling of his present intended to produce the perfected Gatsby of his future ('study electricity, etc.'), must themselves be transformed into efforts to reconstruct his past" (26). Put another way, "Gatsby does not want to be praised for what he is, but for what he is not" (Berman, "*The Great Gatsby* and the Twenties" 87). While Gatsby certainly wants to "reconstruct" his past, as Michaels has said, he also wants to *repeat* the past once he has revised its premises and live out the fantasy that his socially and racially muddled pedigree has prevented. Gatsby's symbolic transformation from James Gatz to Jay Gatsby has already set his desire in motion before he meets Daisy; she simply becomes its objective manifestation, or *objet a.*[6]

Lacan describes *objet a* as "something from which the subject, in order to constitute itself, has separated itself off as organ. This serves as a symbol of the lack, that is to say, of the phallus, not as such, but in so far as it is lacking. It must, therefore, be an object that is, firstly, separable and, secondly, that has some relation to the lack" (*Four Fundamental Concepts* 103). Prior to the mirror stage, the object of the child's desire is the mother; the child—who has not yet imagined him- or herself as subject(ed)—sees the mother as a physical extension of its own body. The "moment at which the mirror stage comes to an end," however, "decisively tips the whole of human knowledge [*savoir*] into being mediated by the other's desire, constitutes its objects in an abstract equivalence due to competition from other people, and turns the *I* into an apparatus to which every instinctual pressure constitutes a danger, even if it corresponds to a natural maturation process. The very normalization of this maturation is henceforth dependent in man on cultural intervention, as is exemplified by the fact that sexual object choice is dependent upon the Oedipus complex" (Lacan, *Écrits* 79). Following the mirror stage, the initial desire for the mother (Other) becomes a repressed unconscious desire for which the subject seeks substitutes, now symbolized in objects, or the "little things"—*objets petit a*—that represent the mother/Other that has been lost (Mellard, *Using Lacan* 147). While the process of subject formation is initiated in childhood, it is ongoing throughout adult life.

In adopting this Lacanian terminology, we must make a crucial differentiation between *Autre* ("Big" Other) and *autre* ("little" other). According to Lacan, the status of the Other is interminable. The subject's desire for the Other is an unending and impossible attempt to fill the void left by the loss of the mother; it is this interminability that causes the subject to seek substitutes in objects that can take virtually any form:[7] "Objet *a* can take on many different guises. It may be a certain kind of look someone gives you, the timber of someone's voice [i.e., 'full of money'], the whiteness, feel, or smell of someone's skin, the color of someone's eyes, the attitude someone manifests when he or she speaks—the list goes on and on. Whatever an individual's characteristic cause may be, it is highly specific and nothing is easily put in its place. Desire is fixated on this cause and this cause alone" (Fink, *Clinical Introduction* 52). *Objet a* produces an elusive/illusory duality since its value is not inherent but is rather a product of the metonymic process of desire, "indicating that it is the signifier-to-signifier connection that allows for the elision by which the signifier instates lack of being [*le manque de l'être*] in the object-relation, using signification's referral [*renvoi*] value to invest it with the desire aiming at the lack that it supports" (Lacan, *Écrits* 428). As Lacan famously says, desire is ultimately "caught in the rails of metonymy, eternally extending toward the *desire for something else*" (428, emphasis in original).

In order to understand Gatsby's fundamental desire to rewrite his ethnological history, we must further unpack the metonymic chain of Gatsby's desire and the process through which Daisy becomes the essential link. The key moment in this process is their first kiss: "His heart beat faster and faster as Daisy's white face came up to his own. He knew that when he kissed this girl, and forever wed his unutterable visions to her perishable breath, his mind would never romp again like the mind of God. So he waited, listening for a moment longer to the tuning fork that had been struck upon a star. Then he kissed her. At his lips' touch she blossomed for him like a flower and the incarnation was complete" (117). The ineffability of the dream—"his unutterable visions"—collides here with a very specific "object": "her perishable breath," culminating in an aptly described "incarnation" that transforms the various components of Gatsby's desire (which are joined through metonymy) into a Borromean knot that entwines each fiber of Daisy's symbolic overdetermination. Hilgart has made a similar observation: "His portrait shows Gatsby's consciousness to be so completely reified that desire's substitutional, symbolic process has become a loop, repeatedly attempting to exceed itself yet ever diverted back to the sig-

nifiers of the commodity" (99). In highlighting the process of reification, Hilgart perceptively demonstrates the way in which commodities
in the novel act as signifiers of deeper desires rather than ends in themselves. Ronald Berman recognizes this distinction as well, noting that
"the central irony developed by the novel is that our largest feelings,
love and faith, can only be directed at objects unable to contain them"
(*"The Great Gatsby" and Modern Times* 50). In turn, when Gatsby says to
Nick that "'her voice is full of money'" (127), he employs not a simile
but a direct metaphor; her voice is not *like* money, it *is* money.[8] According to Richard Godden, "Daisy's quality has a tendency to become
a quantity: how many bedrooms, how many men, what make of car?
Even as the object of Gatsby's desire is translated into 'commodity,' so
Gatsby's desire is commodified" (*Fictions of Capital* 83).

While commodification plays an integral role in the process of
Gatsby's desire, it is crucial that we recognize the role of objects in
the novel—and here I include Daisy—as mere placeholders (*objets a*)
for Gatsby's deeper desire. After all, love of objects, or even people,
always entails loss. Many objects are lost, for example, and all people
eventually die. But there is also ironically a loss at the moment of ob-
taining one's desire; for as soon as one obtains what he or she has been
desiring, the visceral power of the initial desire can never be replicated.
This is why there is such a tragic tinge to the passage above, in the fact
that Gatsby's "mind would never romp again like the mind of God." As
Marcel Proust tells us, the most powerful love is unrequited love.

Desire and Repetition

The first kiss not only marks the moment when Daisy as commodity
fetish and as object manifestation of Gatsby's preexisting desire intersect but also closely precedes the moment when Gatsby symbolically
reinitiates the Oedipal drama. Just before describing the first kiss, Nick
recounts the following: "Out of the corner of his eye Gatsby saw that
the blocks of the sidewalk really formed a ladder and mounted to a
secret place above the trees—he could climb to it, if he climbed alone,
and once there he could suck on the pap of life, gulp down the incomparable milk of wonder" (117). In his Freudian reading, A. B. Paulson
glosses this passage by arguing that "Gatsby must 'climb' alone because
Fitzgerald's metaphor—despite its conventionality—is true to the psy-

chic realities of nursing infants and mothers' breasts; at some deep level Gatsby pursues a source of nourishment in which the self and the world merge, fuse, and expand to colossal proportions" (313). Bruce Fink can help us take this analysis one step further: he explains that "when Freud says in the *Three Essays on the Theory of Sexuality* that '[t] he finding of an object is in fact a refinding of it,' he is referring to the fact that object-choice after the latency period repeats the child's first object-choice: the breast. Here too, an initially encountered object is found anew at some later point in time" (*Lacanian Subject* 94).

Read in the context of Freud's insights on repetition, Gatsby's encounters with Daisy emerge as repetitions of his childhood relationship with his mother. The maternal language that appears throughout the novel—of which more will be said later—suggests Daisy as a substitute for the biological mother whom Gatsby has forsaken, and who is conspicuously absent from the text. When, in the final lines of the novel, the green light at the end of Daisy's dock is symbolically linked to the "fresh, green breast of the new world" (189), the incarnation that becomes "complete" with the first kiss is now wholly consummated in the novel's broader symbolic configuration. The final page of the novel thus underscores repetition as its textual, thematic, and symbolic axis. Gatsby's attempt to repeat his past with Daisy is finally equated with a collective cultural desire to relive a fantasized American past when "man must have held his breath in the presence of this continent, compelled into an aesthetic contemplation he neither understood nor desired, face to face for the last time in history with something commensurate to his capacity for wonder" (189). While not understood or desired at the time—when the future had not been foreseen—it is the nostalgia to recover the (imagined) vanished moment that underlies the compulsion to repeat.

In order to make sense of this compulsion, it will be useful here to review Freud's identification of four types of repetitive behavior in *Beyond the Pleasure Principle*. The first involves "dreams occurring in traumatic neuroses [that] have the characteristic of repeatedly bringing the patient back into the situation of his accident, a situation from which he wakes up in another fright" (11). The second is the *fort/da* (gone/there) game played by children, in which the child throws a toy from its crib, reels it back in, and then repeats the process: "The interpretation of the game was related to the child's great cultural achieve-ment—the instinctual renunciation (that is, the renunciation of in-stinctual satisfaction) which he had made in allowing his mother to go away without protesting. He compensated himself for this, as it were, by himself staging the disappearance and return of the objects within his reach" (14). The third type of behavior occurs when an analysand is exploring his or her repressed past and "is obliged to *repeat* the re-pressed material as a contemporary experience instead of, as the physi-cian would prefer to see, *remembering* it as something belonging to the past" (19). The fourth is a more generalized "compulsion of destiny," in which the subject possesses "an essential character-trait which al-ways remains the same and which is compelled to find expression in a repetition of the same experiences" (23–24). Freud concludes that "if we take into account observations such as these . . . we shall find cour-age to assume that there really does exist in the mind a compulsion to repeat which overrides the pleasure principle" (24). Because the rep-etition compulsion acts counter to the pleasure principle, Freud goes on to explain, it must therefore represent something "more primitive, more elementary, more instinctual than the pleasure principle which it over-rides" (25). This compulsion to act against the pleasure principle underlies Derrida's proclamation in *Writing and Difference* (1967) that "what is tragic is not the impossibility but the necessity of repetition" (248). In other words—as we see in the novel—repetition acts through language as it does through desire.

Gatsby's tragedy, in both a classical and a psychological sense, is en-capsulated in his "incredulous" response to Nick's suggestion that one cannot repeat the past: "Can't repeat the past? . . . Why of course you can!'" (116). Gatsby epitomizes the repetition compulsion; he attempts to relive his affair with Daisy "as a contemporary experience instead of . . . *remembering* it as something belonging to the past." And as we have seen, Daisy is only an object manifestation of Gatsby's deeper de-sire; because it is not Daisy, but a reconstituted version of *himself* that he seeks, Gatsby's dream inevitably "fails" shortly after he and Daisy reunite: "He had passed visibly through two states and was entering upon a third. After his embarrassment and his unreasoning joy he was consumed with wonder at her presence. He had been full of the idea so long, dreamed it right through to the end, waited with his teeth set, so to speak, at an inconceivable pitch of intensity. Now, in the reaction, he was running down like an overwound clock" (97). The image of the overwound clock aptly describes the inevitable failure of the dream to live up to the reality and brings us back to the crucial role of repetition—both psychological and temporal—in the novel, back to the "orgastic future" that has always already eluded us. As we saw above, Gatsby's vision of Daisy cannot possibly live up to the image of her that he has constructed. "In invoking the Oedipus complex," Mellard says of "Winter Dreams," "when Judy situates Dexter within the dialectic of desire, she places him between the polarities of desire and *jouissance*, alienation and separation, Oedipus and Narcissus" ("Oedipus against Narcissus" 62). The same could be said of Gatsby, whose reunion with Daisy sends him symbolically "beyond the pleasure principle" into the realm of *jouissance*, which functions as a surplus desire not unlike Marx's surplus value and is experienced as a form of pain.

The Lacanian concept of *jouissance* offers us a particularly illuminating way of interpreting Gatsby's desire. One especially useful way of thinking about *jouissance* comes from Slavoj Žižek's *The Sublime Object of Ideology*, in which he describes the *Titanic* as "a Thing in the Lacanian sense: the material leftover, the materialization of the terrifying, impossible *jouissance*. By looking at the wreck we gain an insight into the forbidden domain, into a space that should be left unseen: visible fragments are a kind of coagulated remnant of the liquid flux of *jouissance*, a kind of petrified forest of enjoyment" (71). If we appropriate Žižek's metaphor in respect to Gatsby's desire, we might read Daisy in place of the *Titanic*. Because she cannot possibly live up to her symbolic overdetermination, she comes to represent not Gatsby's dream—which requires the whitewashing of his racial past—but the impossibility of its realization. Lacan tells us that we can never actually "obtain" the object of desire; we can only circle around it in a never-ending repetition. What is perhaps most tragic in the novel—if we lend some credence to Nick's insight—is that Gatsby appears to realize this fact. Just after the reunion with Daisy, Nick makes the following observation: "Possibly it had occurred to him that the colossal significance of that light had now vanished forever. Compared to the great distance that had separated him from Daisy it had seemed very near to her, almost touching her. It seemed as close as a star to the moon. Now it was again a green light on a dock. His count of enchanted objects had diminished by one" (98). The light at the end of the dock serves as a perfect metaphor here, bringing Daisy closer to Gatsby in a process of optical magnification; because the light is physically close but also "as close as a star to the moon," the description fittingly analogizes Gatsby's relationship to his dream: in one sense it feels as close as an object across a bay, but from another perspective the distance is unfathomable. In (re)obtaining Daisy, Gatsby appears to ironically recognize what he has lost. This is why psychoanalysis often tells us that we do not actually want to obtain that which we desire; our most profound enjoyment comes from desire itself. The great tragedy of Gatsby's achievement is that even as he attempts to relive his past with Daisy, he realizes that his compulsion to repeat has already taken him beyond the pleasure principle and into the realm of pain and Oedipal punishment.

We should add that Žižek's *Titanic* metaphor proves useful in relation to other aspects of the novel as well, and thus the lesson about the proximity of pain to desire is not confined to Gatsby but is in fact wide reaching. Consider, as another example, Nick's description of the valley of ashes: "About half way between West Egg and New York the motor-road hastily joins the railroad and runs beside it for a quarter of a mile so as to shrink away from a certain desolate area of land. This is a valley of ashes—a fantastic farm where ashes grow like wheat into ridges and hills and grotesque gardens, where ashes take the forms of houses and chimneys and rising smoke and finally, with a transcendent effort, of men who move dimly and already crumbling through the powdery air" (27). Nick's Bosch-like imagery recalls Žižek's description of the *Titanic's* wreckage. The valley rests in a liminal zone between the novel's two geographical poles, Manhattan and Long Island, and serves as a repository for the excreta of society's unconscious, "the material leftover" that Žižek describes above. The imagery of "a fantastic farm" suggests an inversion of America's idealized pastoral past. It also calls to mind Žižek's (re)formulation of the Thing (*das Ding*), a concept used by Freud and later Lacan, as "the Space (the sacred/forbidden zone) in which the gap between the Symbolic and the Real is closed, i.e. in which, to put it somewhat bluntly, our desires are directly materialized (or, to put it in the precise terms of Kant's transcendental idealism, the Zone in which our intuition becomes directly productive—a state of things which, according to Kant, characterizes only infinite divine Reason)" ("Thing from Inner Space" 221). For Žižek, the Thing is an "Id-Machine," "a mechanism that directly materializes our unacknowledged fantasies" (221). This characterization lays the groundwork for a Lacanian analysis of the valley of ashes. The Thing, like Marx's surplus-value and Lacan's *jouissance,* represents a surplus-desire, a desire that has gone "beyond the pleasure principle and into the realm of pain," as does Gatsby's desire for Daisy.

While Žižek's *Titanic* serves "as a condensed, metaphorical representation of the approaching catastrophe of European civilization itself" (*Sublime Object of Ideology* 70), Fitzgerald's valley of ashes can be said to serve the same function in relation to American civilization as manifested in the views of Tom and other nativists of the time. "'Civilization's going to pieces,'" Tom says in the first chapter of the novel, before referencing "The Rise of the Coloured Empires." The valley of ashes thus becomes a symbolic reservoir for society's abject, a fact that is compounded by the eyes of Doctor T. J. Eckleburg, which "look out of no face but, instead, from a pair of enormous yellow spectacles which pass over a nonexistent nose" and "brood on over the solemn dumping ground" (27–28). Spectral and uncanny, the eyes surveil and judge those living beneath. Moreover, it is overlooking the valley where the novel's most notable confrontation with race occurs as Nick and Gatsby cross over the Queensboro Bridge:

> As we crossed Blackwells Island a limousine passed us, in which sat three modish Negroes, two bucks and a girl. I laughed aloud as the yolks of their eyeballs rolled toward us in haughty rivalry.
>
> "Anything can happen now that we've slid over this bridge," I thought; "anything at all. . . ." Even Gatsby could happen, without any particular wonder. (73)

Greg Forter observes that "the sight of racial inversion gives rise to the thought that 'Anything can happen now'; that thought then produces the reflection that 'Even Gatsby could happen.' Such a sequence gives an explicitly racial cast to the social fluidity and sense of possibility that Gatsby exploits in his self-making" (47). As in his descriptions of Meyer Wolfsheim, which exploit anti-Semitic stereotypes of wealth, physiognomy, and crime, Nick is an active participant in constructing the racial caricatures that the novel perpetuates. Broadly speaking, the valley is figuratively racialized through Nick's account, as crossing through it comes to suggest the prospect (and fear) of miscegenation. This fear, particularly on Tom's part, erupts when the characters again make the crossing in chapter 7, where the novel's final tragic events are set in motion and where the violent scene in the hotel room takes us back once again to the Oedipal conflict.

Resolution of the Oedipal Conflict

Purposively reading Gatsby's desire through Lacan's fundamental fantasy means that we must account for the moment in the novel when Gatsby's symbolic castration first takes place. This occurs when his initial affair with Daisy is interrupted by his deployment and he is subsequently usurped by Tom, who marries Daisy in his absence. Nick's first description of Tom supports a reading of his role in the novel as a symbolic father: "Two shining, arrogant eyes had established dominance over his face and gave him the appearance of always leaning aggressively forward. Not even the effeminate swank of his riding clothes could hide the enormous power of that body—he seemed to fill those glistening boots until he strained the top lacing and you could see a great pack of muscle shifting when his shoulder moved under his thin coat. It was a body capable of enormous leverage—a cruel body" (11). Whereas Gatsby's foppish ways of dressing and speaking are meant to suggest effeminacy, Tom's muscular body shatters "the effeminate swank of his riding clothes" and highlights both a body and a demeanor that are driven by aggressivity and cruelty. In the subsequent paragraph, Nick observes in his voice "a touch of paternal contempt" (11). As a symbolic father figure, Tom stands in the way not only of Gatsby's desire for Daisy but of her desire for—or recognition of—Gatsby, which is crucial to his achieving his dream. Tom's nativist views put him squarely in opposition to Gatsby, whom he addresses repeatedly in racially charged terms. "For Tom, as for Stoddard," Michaels explains, "Gatsby (né Gatz, with his Wolfsheim 'gonnegtion') isn't quite white, and Tom's identification of him as in some sense black suggests the power of the expanded notion of the alien. Gatsby's love for Daisy seems to Tom the expression of something like the impulse to miscegenation" (25). As the novel's figurative paternal figure, Tom assumes the role of guardian against the threat that white, female innocence will be defiled by the ethnic other.

In that sense, both Gatsby and Tom rely on Daisy as a talisman in relation to which their sense of (ethnic) self is constructed. The conflict between the men thus takes on a broader significance as a Hegelian battle for recognition in which each man seeks to not only possess Daisy but annihilate the other. The conflict between the men reaches its climax in the hotel-room altercation in which Gatsby insists that Daisy never loved Tom: "Your wife doesn't love you. . . . She's never loved you. She loves me. . . . She only married you because I was poor and she was tired of waiting for me. It was a terrible mistake, but in her heart she never loved anyone but me!" (137). In their battle for recognition, Gatsby wishes to symbolically kill Tom—the father figure—so that he can decisively possess Daisy; it is not until he has eliminated the symbolic influence of the father figure that Daisy's desire for him will be pure and uncorrupted. And it is by proximity to and ownership of Daisy that Gatsby can become fully white. Instead, the humiliating rejection that he suffers when Daisy refuses to declare that she never loved Tom—"'Oh, you want too much!' she cried to Gatsby. 'I love you now—isn't that enough?'" (140)— amounts to another symbolic castration and a further splintering of Gatsby's dream, as she ironically exclaims that she "can't help what's past" (140). It is not enough for Gatsby that Daisy loves him *now;* until the castration is undone and Gatsby's sense of (white) manhood is restored his dream will remain incomplete. It is thus a crucial but too often overlooked fact of the novel that if winning back Daisy's love is truly Gatsby's goal, then he achieves victory when Daisy first tells Tom that she loves Gatsby and plans to leave her marriage. If Gatsby were to simply leave with Daisy at this moment, then she would be his; it is only when she realizes that he "want[s] too much" that Gatsby's plan—and with it his persona—begins to shatter ("Jay Gatsby had broken up like glass against Tom's hard malice" [148]).

The deeper symbolic and psychological consequences of Gatsby's Oedipal desire then begin to unfold when Daisy kills Myrtle Wilson with Gatsby's car. Paulson's analysis of Freudian splitting in the novel has been valuable here in drawing the symbolic connection between

Daisy and Myrtle that fits her into the Oedipal reading as well. "Here," Paulson explains, "the novel's contrary movement—toward synthesis—appears as a function of androgeny [sic]; that is, the mythical dream of the hermaphroditic being. . . . The image of the 'fresh green breast' makes a good beginning because I see both androgeny [sic] and splitting as grounded in a special relationship to the mother" (312). My sense is that the importance of the mother figure in the text is twofold. First, as Paulson argues, "mothers are conspicuous by their very absence" (312). Daisy is the only mother in the novel, but she can be described at best as disinterested. Aside from the opening scene of the novel, in which she briefly parades her daughter in front of Nick before shuffling her away, the child does not appear again, and one otherwise would not even notice that Daisy has a child at all. At the same time, it is arguably all the more significant that Daisy is the only mother in the novel, for it seems a natural extension to symbolically tie her to Myrtle's physical violation, with her breast "swinging loose like a flap" (145). Together with the breast imagery of the "incomparable milk of wonder" that Gatsby imagines consuming when he first kisses Daisy and the "fresh, green breast of the new world" that Nick contemplates at the end of the novel, Myrtle's mutilated breast symbolizes the death of Gatsby's dream. And by extension, if we accept the symbolic tie that links Daisy and Myrtle, the mutilated breast also symbolizes the corruption of the promise once carried by the American landscape as it has been embodied in our collective cultural fantasies. Once again recalling Žižek's *Titanic*, Myrtle's disfigured body may also serve as "the material leftover, the materialization of the terrifying, impossible *jouissance*" that has been Gatsby's relationship with Daisy. Like the *Titanic*, Myrtle's body becomes a spectacle, first lying mutilated in the street and then splayed out on a table in Wilson's garage. The novel's climactic scene invests the valley of ashes with its full significance, as "a condensed, metaphorical representation of the approaching catastrophe of [American] civilization," and sets in motion the events that lead to Gatsby's ultimate punishment, inflicted by Wilson but precipitated by Tom.

"It eluded us then . . ."

The final lines of *The Great Gatsby* unify its themes with an overwrought precision rivaled by few short passages in fiction. Although they have accordingly been the subject of much discussion, they contain a striking temporal irregularity that has gone unmentioned in previous criticism of the novel: "Gatsby believed in the green light, the orgastic future that year by year recedes before us. It eluded us then, but that's no matter—" (189). If we are to assume that the referent of the pronoun *It* that begins the second sentence is "the orgastic future that year by year recedes before us," then we are encountering a temporal disjunction in the text—what Thomas Pendleton has called a "chronological incoherence" (12). The text is telling us that "It" ("the orgastic future") "eluded us *then*," and the context in which *then* is used suggests that the elusion occurred in the past. But how can "the orgastic future *that year by year recedes before us*"—in a continual, ongoing action—have eluded us *then,* in the completed past? This paradox produces the polysemous doubling elusion/illusion mentioned above. The orgastic future eludes us precisely because it is illusory. And just as the orgastic future eludes us, so too does the certainty of meaning.

We can view this temporal disjunction as what Derrida calls an *aporia,* a paradox or contradiction that threatens to unravel the meaning of the text. And yet this contradiction also *produces* meaning in the final lines of the novel. It is through this temporal paradox that the meaning of the text is disseminated; or, perhaps more acutely stated, the literal meaning is dislocated, allowing the symbolic to finally emerge. The final sentence of the book, "So we beat on, boats against the current, borne back ceaselessly into the past" (189), offers an inviting analogy to the concept of the floating signifier developed by Lévi-Strauss and later adopted by Lacan. Each individual word in a sentence acts as a floating signifier because its meaning cannot be fully known or comprehended until the sentence is completed and the broader meaning crystallizes.

This brings us back to the connection between subjectivity, language, and temporality that pervades the novel. I suggest that we approach the temporal disjunction and linguistic uncertainty of the final lines through Lacan's notion of the future anterior: "I identify myself in language, but only by losing myself in it as an object. What is realized in my history is neither the past definite as what was, since it is no more, nor even the perfect as what has been in what I am, but the future anterior as what I will have been, given what I am in the process of becoming" (*Écrits* 247). Lacan suggests that the subject must con-

tinually reinvent itself by anticipating what it will become in a future
moment of psychological harmony. But this unified conception of self
can only be recognized retrospectively, which sends the subject into
a repetitive rummaging of the past. It is this compulsion to repeat,
or more deeply to reconstitute his past and rewrite his questionable
lineage as racial outsider, that plunges Gatsby back into the Oedipal
drama that ultimately punishes him for transgressing not only the law
of the Name-of-the-Father but the racial boundaries that have been
erected against him.

Chapter 4

SPATIALIZED SUBJECTIVITY

Los Angeles and the Post/Modern Subject
in Fitzgerald, West, and Huxley

Scattered among these masquerades were people of a different type. Their
clothing was somber and badly cut, bought from mail order houses. While the
others moved rapidly, darting into stores and cocktail bars, they loitered on the
corners or stood with their backs to the shop windows and stared at everyone
who passed. When their stare was returned, their eyes filled with hatred. At
this time Tod knew very little about them except that they had come to California to die.

—NATHANAEL WEST, *The Day of the Locust*

All of them had come to California as to a promised land; and California had
already reduced them to a condition of wandering peonage and was fast transforming them into Untouchables.

—ALDOUS HUXLEY, *After Many a Summer Dies the Swan*

I seem to be a little mixed up. This doesn't seem to be quite the girl who came
out to California for a new life.

—KATHLEEN MOORE, from F. Scott Fitzgerald's *The Love of the Last Tycoon*

After *The Great Gatsby* received a lukewarm response from readers and
critics following its publication in April 1925, Fitzgerald did not publish another novel until *Tender Is the Night* in 1934. He was deeply de-
pressed that *Gatsby* did not catapult his career as he had hoped, and
the ensuing years were some of the worst of his life. Although he began
writing his new novel immediately after *Gatsby*'s publication, he strug-
gled continually. While he wrote several chapters in 1925 and 1926
that would eventually be revised and incorporated into *Tender*, he was
unable to complete the book at the time. In 1927, after he returned

with his family from Europe, Fitzgerald moved to Hollywood and had
his first stint as a writer for motion pictures. His time there provided
him with further ideas for *Tender,* particularly the inspiration for Rose-
mary Hoyt in actress Lois Moran. "Fitzgerald was fascinated by Moran," writes Arthur Mizener, "and she by him" (204). The Fitzgeralds'
short stay in Hollywood would be defined more, however, by "a whirl
of parties, night clubs, and practical jokes" (204) than by Scott's rejected script for *Lipstick.* The Fitzgeralds left Hollywood as soon as the
script was finished, but Scott would return several times and eventually spend most of the last four years of his life there. But Hollywood
never quite seemed a natural fit for Fitzgerald. One friend, the film-
maker Billy Wilder, once said that "he made me think of a great sculp-
tor who is hired to do a plumbing job. He did not know how to connect
the fucking pipes so the water would flow" (qtd. in Zolotow 72).

His final trip came about as a result of serious financial hardship
in the early and mid-1930s. Mizener writes that "ever since he had got
into financial straits, Fitzgerald had thought of trying to get to Hollywood again. During 1936 he had worked to find a job there. . . . His
income reached a new low in 1936 ($10,180) and would have fallen to
half of that in 1937 had he not gone to Hollywood" (270). This was in
addition to his massive debts, which "amounted, according to his own
estimate, to something like $40,000 at the time" (272). Fortunately,
those final years in Hollywood would prove more successful, and his
income increased considerably. Much of the money came from his pro-
lific short-story writing, but he enjoyed more success as a screenwriter
as well. Along with this financial success, according to Mizener, "he
was in love with someone in Hollywood, really in love for the first time
since his feeling for Zelda had, with separation and time [Zelda was
institutionalized in North Carolina], become a memory rather than a
fact. The best evidence there will ever be of how he felt is the story of
Stahr and Kathleen in *The Last Tycoon*" (275). Indeed, *The Love of the
Last Tycoon*—which critics now agree was Fitzgerald's preferred title—
had the potential to equal the best writing he had done in his career,
but a lifetime of alcoholism and generally self-destructive behavior
caught up to him and he died before he could complete the novel.

Fitzgerald was one of many celebrated American novelists who
tried their hand as screenwriters in Hollywood in the first half of the

twentieth century. William Faulkner, Raymond Chandler, John Steinbeck, Dalton Trumbo, and Nathanael West all wrote for the movies,
mostly because it paid better than writing fiction. A fair share of European and British writers made the move to Hollywood as well, including Thomas Mann, Bertolt Brecht, and Aldous Huxley, who ar-
rived in 1937, around the time when Fitzgerald made his final return.
As it happens, while the birthplaces of Fitzgerald, West, and Huxley
were geographically and culturally distinct from one another—St. Paul,
Minnesota, New York City, and Surrey, England, respectively—they all
died in California: Fitzgerald in Hollywood on December 21, 1940, of
a heart attack, West the very next day with his wife in an automobile
accident outside El Centro while returning from a hunting trip in Mexico, and Huxley in Los Angeles in 1963.[1] I call attention to this fact not
because it is particularly significant in itself but because it illustrates
a long-standing propensity for assigning California, and Hollywood in
particular, a symbolic weight as American's final frontier. We might
think about the epigraph from West above, particularly the remark
about people who "had come to California to die," as a representative
illustration for the many writers who came to California in the first
half of the twentieth century as a last resort and for those who came in
search of new opportunities but instead became disenchanted.

But I do not simply wish to make a point about California. Rather,
in focusing on these three modernist writers,[2] I would like to redirect
what has been a common focus in literary and cultural studies on California—and Los Angeles in particular—as an archetypal *post*modern
locale and ask instead what it might tell us about the symbolic "death"
of modernism, particularly as it relates to notions of subjectivity. Each
of the three novels that make up this chapter—*The Day of the Locust*
(1939), *After Many a Summer Dies the Swan* (1939), and *The Love of the
Last Tycoon* (1941)[3]—were published in the waning years of the modernist period as it is commonly conceived. Locating an "endpoint" to
modernism is, as I have shown, a highly contentious task. For the sake
of convenience, perhaps, the most commonly accepted year is 1945,
when World War II comes to an end. There is also some literary justification for choosing the year 1939, as it saw the publication of James
Joyce's *Finnegans Wake*, after which for many modernism as such could
no longer exist. Such specific lines of demarcation have contributed to

the notion of a postmodern "divide." Andreas Huyssen, one of the most   109

SPATIALIZED SUBJECTIVITY
notable critics to take up this notion, adopts mass culture as a central
concern:

> Mass culture indeed seems to be the repressed other of modern-
> ism, the family ghost rumbling in the cellar. Modernism, on the
> other hand, often chided by the left as the elitist, arrogant and
> mystifying mater-code of bourgeois culture while demonized by
> the right as the Agent Orange of natural social cohesion, is the
> straw man desperately needed by the system to provide an aura
> of popular legitimation for the blessings of the culture industry.
> Or, to put it differently, as modernism hides its envy for the
> broad appeal of mass culture behind a screen of condescension
> and contempt, mass culture, saddled as it is with pangs of guilt,
> yearns for the dignity of serious culture which forever eludes
> it. (16–17)

But like Hassan's and McHale's, Huyssen's attempt to draw a dividing
line between modernism and postmodernism is problematic on account of the flawed assumptions he makes about modernism. While
modernism surely had its share of elitists, more recent studies have
shown that modernist writers and artists engaged with popular and
mass culture far more, and to a more significant degree, than has been
previously recognized.[4] That these three novels are set in and around
Hollywood places them at the hub of mass culture in America, or perhaps even worldwide, in the late 1930s. West's and Fitzgerald's novels,
in particular, are steeped in popular and mass culture in ways that were
in fact far more common to modernist writers than critics like Huyssen
have allowed.

Much of the popular- and mass-culture mood in these novels comes
through their depiction of Hollywood in the 1930s and the political
climate of the film industry. In his book *Hollywood Modernism* (2001),
Saverio Giovacchini insists upon "the necessity of recasting the history
of the Hollywood community and its cinema from the 1930s to the end
of World War II within the cultural context of an increasingly politi-
cized modernism. A modernism that was concerned with the necessity to open up its message to the masses insofar as it was increasingly

aware that the work of the previous generation of modernists had been hampered by the narrowness, elitism, and overall fragmentation of its audience" (5). In other words, the appeal of each of these three novels to mass culture represents a gesture that has typically been associated with the postmodern and does not do justice to the extent to which these late modernist writers sought to contextualize their fiction alongside contemporary popular culture.

It is for reasons like these that critics have increasingly come to view modernism and postmodernism less as divided, more as continuous with one another. Given that Los Angeles has long been associated with so many different elements of postmodernism, it has conventionally been seen as a fault line that runs through the postmodern divide. This may be a useful metaphor, but it is not very accurate. Instead, we ought to view the city as a place where modernism and postmodernism come together and intermix. The novels taken up in this chapter challenge the classic view of Los Angeles as postmodern city by showing how many of the elements that critics have used in justifying that moniker, like the city's geographical, architectural, and cultural peculiarities, are in fact pre–World War II phenomena. These novels cross Huyssen's great divide and transcend Hassan's columns, showing how pre–World War II Los Angeles produces new ways of thinking about subjectivity that have been so commonly and casually associated with postmodernism.

At the turn of the twentieth century, the population of Los Angeles was 102,479, which was itself a stretch on the city's resources at the time and made it the thirty-sixth most populous city in the United States. By 1910 it was the nation's seventeenth most populous city, with 319,198 residents. In 1920 it became the tenth largest city, with a total population of 576,673, and by 1930 that number had ballooned to 1,238,048 and Los Angeles was suddenly the fifth most populous city in the country (United States Census Bureau). While urban metropolises like New York were short on space and had to be built up vertically, Los Angeles sprawled out ever further from the Pacific Ocean and did not, like other major cities, maintain a discernible "center." This chapter argues that the city's geographical decenteredness intersects with the individual subjectivities that inhabit it in the novels of West, Fitzgerald, and Huxley. Consequently, in each of the three novels discussed in this chapter, Los Angeles is represented as "the end of the road," an ideological wasteland whose inhabitants tragically and endlessly attempt to remake themselves in the image of their collective cultural fantasies.[5] The subject in each of these novels is pushed to both a geographical edge, where the American frontier is driven up against the Pacific Ocean, and to the psychological edge of sanity, where the self violently fractures. These novels collectively invite a critical reevaluation of the post/modern subject and offer a potentially fruitful new avenue of investigation in the study of modernist fiction.

Los Angeles: Post/Modern City

Many postmodern theorists have turned to Los Angeles as a paradigmatic example of the postmodern city. Jean Baudrillard writes that "there is nothing to match flying over Los Angeles by night. A sort of luminous, geometric, incandescent immensity stretching as far as the eye can see, bursting out from the cracks in the clouds. Only Hieronymus Bosch's hell can match this inferno effect" (*America* 51). Edward Soja, in the words of Casey Shoop, "effects what is perhaps the ultimate consolidation of the many postmodern encounters with Los Angeles when he characterizes the city in Borgesian terms as the 'Aleph': Los Angeles becomes the space that contains all spaces" (206). Rachel Adams even suggests that we look *beyond* the postmodern, asking, "If Los Angeles is the city that taught us how to be postmodern, might it also be the place where we begin to imagine what comes after?" (248). And the title alone of Norman M. Klein's quintessential *The History of Forgetting: Los Angeles and the Erasure of Memory* (1997) reflects the continually adapted and persistent notion that Los Angeles is a city "without a past." These and other examples reinforce Fredric Jameson's alignment of postmodernism with the "weakening of historicity, both in our relationship to public History and in the new forms of our private temporality" (*Postmodernism* 6). This view of Los Angeles as postmodern seems fitting for a number of reasons, one of the most apparent being its patchwork of disparate architectural styles. Jameson observes that "it is in the realm of architecture . . . that modifications in aesthetic production are most dramatically visible, and that their theoretical problems have been most centrally raised and articulated" (2), and, as he goes on to explain, his own conception of postmodernism grows largely out of architectural debates. These "modifications in aesthetic production" are related to the evolving demands of industrial capitalism and the evolution of humanity's connection to space, which in turn develops alongside the changing aesthetics of the post–World War II cultural landscape.

One prominent feature of greater Los Angeles that has been commonly remarked upon is its endless variety of building styles. These various styles did not, as one might suspect, emerge after World War II, when postmodern architectural styles first became popular, but much earlier. A 2008 draft of the La Fayette Square Preservation Plan developed by the City of Los Angeles Planning Department characterizes the architecture of the city *between* the world wars (*not* post–World War II) as follows:

> The period between the World Wars was one of intense building activity in Los Angeles, and a wide range of revival styles were built in the area during this period. The Eclectic Revival styles popular in Los Angeles between the First and Second World Wars include the Colonial Revival, Dutch Colonial Revival, Spanish Colonial Revival, Mission Revival, French Eclectic, Chateauesque, English and Tudor Revival, Italian Renaissance Revival, Mediterranean Revival, Neoclassical Revival, Egyptian Revival, Monterey and Hispano-Moresque styles. The Craftsman and Craftsman Bungalow styles continued to develop as popular styles through this period. Many of these styles were popular both as residential and commercial styles, with a few, particularly the Egyptian Revival and Chateauesque styles, being particularly popular for use in small and large scale apartment buildings. (18)

This litany of architectural styles anticipates the ironic relationship to history described by Jameson and suggests the rejection of the "new" in favor of a replicative mining of past styles in an almost parodic fashion. And while one might insist that such heterogeneous building is a reflection of high modernism, which according to Jameson is "credited with the destruction of the fabric of the traditional city and its older neighborhood culture" (2), we should also observe that the architecture of Los Angeles was in fact reviled by many architects of high modernism themselves. In a piece entitled "Architect Wright Doesn't Like This City and Bluntly Says So," on the front page of the Saturday morning edition of the *Los Angeles Times* on January 20, 1940, Frank Lloyd Wright famously remarked of Los Angeles that "it is as if you tipped the United States up so all the commonplace people slid down here into Southern California" (qtd. in Turner 1). The author of the piece, Timothy G. Turner, says of Wright that "he looks over its architecture and laments. One notable example of business building, modern in architecture, he calls 'a dish of tripe.'" These sentiments are picked up by cultural critics as well. One notable example is Edmund Wilson, who expresses a number of strong reactions to Los Angeles—and California in general—in his 1932 book *The American Jitters: A Year of the Slump:* "Now we motor agreeably and speedily along the beautiful residential boulevards. The residential people of Los Angeles are cultivated enervated people, lovers of mixturesque beauty—and they like to express their emotivation in homes that symphonize their favorite historical films, their best-beloved movie actresses, their luckiest numerological combinations or their previous incarnations in old Greece, romantic Egypt, quant Sussex or among the priestesses of love of old India" (226). Although Wilson was writing well before critics began thinking about postmodernism, he was attuned to many of the concerns that later critics like Jameson would take up. He suggests, for example, that Angelinos are more interested in surface than depth, which is an essential distinction for Jameson between postmodernism and modernism, respectively. Angelinos, Wilson maintains, style themselves and their lives after such trivialities as their favorite films, movie stars, or astrological/mystical symbols. Wilson picks up on the mishmash of revival architecture around Los Angeles—referring to it as "mixturesque"— and, anticipating Jameson, draws the connection to a shallow appropriation and lack of appreciation for actual history. We find anticipated in Wilson the "weakening of historicity" that forms an essential part of Jameson's definition of postmodernism.

Wilson's observations are also notably similar to those in the opening chapters of both *The Day of the Locust* and *After Many a Summer;* the passages are so similar, in fact, that one wonders whether West and Huxley may have actually read and been influenced by Wilson's account.[6] *After Many a Summer* begins with a comparable automobile ride following Jeremy Pordage's arrival in Los Angeles: "Through trees, Jeremy saw the facades of houses, all new, almost all in good taste—elegant and witty pastiches of Lutyens manor houses, of Little Trianons, of Monticellos; light-hearted parodies of Le Corbusier's solemn machines-for-living-in; fantastic adaptations of Mexican haciendas and New England farms" (11–12). Huxley's references to pastiche and parody in relation to the architecture of Los Angeles anticipate Jameson, who points to the two as important characteristics of the postmodern. The parody of modernist architecture here, however, comes from a modernist source itself. As Michael Snyder explains, "A parody of modernism has, by definition questioned the sensibilities of the International Style: geometric purity, clean lines, austerity, and lack of ornamentation." As such, he goes on, "parody constitutes a proto-postmodern design which is informed by modernism, but injects humor and irony, as called for later by postmodern architectural theorists like Robert Venturi, Jencks, and Moore" (175).

Stoyte's castle, in particular, evokes the type of play and excessiveness with which postmodernism is often aligned: "The thing was Gothic, mediaeval, baronial—doubly baronial, Gothic with a Gothicity raised, so to speak, to a higher power, more mediaeval than any building of the thirteenth century. For this . . . this object, Jeremy was reduced to calling it, was mediaeval, not out of vulgar necessity, like Coucy, say, or Alnwick, but out of pure fun and wantonness, platonically, one might say. It was mediaeval as only a witty and irresponsible modern architect would wish to be mediaeval, as only the most competent modern engineers are technically equipped to be" (Huxley, *After Many a Summer* 18). It is, in other words, even *more* Gothic than an authentic Gothic cathedral, like some sort of gaudy modern-day Las Vegas hotel—the New York, New York or the Paris—that is actually *more* like the actual place (because it so blatantly accentuates its stereotypical features) than the place itself, thus entering into the realm of the hyperreal. Kevin Starr adeptly encapsulates Huxley's vision of Los Angeles in his classic study *The Dream Endures* (1997), where he describes it as "the most sweeping, comprehensive, and . . . successful description of Los Angeles as idiosyncratic cityscape. . . . Huxley's evocation announced to the English-speaking world the palpable presence of a new metropolis on the planet, in which distinctions between fantasy and reality, eccentricity and the norm, dissolved in the tense complexity of a new and vital genre of urban theatre" (158). It would seem that Huxley's novel, which is not often taught or written about, has slipped under the radar, given that it anticipates in so many striking ways the aesthetics of postmodern architecture described by Jameson. And as we will later see, Huxley's concern is not mere aesthetics but rather the intersection of these aesthetics with the philosophical questions that the novel pursues.

Although it is a very different novel than *After Many a Summer* by a very different kind of writer, Fitzgerald's *The Love of the Last Tycoon* is similar in how it blurs the lines between façade and fantasy. Consider the following description of a major Hollywood studio's film lot: "Under the moon the back lot was thirty acres of fairyland—not because the locations really looked like African jungles and French chateaux and schooners at anchor and Broadway by night, but because they looked like the torn picture books of childhood, like fragments of stories dancing in an open fire" (25). Like Wilson and Huxley, Fitzgerald looks beyond the mere aesthetic dimensions of the setting and into the realm of identity; there is a continuity, in other words, between the aesthetic and the subjective. And Nathanael West, finally, uses essentially the same strategy as Huxley in establishing the narrative setting in *The Day of the Locust,* though in this case the trip is ambulatory and follows Tod Hackett on his walk from the movie studio where he works to his apartment building: "But not even the soft wash of dusk could help the houses. Only dynamite would be of any use against the Mexican ranch houses, Samoan huts, Mediterranean villas, Egyptian and Japanese temples, Swiss chalets, Tudor cottages, and every possible combination of these styles that lined the slopes of the canyon" (262). Across these descriptions from each of the three novelists we find a tone of contempt that lines up with Edmund Wilson's observations. These real and fictional accounts of Los Angeles throughout the 1930s and 1940s suggest that observers were acutely aware of the air of artificiality, unreality, and fantasy surrounding the city.

We might best describe the architecture of Los Angeles since the turn of the twentieth century as pastiche, which is another hallmark of Jameson's characterization of postmodernism and one that ties into the broader connections with history and space that he relates back to Baudrillard and Guy Debord. He writes that the "new spatial logic of the simulacrum can now be expected to have a momentous effect on what used to be historical time. The past is thereby itself modified. . . . Guy Debord's powerful slogan is now even more apt for the 'prehistory' of a society bereft of all historicity, one whose own putative past is little more than a set of dusty spectacles" (18). We see this "society bereft of all historicity" in each of the three literary passages above. In turn, we might say that twentieth-century Los Angeles represents "the New spatial logic of the simulacrum." One of the primary characteristics of this new spatial logic, as the above postmodern critics attest, is that it is decentered. This reflects the spatial organization of Los Angeles, but it also more broadly reflects one of postmodernism's most recognizable characteristics, and one that branches out into a number of realms. Snyder, for example, points out that "the decentering of postmodernity affects subjects, interpretations, disciplines, and even cities. During the 1930s in Los Angeles, the downtown city center lost supremacy over other outlying areas, and by the end of the thirties Los Angeles was literally an idiosyncratically decentered city" (169). In fact, however, the notion of decentering is critical in studies of modernism as well (recall Yeats's "the centre cannot hold"). Edmund Wilson picks up on this notion as well, writing that "everyone who has ever been to Los Angeles knows how the mere aspect of things is likely to paralyze the aesthetic faculty by providing no *point d'appui* from which to exercise its discrimination, if it does not actually stun the sensory apparatus itself, so that accurate reporting becomes impossible" (*Classics and Commercials* 53). Again in Wilson's description we find suggestions of the intersection between the aesthetic and the subjective, as the images of paralysis and distortion suggest an endless play of subjectivity. Altogether, this collection of evidence suggests that Los Angeles and its decenteredness is *not* a distinctly postmodern phenomenon but rather one that has firm origins in the pre–World War II history of the city.

What further deepens this connection is the presence within Los Angeles of the district of Hollywood, which was formally absorbed as part of the city in 1910. Much of the tenor of Los Angeles since at least World War I has been set by Hollywood, which was home to more than 80 percent of the world's film industry by 1921 (Buntin). The decentering of Los Angeles has to do not just with its geographical layout but with its role in the birth and development of the film industry, particularly in the interwar years. More than any artistic medium before it, film produced new and complex relationships to time and space, and set the stage for the phenomenon that would later come to be known as simulacrum. In 1946, long before Baudrillard's *Simulacra and Simulation* (1981), the great historian of Southern California Carey McWilliams wrote that Hollywood "exists only as a state of mind, not as a geographical entity. . . . The concentration of the motion-picture industry in Los Angeles is what gives Hollywood its real identity. As Jerome Beatty once said, Hollywood exists as 'a kingless kingdom without a kingdom,' an island within an island" (330). McWilliams's portrayal is strikingly Baudrillardian, particularly evoking the Borges fable "On Exactitude in Science," which Baudrillard draws upon in describing his notion of simulacrum. "Today abstraction is no longer that of the map, the double, the mirror, or the concept," Baudrillard writes. "Simulation is no longer that of a territory, a referential being, or a substance. It is the generation by models of a real without origin or reality: a hyperreal" (1). McWilliams's description of Hollywood suggests such an environment in which the idea, model, or "state of mind" precedes the thing itself, the "geographical entity," testifying to Hollywood's symbolic value as a liminal space between reality and unreality.[7]

While it may seem surprising to find premonitions of Baudrillard in Fitzgerald, in fact we find examples of the simulacrum in *Tycoon*, again with specific ties to geography. Geography in *Tycoon* functions in much the same way as it does in *The Great Gatsby*, only the poles have been reversed and the focus is the West Coast rather than the East. While Nick makes continual reference to the "Middle-West" as a point of contrast to New York City, *Tycoon* begins with our narrator, Cecilia, outside Hollywood—which serves to contextualize its unreality. The opening sequence of the novel, which takes place on a transcontinental commercial airline flight and in Nashville, Tennessee, where it is diverted due to a storm, is essential in establishing the contrast between Hollywood and the rest of America. This is particularly apparent when Cecilia, Wylie White, and Mannie Schwartze take a long middle-of-the-night taxi ride to visit the Hermitage: "I could feel even in the darkness that the trees of the woodland were green—that it was all different from the dusty olive-tint of California. Somewhere we passed a Negro driving three cows ahead of him, and they mooed as he scatted them to the side of the road. They were real cows, with warm fresh, silky flanks and the Negro grew gradually real out of the darkness with his big brown eyes staring at us close to the car, as Wylie gave him a quarter" (9). Having been conditioned by Hollywood's unreality, where everything consists of mere façade without depth, she is struck by how "real" things appear in Middle America. Perhaps someone with her familial connection to Hollywood might see "real" cows there, but they would likely be on a film set, where even in their materiality they would become merely a set piece. This feeling of unreality is one that is pervasive across the literature of Los Angeles, especially for those who, like Fitzgerald, came from the East. According to Edmund Wilson, "All visitors from the East know the strange spell of unreality which seems to make human experience on the Coast as hollow as the life of a troll-nest where everything is out in the open instead of being underground" (*Classics and Commercials* 45–46). In a sense, we might take Wilson's observation literally: the West Coast of the time did not have developed subway systems like those of the East, particularly New York City. But there is also a suggestion, which again anticipates the postmodern, that the West Coast (and Wilson is certainly thinking especially of Los Angeles here) is all façade and no depth. And this could be applied to the people as much as to the architecture.

The opening scene of *Tycoon* also brings us back to Jameson's notion of a "weakening of historicity." Upon landing in Nashville, Cecilia observes that "airports lead you back in history like oases, like the stops on the great trade routes" (7–8). Symbolically speaking, it is as though Cecilia and the others have been taken back in time to a period when America was dominated by large swaths of rural landscape. The pastoral scene that Cecilia observes would not have been at all unusual at this time, but she belongs to a new, urbanized generation for whom this type of quaint scene has become a novel slice of America's past. Cecilia, for her part, seems acutely aware of this. "In the big transcontinental planes we were the coastal rich," she remarks, "who casually alighted from our cloud in mid-America" (8). As she goes on to explain, however, she herself—along with her coastal compatriots—is not necessarily what she seems: "High adventure might be among us, disguised as a movie star. But mostly it wasn't. And I wished fervently that we looked more interesting than we did—just as I often have at premiers, when the fans look at you with scornful reproach because you're not a star" (8). The early pages of the novel suggest a narrator in Cecilia who is acutely aware of the complex relationship between surface and depth that informs the film industry with which she is involved. And one of the things that makes her such a fitting narrator for Fitzgerald's novel is that she is, as Nick Carraway says in *Gatsby*, "within and without, simultaneously enchanted and repelled by the inexhaustible varieties of life" (40)—particularly those found in the Hollywood film industry.

These and other accounts testify to the fact that Los Angeles, back to nearly its earliest beginnings, has carried more symbolic than real value. This fact was becoming especially evident in the 1930s, when Hollywood was on its upward rise to power. In their book *Los Angeles in the Thirties*, David Gebhard and Harriette Von Breton explain that during the Depression Los Angeles, and Hollywood in particular, was the only place that "seemed to retain and even to continue the optimism of former decades. . . . The Los Angeles scene, as portrayed in films, weekly radio broadcasts, and the press, seemed to mirror just what most Americans throughout the country felt their world should be like" (5). In other words, in a time when so many Americans were suffering in their day-to-day lives, Los Angeles was becoming a profound ideological force in the collective cultural unconscious, more significant for what it represented in the public imagination than for what it actually offered in reality. It makes sense, as Cecilia observes, that those attending movie premiers would be disappointed upon seeing "ordinary" people like her who are not stars; after all, they are chasing the glorified image of Hollywood, not those individuals behind the scenes who actually turn the wheels. One of the things that both Fitzgerald and West capture so well is the long-held notion that the West might offer a new and glamorous life, a notion that both writers juxtapose without mercy to the common sense of disillusionment experienced by those who chase the dream. Edmund Wilson is especially caustic in this regard:

> Here these people, so long told to "go West" to escape from poverty, ill-health, maladjustment, industrialism and oppres-

sion, discover that, having come West, their problems and diseases still remain and that there is no further to go. Among the sand-colored power plants and hotels, the naval outfitters and waterside cafés, the old spread-roofed California houses with their fine close grain of gray or yellow clapboards—they come to the end of their resources in the empty California sun. Brokers and bankers, architects and citrus ranchers, farmers, housewives, building contractors, salesmen of groceries and real estate, proprietors of poolrooms, music stores and hotels, marines and supply-corps lieutenants, molders, machinists, oil-well drillers, auto mechanics, carpenters, tailors, soft-drink merchants, cooks and barbers, teamsters, stage drivers, longshoremen, laborers—mostly Anglo-Saxon whites, though with a certain number of Danes, Swedes and Germans and a sprinkling of Chinese, Japanese, Mexicans, Negroes, Indians and Filipinos—ill, retired or down on their luck—they stuff up the cracks of their doors in the little boarding-houses that take in invalids, and turn on the gas; they go into their back sheds or back kitchens and swallow Lysol or eat ant-paste; they drive their cars into dark alleys and shoot themselves in the back seat; they hang themselves in hotel bedrooms, take overdoses of sulphonal or barbital, stab themselves with carving-knives on the municipal golf-course; or they throw themselves into the placid blue bay, where the gray battleships and cruisers of the government guard the limits of their enormous nation—already reaching out in the eighties for the sugar plantations of Honolulu. (*American Jitters* 259–60)

Against the glamour of Hollywood and American life as it was portrayed on the big screen, Wilson's stark description of the West's brutal reality is all the more powerful. He identifies suicide as a major problem in the West, particularly in San Diego, which had the highest suicide rate in the nation at one time.[8] Although one would not know it from the depiction of American life in popular films, many saw California not as an untapped land of opportunity but as the end of the road for the tragically desperate and hopelessly deluded.

This storyline forms the backbone of *The Day of the Locust,* which features a cast of disenchanted and dejected characters. West captures

their general state of being as follows: "All their lives they had slaved at
some kind of dull, heavy labor, behind desks and counters, in the fields
and at tedious machines of all sorts, saving their pennies and dream-
ing of the leisure that would be theirs when they had enough" (411).
Los Angeles thus becomes for them a means of escape, an opportunity to overcome their lives of banal enslavement to industrial capitalism. But eventually they become bored and "realize that they've been
tricked and burn with resentment" (411). The newspapers and movies
that they turn to for entertainment instead feed them on "lynchings,
murder, sex crimes, explosions, wrecks, love nests, fires, miracles, revolutions, war. . . ." "They have been cheated and betrayed," the novel
laments. "They have slaved and saved for nothing" (412). While early
Hollywood suggests a glamorous land of opportunity in Los Angeles,
the reality simply does not live up to the filmic depictions. *The Day of
the Locust* emphasizes this fact in its opening pages, when Tod Hackett
first steps off the streetcar at Vine Street, near his apartment:

> A great many of the people wore sports clothes which were not
> really sports clothes. Their sweaters, knickers, slacks, blue flan-
> nel jackets with brass buttons were fancy dress. The fat lady in
> the yachting cap was going shopping, not boating; the man in
> the Norfolk jacket and Tyrolean hat was returning, not from a
> mountain, but an insurance office; and the girl in slacks and
> sneaks with a bandana around her head had just left a switch-
> board, not a tennis court.
>
> Scattered among these masquerades were people of a dif-
> ferent type. Their clothing was somber and badly cut, bought
> from mail-order houses. While the others moved rapidly, dart-
> ing into stores and cocktail bars, they loitered on the corners
> or stood with their backs to the shop windows and stared at
> everyone who passed. When their stare was returned, their eyes
> filled with hatred. At this time Tod knew very little about them
> except that they had come to California to die. (261)

In West's novel many of the people, like the architecture, are mere
façade, dressing as though they are preparing to engage in exclusive

recreational activities practiced by the wealthy, when in fact such a life-style is beyond their means. But West also shows the underside of the façade, which is illustrated in the striking juxtaposition between the two paragraphs quoted above. Alongside the "masquerades" are a sub-section of the population who are so disillusioned that their bitterness and hatred are plainly evident in their dress and physiognomy. West depicts openly what Fitzgerald only hints at. Compare the above de-scription to the more moderate one from *Tycoon:* "There was lassitude in plenty—California was filling up with weary desperadoes. And there were tense young men and women who lived back East in spirit while they carried on a losing battle against the climate" (80). Fitzgerald's description, while more moderate, similarly captures the feeling of dis-enchantment felt by so many who moved to California from the East in the first half of the twentieth century. In all three novels explored in this chapter, we find a stark contrast between the expectations of what California will offer and what the actual experience of living there is like. While the plots of their three novels move in very different direc-tions,[9] West's, Huxley's, and Fitzgerald's characters all undergo psycho-logical crises that lead us to consider what we call "identity" as merely a projection of our own desire. Consequently, their divergent plots in-evitably venture into the realms of tragedy, violence, and the grotesque.

The Lost Tycoon

In one of his oft-quoted descriptions, Nick says of Gatsby that "if per-sonality is an unbroken series of successful gestures, then there was something gorgeous about him, some heightened sensitivity to the promises of life, as if he were related to one of those intricate machines that registers earthquakes ten thousand miles away" (6). Indeed, as we have seen above, Gatsby's "identity" is in fact a meticulously con-structed façade that he employs in an attempt to hide the true chaos at work in his subconscious mind. Although there are distinctions to be made between their various depictions of personality, ultimately our three novels take a similar view of identity as multifarious and elusive rather than singular.

Tycoon, like *Gatsby,* is narrated from the periphery. While Cecilia is involved in the action at times, she acts mostly as an observer rather than a direct influence.[10] Like Nick Carraway, she interacts with the central characters and colors the narrative with her own subjective point of view, but her essential purpose in the novel is to tell the story of Monroe Stahr and his relationship with Kathleen Moore. In keeping with this narrative framing, Cecilia tells us from the outset that she's unable to get fully inside the world of Hollywood herself and instead will take us there through her proximity to Monroe Stahr. "You can take Hollywood for granted like I did," she says, "or you can dismiss it with the contempt we reserve for what we don't understand. It can be understood too, but only dimly and in flashes. Not half a dozen men have ever been able to keep the whole equation of pictures in their heads. And perhaps the closest a woman can come to the set-up is to try and understand one of those men" (3). Cecilia is essentially a marginalized figure, not only in her role as peripheral narrator but in her inability to get Stahr to see her in the way that she wishes he would. As she remarks in the scene on the plane, she wishes that she looked more interesting and captivated more of Stahr's attention. But like Nick Carraway, she is overshadowed by the colossal stature of the man about whom she writes.

Monroe Stahr resembles Gatsby in a number of ways; both are wealthy, self-made, and charismatic young men seeking to recover a lost love. As Bruccoli points out, however, Stahr achieves greater "success" than Gatsby: "Monroe Stahr is an archetypal American hero," Bruccoli explains, "the embodiment of the American Dream: a Jay Gatsby with genius" (vii). Stahr, for one thing, amasses his fortune legally. And while he is not universally liked, unlike Gatsby he *is* universally feared, and his power is virtually unquestioned. We find in Stahr's character an apt example of the "cult of personality" typically associated with political dictators. Note Cecilia's description of him when a crowd spots him on the studio lot:

He spoke and waved back as the people streamed by in the darkness, looking I suppose a little like the Emperor and the Old Guard. There is no world so but it has its heroes and Stahr was the hero. Most of these men had been here a long time—through the beginnings and the great upset when sound came and the three years of Depression he had seen that no harm came to them. The old loyalties were trembling now—there were clay feet everywhere—but still he was their man, the last of the princes. And their greeting was a sort of low cheer as they went by. (27)

Crowds obviously flock to Gatsby as well, but we find that Stahr is more deeply implicated in the actual lives of those around him. He is treated and thought of as royalty and as a hero who is carrying on a historical legacy of sorts; he is seen as a man of mythic proportions. Whereas the mythology surrounding Gatsby leads to cynical speculation about a nefarious past, Stahr evokes all the glamour and glory of an idealized Hollywood film industry. Without Stahr, the novel implies, the system itself would implode: "Stahr must be right always, not most of the time, but always—or the structure would melt down like gradual butter" (56). There is certainly a hint of paternal arrogance in Stahr (evoking more Tom Buchanan than Gatsby in that respect). As another example, when asked what makes the "unity" of his studio system, Stahr, whose "face was grim except that his eyes twinkled" (58), replies, "I'm the unity" (58). Even Stahr's name is suggestive, as he is a star in the many different senses of the word. He is not only the star of the novel and a star in the sense of celebrity but also, like a celestial star, a collection of matter held together by his own gravity. We might even add another meaning of *star* from the *Oxford English* Dictionary: "a crack or fissure in the skin." Ironically, then, *star* implies both centripetal and centrifugal force. It is thus a fitting metaphor for personality, which implies cohesion but is always in danger of fracturing. Like Gatsby, Stahr is struggling with his own sense of identity and attempting to reconstruct it by repeating his past with a proxy for his deceased wife, Minna Davis.

Early in the novel, Stahr appears as a strikingly confident figure who is entirely in control of his thoughts and actions; but when he first sees Kathleen and notices her uncanny resemblance to Minna, his personality begins to fracture. This begins, in the first instance, with his fragmented vision of Kathleen, as seen here during their first consequential meeting in the novel: "When she came close his several visions of her blurred; she was momentarily unreal. Usually a girl's skull made her real but not this time—Stahr continued to be dazzled as they danced out along the floor—to the last edge, where they stepped through a mirror into another dance with new dancers whose faces were familiar but nothing more. In this new region he talked, fast and urgently" (73). Kathleen appears to Stahr as "unreal" (like Hollywood itself), and he is unable to process his experience with her as he does other things in his life. His "several visions of her" also suggest that like Daisy, she is symbolically overdetermined. And like the reunion between Daisy and Gatsby, Stahr's moment of ecstasy is fleeting, which becomes apparent to him the next day: "Last night was gone, the girl he had danced with was gone" (78). Like Gatsby, Stahr is fixated on irretrievable moments from the past, and as is the case elsewhere in Fitzgerald, personality is depicted as something that is fleeting and changeable from one moment to the next. The major difference between Gatsby and Stahr is that while Gatsby is true to his illusion until the end, Stahr gains a level of self-awareness and self-consciously desires to break the pattern of his life (a notion that recalls Nick's notion of personality as "a series of successful gestures"):

> "Don't be a mother," he [Stahr] said.
> "All right. What shall I be?"
> Be a trollop, he thought. He wanted the pattern of his life broken. If he was going to die soon, like the two doctors said, he wanted to stop being Stahr for a while and hunt for love like men who had no gifts to give, like young nameless men who looked along the streets in the dark. (90–91)

Stahr's response evokes Freud's Madonna-whore complex, which identifies men who can only see women as either virginally pure or as sexually debased. This distinction is in keeping with Stahr's tendency to view people not as individuals but as either objects with something to offer or obstacles that must be overcome on the path to success. But it also suggests that like Gatsby, Stahr ultimately desires a mother figure, although he eventually wants to break that pattern of desire. The implication is that Stahr seeks to break the cycle of his desire for a mother figure because he wants to become someone other than who he has been. While Kathleen helps him experience this, the experience is fleeting and temporary: "Now they were different people as they started back. Four times they had driven along the shore road today, each time a different pair. Curiosity, sadness and desire were behind them now; this was a true returning—to themselves and all their past and future and the encroaching presence of tomorrow" (94–95). Once again Fitzgerald reminds us that these instances of figuratively stepping outside oneself are only temporary and situational, limited to the specific moments in which they occur. It is for this reason that both Gatsby and Stahr seek to repeat their past, but under the guise of a new sense of self.

What makes it so difficult for Stahr to "escape himself" is that his sense of his own identity is so firmly entrenched in his work in the film industry, which ensnares him in a world of illusion and deception. Even when he experiences one of his most emotional moments, it is mediated through the language of film:

> Winding down the hill he listened inside himself as if something, by an unknown composer, powerful and strange and strong, was about to be played for the first time. The theme would be stated presently but because the composer was always new, he would not recognize it as the theme right away. It would come in some such guise as the auto-horns from the technicolor boulevards below or be barely audible, a tattoo on the muffled drum of the moon. He strained to hear it, knowing only that music was the beginning, new music that he liked and did not understand. It was hard to react to what one could entirely compass—this was new and confusing, nothing one could shut off in the middle and supply the rest from an old score. (95–96)

This experience with Kathleen is so entirely new to Stahr that he finds himself unable to neatly fit it into any paradigm that he already knows. This lack of control becomes frightening for him, and when he finds the letter that Kathleen accidentally dropped in his car he cannot resist opening it: "He was proud of resisting his first impulse to open the letter. It seemed to prove that he was not 'losing his head.' . . . 'Falling for dames' had never been an obsession—his brother had gone to pieces over a dame, or rather over dame after dame after dame" (97). Although Stahr desires to break the pattern of his life and become someone new, he is, paradoxically, afraid of losing his head or "going to pieces," which he associates with a lack of self-control. Nonetheless, this is precisely what happens when he meets Kathleen. The raw reality of the emotions he experiences for the first time (that we know of) challenges his sense of identity as Monroe Stahr, and he realizes how difficult, even impossible, it is to escape the public identity that he has created for himself and that he has allowed to entirely consume his own personal thoughts. And while he begins to inevitably recognize the incoherence of his own identity, he finds himself deconstructing Kathleen's in order to justify opening her letter: "Kathleen was really far away now with the waning night—the different aspects of her telescoped into the memory of a single thrilling stranger bound to him only by a few slender hours. It seemed perfectly all right to open the letter" (98). While Stahr allows himself to be seduced by the notion that Kathleen can act as a replacement for Minna, ultimately he realizes that she is merely a projection of his own desire, just as he has been a projection of Cecilia's: "I'll always think of that moment, when I felt Miss Doolan behind me with her pad, as the end of childhood, the end of the time when you cut out pictures. What I was looking at wasn't Stahr but a picture of him I cut out over and over. . . . He was my picture, as sure as if he was pasted on the inside of my locker in school" (71). Cecilia's realization illustrates the central difference between her and Stahr: she realizes and accepts that her "picture" of Stahr is only a simulacrum, while he acknowledges that Kathleen is only a simulacrum of his dead wife but is never able to reconcile this fact with his obsessive desire. What we find in the relationships throughout the novel is a great deal of blurring between the various conceptions that the characters have of one another and of themselves. By continually calling attention to this confusion, Fitzgerald creates an ironic characterization of identity in which each character projects his or her desire on an other in an endless cycle, which creates a feeling of radical decenteredness in relation to the novel's subjects.

This brings us back full circle to the geography of Los Angeles. There is a popular conception that Hollywood is the lifeblood of the city, when in fact it is merely a vacuum filled by the illusions and fantasies of its inhabitants. When we speak of Los Angeles as "decentered," we mean literally, as a result of its endless sprawl, but also figuratively. Monroe Stahr, the center of Hollywood in the novel, functions in the same way. While he is decentered himself, ironically the other characters depend upon him for their own senses of identity. A perfect example of this is Mannie Schwartze, who, although he appears in the novel only briefly, is a crucial figure in establishing both Stahr's profound power over the other characters and some of the deeper themes that the novel develops in relation to American ideology.

When we first meet him, Schwartze is on the tail end of a downfall from a powerful position in Hollywood as a studio head. His suicide, while not actually described, is imagined by Cecilia after she and Wylie leave him at the Hermitage in a scene that establishes a number of deep symbolic connections to American history: "Mannie Schwartze and Andrew Jackson—it was hard to say them in the same sentence. It was doubtful if he knew who Andrew Jackson was as he wandered around, but perhaps he figured that if people had preserved his house Andrew Jackson must have been someone who was large and merciful, able to understand. At both ends of life man needed nourishment—a breast—a shrine. Something to lay himself beside when no one wanted him further, and shoot a bullet into his head" (13). The passage recalls the maternal imagery from *Gatsby,* which uses both the breast and the idea of nourishment, particularly in the description of the scene just before Gatsby and Daisy share their first kiss: "Out of the corner of his eye Gatsby saw that the blocks of the sidewalk really formed a ladder and mounted to a secret place above the trees—he could climb to it, if he climbed alone, and once there he could suck on the pap of life, gulp down the incomparable milk of wonder" (117). And just as Daisy and the maternal imagery of Gatsby establish a connection between Gatsby and the American landscape and its history, a similar connection is made here between the Jewish Schwartze and Andrew Jackson, one of America's most enduring historical figures, although one who was not particularly merciful or understanding. But as we have continually been reminded, the object does not matter in itself but only insofar as it provides a center around which we can orbit.

For several characters in the novel, including Schwartze, Stahr occupies the central role. This is demonstrated in the case of Schwartze's suicide letter, which reads, "Dear Monro, You are the best of them all I have always admired your mentality so when you turn against me I know it's no use! I must be no good and am not going to continue the journey let me warn you once again look out! I know" (16). Stahr, also not particularly merciful or understanding, at least professionally, is godlike in the power that he exercises over the other characters in the novel. Cecilia tells us early on that "some of my more romantic ideas actually stemmed from pictures—'42nd Street,' for example, had a great influence on me. It's more than possible that some of the pictures which Stahr himself conceived had shaped me into what I was" (18). We see, in short, a troubling sense of dependency among those characters who satellite around Stahr and depend on him for their own senses of identity. We might say that Stahr himself functions as a shrine—certainly for Cecilia. In addition to forming their identities in relation to notions of Hollywood success, the characters actually construct their own ideas of personal identity in relation to Stahr. This is ironic, of course, given that Stahr himself orbits around Kathleen, who satisfies both his desire for a mother figure and his desire to reconstruct his own identity. These relationships show how identity in *Tycoon,* as in Conrad, is intersubjective in nature.

Throughout *Tycoon,* Fitzgerald shows a keen awareness of the ways in which Hollywood problematizes notions of personal identity. This is true of Cecilia, as we have already seen, but we find similar anxieties in every other notable character as well. Wylie White, for example, tells Cecilia wearily that Hollywood is "a good place for toughies but I went there from Savannah, Georgia. I went to a garden party the first day. My host shook hands and left me. It was all there—that swimming pool, green moss at two dollars an inch, beautiful felines having drinks and fun—" (11). His first impression is just what one expects from Hollywood; the appearance is just as one would imagine it. He goes on, however: "—And nobody spoke to me. Not a soul. I spoke to half a dozen people but they didn't answer. That continued for an hour, two hours—then I got up from where I was sitting and ran out at a dog trot like a crazy man. I didn't feel I had any rightful identity until I got back to the hotel and the clerk handed me a letter addressed to me in my name" (11). While Cecilia tells us that she has never had this experience herself, she is not surprised by it. "We don't go for strangers in Hollywood unless they wear a sign saying that their axe has been thoroughly ground elsewhere," she explains, "and that in any case it's not going to fall on our necks—in other words unless they're a celebrity. And they'd better look it even then" (11). Hollywood, of course, is made up largely of actors and writers, and Cecilia makes a notable distinction between the two when she first finds out that Wylie White is a writer: "Writers aren't people exactly. Or, if they're any good, they're a whole *lot* of people trying hard to be one person. It's like actors, who try so pathetically not to look in mirrors. Who lean *back*ward trying—only to see their faces in the reflecting chandeliers" (12). While writers are many people trying to be one, in other words, actors are one trying to be many. Fitzgerald's broader point is that in Hollywood everyone is driven to be something other than who or what they are. And regardless how they manage to present themselves, others will form their own opinions based on the endless gossip that is passed around. In the case of one minor character named Rose Meloney, for example, we are told that she is "a dried up little blonde of fifty about whom one could hear the fifty assorted opinions of Hollywood—'a sentimental dope,' ' the best writer on construction in Hollywood,' ' a veteran,' ' that old hack,' 'the smartest woman on the lot,' 'the cleverest plagiarist in the biz,' and of course in addition a nymphomaniac, a virgin, a pushover, a lesbian and a faithful wife" (36). In Fitzgerald's Hollywood, everyone contains multiple personalities. Ultimately, Fitzgerald paints a picture of a Hollywood that maintains a stark contrast between what is above and beneath the surface, where people are seldom recognized for who they are and are often unsure of their own selves. Although his depiction may not be as appalling as West's, he similarly captures "the emptiness of Hollywood."

The Burning of Los Angeles

Tod's model for "making it" in the early part of *The Day of the Locust* is the "successful screenwriter" Claude Estee (271). Estee's house, like Gatsby's, is a gaudy imitation—akin to the personality of its owner. It is a "a big house," we are told, "that was an exact reproduction of the old Dupuy mansion near Biloxi, Mississippi. When Tod came up the walk between the boxwood hedges, he greeted him from the enormous, two-story porch by doing the impersonation that went with the Southern colonial architecture. He teetered back and forth on his heels like a Civil War colonel and made believe he had a large belly" (271). Aside from the disturbing racial implications of Estee's slave fantasy, one can understand why the glamour and wealth of the motion-picture industry would lead someone like him to develop such an inflated sense of self. Estee's party is just the kind that Fitzgerald's Wylie White might have attended. As contrasted with White, or perhaps a figure like George Boxley, the novelist turned screenwriter in *Tycoon*, Estee demonstrates what success in Hollywood can get you. And like Joe Stoyte, Estee is able to in some sense "repeat the past" by replicating it architecturally—and of course playing the part of a plantation owner. The successful characters in all three novels have a knack for transcending history in ways that are not accessible to the middle-class and poor characters.

While the successful characters in each novel act out in forms of masquerade that are often depicted as more playful than sinister, the middle-class and poor characters are seen as grotesque. A description of Tod Hackett early in the novel tells us that "despite his appearance [he is previously described as appearing "without talent, almost doltish"], he was really a very complicated young man with a whole set of personalities, one inside the other like a nest of Chinese boxes" (260). One side of Hackett that we encounter quite early is a proclivity for violent thoughts. Looking at a photograph of Faye Greener, he muses: "Her invitation wasn't to pleasure, but to struggle, hard and sharp, closer to murder than to love. If you threw yourself on her, it would be like throwing yourself from the parapet of a skyscraper. You would do it with a scream" (271). He reflects bitterly that Faye would never have him, that she is not sentimental and sees Hackett as a "good-hearted man" (270), meaning that he would only be suitable as a friend. Sexual rejection is an important facet of Hackett's inclination toward violence. As he becomes increasingly disillusioned by Hollywood, his sexual fantasies about Faye intensify, and eventually he dreams of violently raping her. Of course, his fantasies are based in misplaced illusions about what Hollywood has to offer its inhabitants—a fact that unites Hackett with "the people who come to California to die."

Throughout the novel, we see a number of these different personalities emerge at various moment, causing Hackett to appear as one (type of) person at one moment, and a completely different one at another. West's descriptions are much like Fitzgerald's, whose characters are described as different people at different points in time: "Now they [Stahr and Kathleen] were different people as they started back. Four times they had driven along the shore road today, each time a different pair. Curiosity, sadness and desire were behind them now; this was a true returning—to themselves and all their past and future and the encroaching presence of tomorrow" (94–95). But while Hackett is described as someone who is more complex than he appears, Kathleen insists that Stahr's personalities are out in the open: "You're three or four different men but each of them out in the open. Like all Americans" (116). The difference in each case is simply one of appearance; on a deeper level, each novel recognizes that the subject exists as an apparently singular entity only at specific moments in time. The subject, according to this conception, has little coherence but rather adapts to situational particularities.

This notion of multiple personalities is not limited to Hackett but spills over into other characters as well. In fact, early descriptions of Homer Simpson demonstrate a lack of stable personality and self-control. Shortly after we first meet him, he is described getting out of bed "in sections, like a poorly made automaton" who, as though not fully in control of his body, "carried his hands into the bathroom" (289). Once there, "he ran hot water into the tub and began to undress, fumbling with the buttons of his clothing as though he were undressing a stranger" (289). This lack of agency becomes more sinister later, when we are told of a former encounter with a drunk and crying Romola Martin: "He caught her in his arms and hugged her. His suddenness frightened her and she tried to pull away, but he held on and began awkwardly to caress her. He was completely unconscious of what he was doing" (293). Strangely enough, when she later lies on her bed and offers herself to him, he suddenly runs out of the room, unable to act upon his obvious sexual impulses. When we are brought back into the present, we are given some indication of his underlying issues: "He got out of the tub, dried himself hurriedly with a rough towel, then went into the bedroom to dress. He felt even more stupid and washed out than usual. It was always like that. His emotions surged up in an enormous wave, curving and rearing, higher and higher, until it seemed as though the wave must carry everything before it. But the crash never came. Something always happened at the very top of the crest and the wave collapsed to run back like water down a drain, leaving, at the most, only the refuse of feeling" (294). These disturbing descriptions of Simpson suggest a deeply crippling emotional impotence that, while it precedes his move to California, eventually reaches a head there and returns in the form of powerful violent acts that culminate in the mob-scene finale.

One of the strangest and most poignant examples of troubled personality in *Locust* is Harry Greener, who epitomizes the tragic downfall of the Hollywood performer. When Greener, a former vaudeville clown who has been reduced to selling silver polish door to door, tries to close a sale with Simpson, we see him shift into "acting" mode: "He jumped to his feet and began doing Harry Greener, poor Harry, honest Harry, well-meaning, humble, deserving, a good husband, a model father, a faithful Christian, a loyal friend" (300). The irony, of course, is that Greener's "acting" is just another version of himself. Like many of the characters in *Tycoon* and *Locust*, Greener has been reduced to a caricature of himself. Once again the masquerade is not playful but tragic, which is emphasized a moment later: "Suddenly, like a mechanical toy that had been overwound, something snapped inside of him and he began to spin through his entire repertoire. The effort was purely muscular, like the dance of the paralytic. He jigged, juggled his hat, made believe he had been kicked, tripped, and shook hands with himself. He went through it all in one dizzy spasm, then reeled to the couch and collapsed" (301). These types of depictions are not unique in modernism, as Martin Rogers explains: "Modernism's ambivalence toward technology often took shape in the critique of the dehumanization of mechanized industry, prophetically so in Karl Capec's play *R.U.R.* (first performed in 1921) as well as Chaplin's *Modern Times* (1936) and [Fritz Lang's] *Metropolis*" (373). West's point, however, stretches beyond a mere critique of mechanized society. Homer's daughter Faye, for example, suffers from a similar obsession with show business that reaches frightening limits. She tells Simpson, "I'm going to be a star some day. . . . It's my life. It's the only thing in the whole world that I want. . . . If I'm not, I'll commit suicide" (309). Faye represents exactly the kind of all-or-nothing attitude that West finds so disturbing among the Hollywood crowd. For West's characters there is no contentment to be found in leading "ordinary" lives; their entire existence is premised around "making it" and living out their fantasies of what show business ought to be. His characters, like many of Fitzgerald's, are so obsessed with their projected images of themselves that they become mere simulations.

What makes Faye's artificiality all the more disturbing is that Hackett actually becomes attracted to it: "Had any other girl been so affected, he would have thought her as intolerable. Faye's affectations, however, were so completely artificial that he found them charming" (316). Faye's artificiality is so consuming and transparent that it is almost as if any sense of "reality" has melted away. "Being with her," the narrator says of Hackett's attraction, "was like being backstage during an amateurish, ridiculous play. From in front, the stupid lines and grotesque situation would have made him squirm with annoyance, but because he saw the perspiring stage-hands and the wires that held up the tawdry summerhouse with its tangle of paper flowers, he accepted everything and was anxious for it to succeed. . . . She didn't know how to be simpler or more honest" (316). Despite his "attraction" to her, Hackett's desire is deeply conflicted and, like Simpson's, is also tinged with a desire for violence. These violent tendencies are a result of Hackett's conflicted emotional state, and he is simultaneously drawn to and repulsed by Faye's fakeness: "If he only had the courage to throw himself on her. Nothing less violent than rape would do. The sensation he felt was like that he got when holding an egg in his hand. Not that she was fragile or even seemed fragile. It wasn't that. It was her completeness, her egglike self-sufficiency, that made him want to crush her" (320). What seems to enrage him so much about Faye is that she thinks of herself as self-assured and level-headed, while he sees through her façade and recognizes that she is the exact opposite. Amid the crowded throngs of people Hackett observes around Los Angeles, it is actually Faye's ignorance of her inconsistency that he finds so infuriating. The very fact that Faye is so content with herself inspires the violent rage that Hackett channels into his art:

In "The Burning of Los Angeles" Faye is the naked girl in the left foreground being chased by a group of men and women who have separated from the main body of the mob. One of the women is about to hurl a rock at her to bring her down. She is running with her eyes closed and a strange half-smile on her lips. Despite the dreamy repose of her face, her body is straining to hurl her along at top speed. The only explanation for this contrast is that she is enjoying the release that wild flight gives in much the same way that a game bird must when, after hiding

for several tense minutes, it bursts from cover in complete, un-
thinking panic. (321)

The painting, which is disturbing enough in its mere depiction of the
naked Faye being chased by an angry mob, is made even more so by its
suggestion that she is actually enjoying her torment. As with Simpson,
it seems inevitable from early on in the novel that Hackett's repressed
desire will eventually be realized in the form of real violence.

Hackett is able to see through the various characters he meets and
recognize that they, like Hollywood, are pure artifice. When one looks
closely enough, it becomes apparent that people fit into various reproduced categories of personality based upon the models presented to
them by the popular culture of the time and Hackett cannot help but
take notice of these phenomena:

> He thought of Janvier's 'Sargasso Sea.' Just as that imaginary
> body of water was a history of civilization in the form of a ma-
> rine junkyard, the studio lot was one in the form of a dream
> dump. A Sargasso of the imagination! And the dump grew
> continually, for there wasn't a dream afloat somewhere which
> wouldn't sooner or later turn up on it, having first been made
> photographic by plaster, canvas, lath and paint. Many boats sink
> and never reach the Sargasso, but no dream ever entirely dis-
> appears. Somewhere it troubles some unfortunate person and
> some day, when that person has been sufficiently troubled, it
> will be reproduced on the lot. (353)

Andrew Lyndon Knighton points out that "the novel is replete with
similar inventories. It is set in a Hollywood where such fetish objects
abound, both on the studio lots and beyond. And it makes the argument that, torn from their homelands and their historical contexts,
such objects share their alienation with those refugees who have
flocked to Los Angeles to pursue dreams of celebrity, wealth, or freedom" (145–46). This description applies directly to Faye, who has built
herself up entirely around the notion of achieving celebrity and fame.
Her beliefs about Hollywood are culled together from various things
she has read and heard: "She went on and on, telling him how careers

are made in the movies and how she intended to make hers. It was all nonsense. She mixed bits of badly understood advice from the trade papers with other bits out of the fan magazines and compared these with the legends that surround the activities of screen stars and executives. Without any noticeable transition, possibilities became probabilities and wound up as inevitabilities" (386). Just as we arrive at a stable sense of identity by transforming our thoughts and experiences into coherent narratives, Faye creates a coherent narrative of future success out of what is, in fact, a patchwork of anecdotes and half-truths. What become for her "inevitabilities" are actually no more than fantasies.

As in *Tycoon,* one potential reaction to this phenomenon is the symbolic return to the maternal. But just as this step represents the end for Mannie Schwartze in his suicide, for Simpson it turns into a devolution toward violence. Unable to bear the stress any longer, near the end of the novel Simpson enters into what Hackett calls a "Uterine Flight," a term that he gleaned from a caption under a picture of a woman in a similar position from a book of abnormal psychology: "But he wasn't relaxed. Some inner force of nerve and muscle was straining to make the ball tighter and still tighter. He was like a steel spring which has been freed of its function in a machine and allowed to use all its strength centripetally. While part of a machine the pull of the spring had been used against other and stronger forces, but now, free at last, it was striving to attain the shape of its original coil" (403). Once again we see the pervasive imagery of machinery; even in his attempt to symbolically return to the safety of the womb, Simpson is unable to escape the influence of the mechanized world around him. Hackett, for his part, sees the tragedy in this, imagining the womb as an idealized space: "What a perfect escape the return to the womb was. Better by far than Religion or Art or the South Sea Islands. It was so snug and warm there, and the feeding was automatic. Everything perfect in that hotel. No wonder the memory of those accommodations lingered in the blood and nerves of everyone. It was dark, yes, but what a warm, rich darkness. The grave wasn't in it. No wonder one fought so desperately against being evicted when the nine months lease was up" (403–4). But clearly one can never find an *actual* replacement for this state. As in the case of Mannie Schwartze, the closest one can get to this return is death. In lieu of that, the inevitable turn is to violence.

Harking back to West's broader focus on mass culture, what is particularly frightening about the violence in the final pages of the novel is the way that it erupts as a result of a spontaneous crowd gathering. West describes the scene in meticulous and horrifying detail, suggesting that the erupting violence wells up from a site of repressed rage:

> New groups, whole families, kept arriving. He could see a change come over them as soon as they had become part of the crowd. Until they reached the line, they looked difficult, almost furtive, but the moment they became part of it, they turned arrogant and pugnacious. It was a mistake to think them harmless curiosity seekers. They were savage and bitter, especially the middle-aged and the old, and had been made so by boredom and disappointment.
>
> All their lives they had slaved at some kind of dull, heavy labor, behind desks and counters, in the fields and at tedious machines of all sorts, saving their pennies and dreaming of the leisure that would be theirs when they had enough. . . . If only a plane would crash once in a while so that they could watch the passengers being consumed in a "holocaust of flame," as the newspapers put it. But the planes never crash.
>
> Their boredom becomes more and more terrible. They realize that they've been tricked and burn with resentment. Every day of their lives they read the newspapers and went to the movies. Both fed them on lynchings, murder, sex crimes, explosions, wrecks, love nests, fires, miracles, revolutions, war. . . . Nothing can ever be violent enough to make taut their slack minds and bodies. They have been cheated and betrayed. They have slaved and saved for nothing. (411–12)

The mob feel "cheated and betrayed" when their actual experience in Los Angeles does not live up to the ideological fantasies that they have been fed. But the final riot scene of the novel is not without wry irony and humor. What makes it so bizarre is that some participants do not even realize that they are part of a riot to begin with and simply gather because they believe Gary Cooper has been sighted. This absurdity makes West's insight into the violence of crowd mentality all the more disturbing, as does the fact that most of the participants do not enter with any violent intent but rather are swept up in the fervor of the moment. Human beings, West suggests, are tragically susceptible to social influence and mob mentality.[11]

Recent critics and historians have drawn major connections between modernism and fascism. The historian Roger Griffin's *Modernism and Fascism* (2010), for example, convincingly argues that modernism—in areas from aesthetics to politics—was integral in setting the stage for the spread of fascism in Europe. Ultimately, West's violent vision anticipates the violence of World War II and the destructive potential of the masses as seen most tragically in the Nazi concentration camps. His vision serves as a warning about the destructive potential of modernity's effects on the individual psyche. Pushed to the edge, the human animal, like any other, will inevitably turn violent.

After Many a Summer Dies the Swan and the Escape from Personality

Given the subject matter of *The Love of the Last Tycoon* and *The Day of the Locust,* Huxley's *After Many a Summer Dies the Swan* is somewhat of an outlier here. It is not a Hollywood novel, strictly speaking, although it does tell the story of a Hollywood millionaire. And although it is less dystopian and less steeped in the conventions of science fiction than Huxley's earlier novel *Brave New World* (1932), *After Many a Summer* is nonetheless a novel that it is difficult to imagine Fitzgerald or West ever attempting, at least successfully. Then there is the obvious fact that Huxley is British, which makes him an "outsider" alongside these two quintessentially American writers. But this fact actually makes Huxley's inclusion here all the more intriguing, as he offers a sardonic outsider's perspective on the ideology of American exceptionalism, which fascinated Fitzgerald and West. Huxley's Joe Stoyte is an obvious caricature of William Randolph Hearst, who does not appear in either Fitzgerald or West but whose colossal presence in Los Angeles inevitably informs their respective novels, particularly their depictions of the gaudy opulence of Southern California's aristocracy.[12] Unlike Fitzgerald and West, who came to Los Angeles at the end of their careers, Huxley would spend more than twenty years in Southern California, mostly in and around Los Angeles (including Hollywood). While Hollywood and the film industry do not play a direct role in the novel, their influence on Huxley is clear. Like those in West's *The Day of the Locust*, Huxley's characters are often described as artificial, or as actors who are meant to play a specific role. The chauffeur, for example, who takes Pordage to Stoyte's mansion at the beginning of the novel, seems entirely aware of the part that he is being asked to play in Stoyte's charade: "Once more the old-fashioned retainer, the chauffeur, taking off his cap, did a final impersonation of himself welcoming the young master home to the plantation, then set to work to unload the luggage" (26). The chauffer is conscious of his own role, understanding that Stoyte is interested not only in his practical employment but in his keeping up the appearance of classical grandeur that feeds Stoyte's narcissism. The reference to Stoyte's mansion as a "plantation," which echoes Claude Estee, reflects Stoyte's desire to possess not only lavish commodities that serve as testament to his vast wealth but people themselves.

Huxley builds upon this notion of acting in his description of Stoyte's face when he and Pordage first meet: "The face wore that shut, unsmiling mask which American workmen tend to put on in their dealings with strangers—in order to prove, by not making the ingratiating grimaces of courtesy, that theirs is a free country and you're not going to come it over *them*" (28). We see echoes here of Fitzgerald's Monroe Stahr; it is not enough that each man possesses wealth and power, but he must play the part of a wealthy and powerful man down to the minutiae of each facial expression. Stoyte maintains a similar countenance throughout the novel, fitting of the archetypal American business tycoon after whom he styles himself. Underneath, however, like Monroe Stahr, Stoyte suffers from an emotional vulnerability, not unlike the less wealthy and powerful characters around him. While the other characters are utterly fooled by Stoyte's act, Pordage comes to recognize Stoyte's façade for what it is: an attempt to mask his deep insecurities. Pordage, in fact, sees beneath the surface of all the other characters in ways that no one else is able to do. Perhaps, we might surmise, this is because Pordage is the novel's only outsider (a proxy for Huxley), an Englishman who has not been so thoroughly corrupted by the intellectually enervating forces of American popular culture. While the other characters in the novel appear to fully buy into the "acts" they perform, Pordage sees them for what they are. In the opening pages of the novel, he observes a number of women walking down the city streets: "Most of the girls, as they walked along, seemed to be absorbed in silent prayer; but he supposed, on second thought, it was only gum that they were thus incessantly ruminating. Gum, not God" (5). Like those in *Locust*, Huxley's characters appear to be doing something meaningful, but upon deeper examination there is in fact nothing behind the façade; the façade itself produces the illusion of meaning. In this case, the juxtaposition is particularly ironic on account of its religious connection; where God appears to exist, there is in fact only meaningless, mechanical action.

Religion is a major theme in the novel, and it straddles the underling paradoxes between mind and body and between faith and science that compose its essential symbolic structure. In the vein of Eliot and Joyce, the novel takes up the classic modernist notion that society's old (namely, religious) value systems have crumbled. Huxley suggests that society is at a critical moral and philosophical juncture, and it is unclear whether salvation will come in the form of faith or of science. While in the cemetery that Stoyte owns, Pordage reads religious messages that accompany the sculptures scattered throughout and reflects upon their meaning in their new modern context. One in particular sets off his interest: "'Death is swallowed up in victory'—the victory no longer of the spirit but of the body—the well-fed body, for ever youthful, immortally athletic, indefatigably sexy. The Moslem paradise had had copulations six centuries long. In this new Christian heaven, progress, no doubt, would have stepped up the period to a millennium and added the joy of everlasting tennis, eternal golf and swimming" (16). Jeremy envisions a materialist heaven rather than a spiritual one, a heaven that resembles the lives led by the rich inhabitants of Los Angeles. Like the girls chewing gum who appear to be ruminating upon God, the cemetery shows all the outward signs of faith, but those buried there have worshiped and coveted their earthly goods rather than the God who is evoked at their gravesites. While Fitzgerald and West do not take up the issue of religion in quite the same way, each novel uses the setting of Los Angeles to symbolize the broader and ever-growing trend of American consumer culture. While Stoyte offers an extreme (and satirical) example, *After Many a Summer* suggests that Americans have become obsessed by the notion that immortality is available for purchase.

For Pordage, the man of history and science, the academic, the idea of faith in a "higher power" runs counter to his distinctly practical character. While "faith" is continually undermined throughout the novel, in Pordage Huxley privileges the importance not only of experience but of recognizing "meaning" as a construct rather than an a priori phenomenon: "For Jeremy, direct, unmediated experience was always hard to take in, always more or less disquieting. Life became safe, things assumed meaning, only when they had been translated into words and confined between the covers of a book" (27). Unlike the novel's other characters, Pordage recognizes the importance of language in structuring "reality." His reference to Stoyte's castle upon first seeing it as "this Object" (19) suggests Lacanian undertones, as though the thing itself cannot be encompassed by the inadequate descriptions of language. This is further emphasized by the word's capitalization, which accentuates its domineering nature. As he comes upon the castle for the first time, he makes the following observation: "The Object impended, insolently enormous. Nobody had dealt poetically with *that*. Not Childe Roland, not the King of Thule, not Marmion, not the Lady of Shalott, not Sir Leoline. Sir Leoline, he repeated to himself with a connoisseur's appreciation of romantic absurdity, Sir Leoline, the baron rich, had—what? A toothless mastiff bitch. But Mr. Stoyte had baboons and a sacred grotto, Mr. Stoyte had a chromium portcullis and the Hauberk Papers, Mr. Stoyte had a cemetery like an amusement park and a donjon like . . ." (27, ellipsis in original). In some sense, for Pordage at least, what Stoyte has created transcends words and history, which makes it especially difficult for him to fit it into the practical paradigm in which he couches his existence. It also, in that sense, stands as a contrast to religion and symbolically sets up Stoyte as a Kubla Khanian figure whose vast material possessions make him a sort of god on earth; though in spite of his godlike stature, we are led to anticipate the erosion of this heretical power.

Running directly counter to the religious theme in the novel, and once again evoking the false belief in a timeless earthly paradise, is Stoyte's obsession with developing a scientific cure for aging. The irony of his wish is that when one turns so entirely from faith to science one must starkly face the realities of the human animal for exactly what it is: abject. Our first glimpse of these implications comes in the form of a description of the gorillas that are housed at Stoyte's residence: "Just opposite the point at which they were standing, on a shelf of artificial rock, sat a baboon mother, holding in her arms the withered and disintegrating corpse of the baby she would not abandon even though it had been dead for a fortnight. Every now and then, with an intense, automatic affection, she would lick the cadaver. Tufts of greenish fur and even pieces of skin detached themselves under the vigorous action of her tongue. Delicately, with black fingers, she would pick the hairs out of her mouth, then begin again" (91–92). This grotesque scene is, first of all, a reminder of human mortality that contextualizes Stoyte's futile pursuit in a far more disturbing light than Coleridge's "Kubla Khan." While Stoyte makes an effort to avoid meaningful emotional attachment, it is also a reminder of the inevitable ("automatic affection") connection that even nonhuman animals feel toward one another. It also suggests the difficulty of understanding and coping with death. We cannot help but see shades of Stoyte in the baboon mother, unable to accept the reality of death and decay. Just earlier, Huxley equates the rich with gorillas, another reminder of the connection between human beings and our primate ancestors. Further, the baby symbolically recalls Virginia (whose name is certainly an ironic joke), who is earlier described as Stoyte's baby, "not only figuratively and colloquially, but also in the literal sense of the word" (50). As two gorillas begin copulating she remarks, "Aren't they cute! . . . Aren't they *human!*" (93). What is so disturbing about the scene is precisely that the gorillas *are* so human and that their actions, although we would not like to think so, are not so far removed from our own.

While the gorillas anticipate the final grotesque scene of the novel, in which we find that the Fifth Earl has devolved into, as Obispo calls him, a "foetal ape" (353), making a horrifying ironic joke of Stoyte's dream, the most truly revealing aspect of the novel comes in the form of Propter's ruminations on personality. By way of contrast, the narrator first explains Propter's notion that "Peter Claver's conception of the world had the defect of being erroneous, but the merit of being simple and dramatic" (108–9). This conception consists of a personal and forgiving God, "heaven and hell and the absolute reality of human personalities" (109), and other qualities that one would typically associate with a Christian worldview. Propter, however, poses the following: "For, if individuality is not absolute, if personalities are illusory figments of a self-will disastrously blind to the reality of a more-than-personal consciousness, of which it is the limitation and denial, then all of every human being's efforts must be directed, in the last resort, to the actualization of that more-than-personal consciousness" (109). It is in this gesture toward something somehow "more-than-personal" that Huxley most closely reaches a postmodern and Lacanian psychoanalytic conception of "identity."

This is supported by other echoes of Lacanian theory elsewhere in the novel, for example, in Dr. Obispo's comments during his first conversation with Pordage, in which he draws a connection between the novel's problematic view of religion and what resembles parts of Lacan's theory of object choice: "Why, you can't even love a woman as she is in herself; and after all, there is some sort of objective physical basis for the phenomenon we call a female. A pretty nice basis in some cases. Whereas poor old Dios is only a spirit—in other words, pure imagination" (61). Like Lacan, Obispo suggests that we do not actually desire objects themselves but rather the meanings that we project upon them. Our desires are primarily narcissistic, and ultimately our only desire is to fill the void opened up by our entry into the realm of the symbolic.

Propter's philosophy is not so different from what we find in Fitzgerald and West, but it is more acutely stated. "To conceive of that all-important ego of his [referring to Stoyte's worker from Kansas] as a fiction," he ruminates, "a kind of nightmare, a frantically agitated nothingness capable, when once its frenzy had been quieted, of being filled with God, with a God conceived and experienced as a more than personal consciousness, as a free power, a pure working, a being withdrawn" (111). There are echoes here of our previous focus on Lacan's three primary modes of sublimation, and of course the novel as a whole travels on the border between science and religion. This is the vision of ideal human identity that Propter lays out, and it is essentially Lacanian in nature. I would like to view Propter's vision, ultimately, as a culmination of the fragmented view of personality collectively laid out by Fitzgerald, West, and Huxley. Together, these novels create a post/modern Los Angeles that imagines not simply an alternative view of subjectivity—as do many modernist novels—but a profound problematization of the conception of personality altogether.

I have tried to suggest that the Los Angeles of the 1930s provided a perfect site for these writers to take up the notion of identity as a construct, rather than an ontological fixity. As for the city's broader symbolic value, there is a great deal of nuance to their view. For *After Many a Summer Dies the Swan* also suggests, as Russell Berman points out, that it is problematic to simply view Los Angeles as a place disconnected from any but its own ephemeral history:

> Stoyte's own obsessive pursuit of youth, which Pordage incorporates into his condemnation of the American West, turns out to draw on a tradition—so we learn from the documents—that leads back to England, and this unsettles Pordage's too comfortable contrast between Old World and New: California youth culture draws on very Old World traditions. Far from endorsing the denunciation of Los Angeles as barbarian, Huxley—not unlike the German exile philosophers Max Horkheimer and Theodor Adorno—uncovers a dialectic in the Enlightenment which finds its starkest expression in his new home. (50–51)

Huxley's Los Angeles, in particular, gives us the paradox of the city's vapidity and artificiality—a weakening of historicity—but at the same time a reminder that even as it seems so completely detached from what has come before, it is in fact built upon the values of its nation and its nation's progenitors. Taken together, Fitzgerald, West, and Huxley seem keenly aware that Los Angeles represents a new phenomenon in American life, a fragmentation of old value systems and of classic notions about identity. But they also maintain a sense of continuity with the past. This chapter is meant to show that what we call postmodernism is not so far removed from its predecessor. In fact, these novelists of the 1930s were already exploring the major themes that postmodern writers would take up following World War II. If we thus make a more concerted effort to trace the lineage of Los Angeles's representation in modernist fiction, we might reclaim it from the realm of postmodernism and instead paint a more accurate picture of its importance to the age of modernism.

Chapter 5

THE NEGATION OF SUBJECTIVITY

Méconnaissance and the Other in Beckett's *Murphy*

The first four chapters of this project have proceeded for the most part chronologically, through the work of Joseph Conrad, James Joyce, Virginia Woolf, F. Scott Fitzgerald, Nathanael West, and Aldous Huxley. I have attempted a sense of continuity in order to suggest a trajectory from early modernist attempts to situate the subject within capitalist ideological structures to later novels that increasingly adopt stylistic and thematic traits typically associated with postmodernism and post-structuralism. Samuel Beckett's *Murphy* (1938) is thus, in a sense, out of sequence here, as its publication precedes that of the three novels from the previous chapter. But like Huxley, who also lived well into the age of postmodernism, Beckett did the bulk of his writing after 1945. His work continues to challenge critics, who have called him the last modernist or the first postmodernist or used countless other monikers in an attempt to classify his elusive writing. Duncan McColl Chesney encapsulates the problem of classifying Beckett, describing him as a "crucial test case" in evaluating the usefulness and validity of postmodernism as a category, style, or, borrowing a term from Jameson, "cultural dominant" (637):

> He follows perhaps the most exemplary of prose modernists, James Joyce, and produces a body of work which is very much unlike that of his famous predecessor and compatriot/co-exile, as well as that of the subject of his youthful scholarly interest (another quintessential prose modernist), Marcel Proust. Beckett clearly, and not just temporally, comes after these modernists and their moment. His defining war is the Second, not the First. His childhood was not that of the *fin-de-siècle*; his abandoned homeland was the *Republic* of Ireland; *his* exile was so

famously marked by the change of language in order to achieve what he called "the right weakening effect" in a clear attempt to escape the style of Joyce in the language of Proust, and thus attain a style all his own. If *post* simply means *after,* then Beckett is perhaps the first great postmodernist. But we all know it is not so simple. (637–38)

Indeed, critics have noted that Beckett has often been cited as an exemplar in justifying just the type of post/modern "break" outlined above.[1] Steven Connor, for instances, writes that "for a while during the 1980s and 1990s, it seemed to make more sense for critics to use Beckett's works to make the case for some kind of break within modernism, moving beyond the forms of order and authority represented by high and classic modernism into a world of unlimited contingency" (2). This is ironic, in some sense, given that, as Chesney points out, Beckett's great influences were modernists. And yet his writing, even as early as *Murphy,* does not feel quite right in company with Joyce, Proust, and his other compatriots (with the exception, perhaps, of Joyce's 1939 novel *Finnegans Wake,* which has itself been used as an emblem to mark the end of modernism). In addition to being influenced by many modernist novelists and poets, Beckett was also profoundly influenced by his radically diverse readings in philosophy, psychology, and other subjects. These disparate influences generate in Beckett a style that is intensely literary, deeply philosophical, and packed with penetrating psychological insight. It is surely in part Beckett's footing in so many different disciplines that gives his prose such a distinctive and unclassifiable character. He is one of those few writers who truly resist comparison.

Murphy was Beckett's second novel, although his first, *Dream of Fair to Middling Women,* which was allegedly written in a matter of weeks in 1932, was rejected by publishers and not actually released until 1992, three years after Beckett's death. While the mid-1930s saw the publication of the short story collection *More Pricks Than Kicks* (1934) and the collection of poems *Echo's Bones and Other Precipitates* (1935),[2] *Murphy* was Beckett's first mature effort. The major event that defined the 1930s for Beckett was the death of his father in 1933, which was extraordinarily traumatic for him. Following his father's death, he began psychoanalytic treatment with Wilfred Bion at the Tavistock Clinic in London. During his treatment Beckett developed an interest in psychology and began his own course of study on the subject. Chris Ackerley explains that "Freud was a major force, Beckett's interest centering upon narcissism, neuroses and the psychopathology of daily life rather than the familiar dreams of totems and taboos. He found in these studies . . . confirmation of his own intrauterine attraction and psychosomatic problems, and insights into the fraught relationship with his mother . . . but he retained a skepticism about their potential" (17). James Knowlson, one of Beckett's biographers, describes some particular influences, writing that "in the course of his therapy, Beckett read widely on the subject of psychology and psychoanalysis. R. S. Woodworth's *Contemporary Schools of Psychology* provided him with the general framework he needed. His detailed notes on this book still exist. In it, he read about behaviorism, gestalt psychology, Freud, Jung, Adler, and William McDougall" (171). These readings, coupled with his own experience, became the inspiration for the Magdalen Mental Mercyseat, where Murphy eventually takes employment. Given this context, it is not surprising that *Murphy* was a deeply personal novel for Beckett. "Above all," according to Knowlson, "*Murphy* expresses in a radical and sharply focused way that impulse toward self-immersion, solitude, and inner peace the consequences of which Beckett was attempting to resolve in his personal life through psychoanalysis" (203). Together with his philosophical readings of Descartes, Spinoza, Leibniz, and others, Beckett's readings in psychology inform *Murphy*'s unique discourse on human subjectivity.

While previous critics have observed the novel's underlying irony, I will focus specifically on what I find to be a central ironic tension out of which the novel's deconstructive critique emerges, which is the juxtaposition of Murphy's belief in a Cartesian dualism to the novel's narrative posture, which suggests a Lacanian view of subjectivity as a symptom of desire. In order to reach his utopian vision of existential transcendence, Murphy attempts to extricate himself from the torment of the subject-object relationship; in other words, he desires the negation of desire. The omnipotent narrative voice, on the other hand, recognizes that desire itself generates subjectivity, and thus Murphy (like Gatsby) finds himself trapped in an endless repetition, which in his case is symbolically represented by his rocking chair. While the rocking of the chair creates physical movement, in a deeper sense Murphy does not go anywhere at all. His vision is further sabotaged by the other characters in the novel, whose ceaseless pursuit of him mocks his attempt to escape the social dimension of subjectivity (we might imagine Lacan's symbolic realm here). As Lacan, Althusser, and others have demonstrated, we are always already subjected through the signifying practice of language and our existence in a physical space populated by other human beings, through whom our desire is mediated. Accordingly, the driving force of Beckett's novel is *méconnaissance,* the persistent misrecognition that sustains the subject's sense of unity and coherence. This leads Murphy continually into the painful realm of *jouissance,* culminating in his encounter with Mr. Endon and his eventual death. While Murphy longs to escape into the realm of the real, the novel reminds us that our entrance into the symbolic forever severs us from this realm.

Head/Space

Just as the novels taken up in the previous chapter emphasize the importance of spatial surroundings in creating a geographical context for the subject's existence, *Murphy* establishes spatiality as a major theme through its meticulous attention to particular spatial details. John Pilling argues that *Murphy* "could be called 'a novel of London' in much the same way as T. S. Eliot's *The waste land* [*sic*] can be seen as a 'poem of London,' and there is perhaps no other single work of Beckett's that fosters, though very much as an incidental by-product, the possibility of a 'literary pilgrimage' to the places mentioned in it" (33). Indeed, *Murphy* is filled with references to particular streets, neighborhoods, and landmarks. As John Pilling goes on to observe, "Without such representational, solid points of reference—quite as important in their way as the 'points' which both the characters and the narrator insist we take note of . . . Murphy's desire to elude definition would itself lack definition" (33). Particularly interesting in Pilling's characterization of the novel is his claim that geography represents an "incidental by-product" in its own right, along with his insistence that it is in fact thematically crucial in that it allows a point of juxtaposition against which Beckett can examine issues of psychology and philosophy. The paradoxical tension underlying Pilling's characterization of geographical specificity in the novel mirrors the ironic tensions that underlie the novel itself, those between virtual and actual, mental and physical, subject and object, presence and absence, and ultimately life and death.

Neary says to Murphy in the opening pages of the novel that "all life is figure and ground" (2), to which Murphy responds, "But a wandering to find home" (3). Taking a cue from Joyce, the novel is pervaded by this desire to "find home," but *Murphy* explores a notion of "home" that is entirely psychological. In these opening pages, as it will do so often throughout, the novel asks us to consider the function of a concept that is generally associated with physicality (wandering) in a less familiar psychological context. In other words, the novel constantly forces us into an uncanny position as readers: whenever we try to establish a footing in physical reality, we are pulled back through the subjective filter of Murphy's consciousness. The notion of wandering is also contrasted with Murphy's obsession with bondage, which is introduced on the opening page of the novel, beginning with a meticulous description of the room in which Murphy feels his deepest pleasure by distancing himself from the outside world: "The sun shone, having no alternative, on the nothing new. Murphy sat out of it, as though he were free, in a mew in West Brompton. Here for what might have been six months he had eaten, drunk, slept, and put his clothes on and off, in a medium-sized cage of north-western aspect commanding an unbroken view of medium-sized cages of south-eastern aspect" (1). The novel gives us in this first paragraph not only the general location of West Brompton but also the directionality of the apartment itself. In mock epic fashion it even begins with a description of celestial positioning, foreshadowing the premonition that Murphy receives from Suk, which he takes as gospel and obsessively follows in his future actions throughout the novel. The irony here is that aside from the fact that he prefers spaces that provide him solitude, physical location is practically meaningless to Murphy, who desires only withdrawal into his own mind. As with the juxtaposition between Murphy's belief in a mind/body dualism and the novel's constant undermining of such a view of subjectivity, one gets the sense that the novel's meticulous spatial details subtly mock Murphy's insistence that place is of no importance to his project of psychological liberation. Of course, this is not entirely true for Murphy, as in fact particular places, like the Cockpit in Hyde Park and, of course, his apartment, become crucial sites of escape for Murphy. It is significant, going along with this fact, that the passage refers to Murphy's state "as though he were free," again highlighting the irony that while Murphy may feel a sense of freedom, we as readers are continually being told that this freedom is illusory. This is emphasized as well in the reference to his apartment as a "cage," suggesting that what Murphy sees as liberating is in fact a form of confinement—in a physical sense but perhaps in a psychological or emotional one as well.

Murphy's fixation on the solitude of his apartment is introduced in stark terms in the following paragraph, which tells us just how unusual his obsession is: "He sat naked in his rocking-chair of undressed teak, guaranteed not to crack, warp, shrink, corrode, or creak at night. It was his own, it never left him" (1). Murphy's nakedness recalls the safety of the womb and his desire to escape the realm of the symbolic. We also learn that Murphy is not only mentally but also physically constrained by the scarves that he has used to fasten himself to his chair: "Seven scarves held him in position. Two fastened his shins to the rockers, one his thighs to the seat, two his breast and belly to the back, one his wrists to the strut behind. Only the most local movements were possible" (1). The fetal metaphor is extended here as the scarves that hold Murphy to his chair suggest an umbilical connection, the security of physical confinement. Later the narrator tells us that "he sat in his chair this way because it gave him pleasure! First it gave his body pleasure, it appeased his body. Then it set him free in his mind. For it was not until his body was appeased that he could come alive in his mind, as described in section six. And life in his mind gave him pleasure, such pleasure that pleasure was not the word" (2). In this initial description of Murphy's occupation, we can already begin to see the novel's underlying irony emerge: while Murphy insists upon the absolute separation of mind and body, he nonetheless must rely upon physical appeasement in order to achieve the psychological pleasure that prepossesses him.

Murphy's Mind

The famous sixth chapter of the novel fully lays bare the philosophical and psychological assumptions according to which Murphy operates. In doing so, it also calls attention to the multiplicity of viewpoints regarding subjectivity that the novel contains. "It is most unfortunate," the narrator explains, "but the point of this story has been reached where a justification of the expression 'Murphy's mind' has to be attempted. Happily we need not concern ourselves with this apparatus as it really was—that would be an extravagance and an impertinence—but solely with what it felt and pictured itself to be" (65). We might interpret "as it really was" here as a scientific or biological description, the implication being that such a description would serve no purpose in this venue. That we are given a description of Murphy's mind according to "what it felt and pictured itself to be" suggests the problem of subjectivity, with which the novel is concerned. There is, first off, an ontological conundrum here: if we accept that "Murphy's mind" carries this conception of itself, are we to assume that we are speaking here of Murphy? In other words, do we assume that Murphy's mind is speaking for him? This once again raises the issue, which the subsequent paragraphs develop, of the Cartesian mind/body dualism:

> Murphy's mind pictured itself as a large hollow sphere, hermetically closed to the universe without. This was not an impoverishment, for it excluded nothing that it did not itself contain. Nothing had ever been, was or would be in the universe outside it but was already present as virtual, or actual, or virtual rising into actual, or actual falling into virtual, in the universe inside it.
>
> This did not involve Murphy in the idealist tar. There was the mental fact and there was the physical fact, equally real if not equally pleasant. He distinguished between the actual and the virtual of his mind, not as between form and the formless yearning for form, but as between that of which he had both mental and physical experience and that of which he had mental experience only. Thus the form of kick was actual, that of caress virtual. (65)

The description is solipsistic in its insistence on absolute subjectivity. Although the "mental fact" and the "physical fact" are said to be "equally real," all physical experiences are filtered through processes of mental activity. At the same time, it is only through mental processes connected with the brain that physical stimuli can be felt. The two are, then, equally real in the sense that both mental and physical sensations are registered through the activity of sensory perception as it is received by the brain. But the virtual, unlike the real, entails that which cannot be seen or felt by the real. The foot that kicks has a physical presence in time and space and is therefore plainly visible; the caress, in the common sense, is physical as well. The hand that caresses us exists in time and space and makes physical contact with the sensing body. But the caress transcends the real in the intangible emotion that it evokes, the immaterial thought, feeling, or desire that has no materiality. The novel plainly recognizes the fundamental subjectivity of human existence. Our experiences, whether mental or physical, are always filtered through our biological selves *and* our psyches.

The Cartesian dualism is more fully developed and muddled by the narrator's description of Murphy's conception of and relationship toward his body and mind, which is rendered problematic by an essential lack of understanding: "Thus Murphy felt himself split in two, a body and a mind. They had intercourse apparently, otherwise he could not have known that they had anything in common. But he felt his mind to be bodytight and did not understand through what channel the intercourse was effected nor how the two experiences came to overlap" (66). While Murphy sees the body and mind as equal—if we may extrapolate this from the previous passage—he also experiences a fundamental disconnect between the two. Interestingly, despite this philosophical notion of separation, Murphy does admit to some sort of fundamental continuity between his body and mind, but he simply chooses to believe that it is enshrouded in metaphysical mystery: "However that might be, Murphy was content to accept this partial congruence of the world of his mind with the world of his body as due to some such process of supernatural determination" (66). We see here Murphy succumbing to ideology in the Žižekian sense of choosing to believe even while the evidence in front of him challenges his belief: "The problem [of reconciling the disconnect between his body and mind] was of little interest. Any solution would do that did not clash with the feeling growing stronger as Murphy grew older, that his mind was a closed system, subject to no principle of change but its own, self-sufficient and impermeable to the vicissitudes of the body. Of infinitely more interest than how this came to be so was the manner in which it might be exploited" (66). In other words, Murphy continues to believe, even though he realizes that he is deceiving himself in doing so. "Any solution would do," as long as he does not have to confront reality as such. In a passage from *The Sublime Object of Ideology* referenced above, Žižek posits "a new way to read the Marxian formula 'they do not know it, but they are doing it'" (32), which encapsulates the classic Marxist view of ideology. "The illusion is not on the side of knowledge," Žižek explains, "it is already on the side of reality itself, of what the people are doing. What they do not know is that their social reality itself, their activity, is guided by an illusion, by a fetishistic inversion. What they overlook, what they misrecognize, is not the reality but the illusion which is structuring their reality, their real social activity" (32). This brings us back to *Nostromo*, where the citizens of Sulaco allow themselves to be victimized by bourgeois ideology and continue to act in ways that obviously run counter to their own interests (supporting successive political dictators, and so on).

While the nature of Murphy's misrecognition is somewhat different, the effect is nevertheless the same: he is unable to recognize his role in social activity through his relationship to others. Despite the obvious and inevitable connections that build between him and the people around him, he persists in the belief that he may simply sever these connections at any time and retreat back into the virtual world of his mind, essentially shutting off the "actual" world. Let us recall that Žižek concludes the above point by reformulating Marx's famous statement: "They know very well how things really are, but still they are doing it as if they did not know. The illusion is therefore double: it consists in overlooking the illusion which is structuring our real, effective relationship to reality. And this overlooked, unconscious illusion is what may be called the *ideological fantasy*" (32–33). While Murphy believes in the liberating potential of freeing his mind from the tethers of his body, the novel makes it clear that his pursuit simply constitutes a fundamental ideological fantasy.

The essence of Murphy's fantasy is the belief that if he extricates himself from the realm of the physical, the realm of bodily sensation, he can then extricate himself from the realm of desire. This is where we, as readers, encounter the disconnect between Murphy's Cartesian view of subjectivity and that of the novel, which recognizes that Murphy has already been inevitably cast into the drama of desire from which his subjectivity has emerged. The notion of subjectivity that the novel suggests resembles that posited by Lacan, who maintains that physical objects are only fleeting material manifestations of our desire, which in fact resides entirely in the psychological realm, or the realm of the mind, as Murphy would have it. Murphy's mistake, in other words, is to think that he can escape the constriction of corporeality by shielding his body, so to speak, from the physical world—thus his tying himself to his chair. The underlying irony in the novel, which functions simultaneously as comedy and tragedy, arises out of the juxtaposition of Murphy's view to the novel's rejection of Cartesianism and its insistence that one cannot escape desire, as it is desire itself that distinguishes us as human. The situational irony in Murphy's case is that his very attempt to escape the realm of desire through physical bondage is actually a symptom of his desire (put in Lacanian terms) to return to the prespecular and prelinguistic subjective fantasy prior to the mirror stage, or, as we have seen, a symbolic return to the safety of the womb. While Murphy becomes increasingly convinced throughout the novel that he can escape the external world, which he loathes, and achieve what might be described as a form of psychological enlightenment, the novel's narrative voice simultaneously deconstructs his attempts.

Daniel Katz explores this issue as well, explaining that "a deconstructive analysis of the 'voice' in Beckett inevitably leads to the broader questions of consciousness, self-presence, and subjectivity. As Beckett's prose closes down the space of phenomenal identification based on the representation of a coherent subjectivity, it likewise eliminates the possibility of psychologizing interpretations" (17). Without question, one of the most difficult characteristics of Beckett's prose for critics is its inherent resistance to interpretation. "It is difficult indeed," Katz writes, "to state the sum of the achievements of an author who so consistently strove for erasure, to constantly say in order to have finally said nothing" (181). This notion of "say[ing] in order to have finally said nothing" encapsulates Beckett's deconstructive discourse throughout the novel. While Murphy is continually denied the negation of desire that he strives for, the novel ironically ends in erasure when his ashes are unceremoniously scattered across a soiled barroom floor.[3]

It is as though Murphy is gradually erased throughout the novel until he is done away with entirely—and of course Beckett further develops this irony by continuing the novel for several chapters after his death.

As we have established, one of the central tensions in the novel is between Murphy's attempt to escape the ensnaring net of desire and the novel's continually recasting him back into it. Murphy's essential problem is that he believes in the uniqueness of his own subjective experience; as the narrator tells us, "Murphy believed there was no dark quite like his own dark" (95). Murphy says to Celia during one exchange early in the novel, "I can't talk against space" and then asks her, "What have I now? . . . I distinguish. You, my body and my mind. . . . In the mercantile Gehenna . . . to which your words invite me, one of these will go, or two, or all. If you, then you only; if my body, then you also; if my mind, then all" (25). Murphy's Cartesian dualism has animated many critical responses to the novel. Ackerley, for example, contends that "the structure of the novel as a whole arises from a distrust of Cartesian rationalism, and its controlling irony from the incommensurability of Murphy's declared goal and its realization in a universe which is unclear and indistinct—in a word, absurd" (18).[4] Thomas J. Cousineau also recognizes this underlying tension in his account of the novel's central ironic structure: "In effect, Beckett uses irony to place in question that very promotion of mental experience at the expense of the physical which is the essence of Murphy's system. The abuse to which he subjects Murphy serves as a vehicle through which he registers his suspicion that, as attractive an option as Murphy's retreat into his mental world may be, it represents in some way a misconception of reality" (225). What I find particularly interesting about Cousineau's account is the way that he characterizes Beckett as subjecting Murphy to the abuse he suffers throughout the novel. One cannot help but feel as though we, as readers, are in on a joke that the novel is perpetrating against Murphy, that the novel is subtly mocking him in his attempts at escape. It is as though, in effect, he is entrapped by the novel—and thus language—itself. While the novels taken up in previous chapters recognize the importance of language in structuring subjectivity, *Murphy* is more assertive in plainly suggesting that subjectivity *is* language. This is why a Lacanian framework is so essential to making sense of the novel's complex project.

Not surprisingly, there is precedent for reading Murphy through a Lacanian lens. Cousineau himself, for instance, addresses the novel's treatment of subjectivity as follows:

> For both Beckett and Lacan a central concern is the process through which the primordial subject moves out of its original undifferentiated experience into the world of customs, cultural norms, and socially sanctioned rationality. The process itself is paradoxical. Positively, it confers upon the subject an identity, through which he perceives himself as an organized unity, and a language, through which he presents himself to the world and forms relations with other language-uttering subjects. Negatively, it substitutes an artificial, socially conditioned self for the original, authentic, pre-cultural subject. Both Beckett's fiction and the psychoanalytical process as envisaged by Lacan are motivated by the desire, ultimately futile though it may be, to reverse this process of alienation and to restore original subjectivity. (225)

Cousineau's account is rooted in Lacan's famous account of the mirror stage, in which the subject first recognizes itself as an autonomous and coherent whole apart from the mother. As Lacan explains, however, this apparent "recognition" is in fact a *méconnaissance,* or "misrecognition." Because this autonomy and coherence are illusory, the subject finds itself forever longing for the lost unity that the mirror stage deceptively suggests. In some sense, then, Murphy's struggle actually brings us back around to Gatsby, who similarly yearns for a symbolic return to the safety of the mother's womb. The primary difference in the two cases is that Gatsby appears to be entirely unaware of his subconscious desire and is so thoroughly immersed in ideological and desiring processes that he believes himself to be striving toward an obtainable goal or idea, while Murphy's attempt is premeditated. Gatsby desires the fulfillment of desire, while Murphy desires its negation.

In outlining the novel's symbolic structure, Cousineau identifies Lacan's symbolic order in the "three zones" that Murphy delineates in his mind, the "light," "half light," and "dark." respectively. "In the first," the novel explains, "were the forms with parallel, a radiant abstract of the dog's life, the elements of physical experience available for a new arrangement. . . . Here the kick that the physical Murphy received, the mental Murphy gave" (67). This first zone corresponds with the realm of the symbolic, where experience is given form and arrangement. "In the second were the forms without parallel. Here the pleasure was contemplation. This system had no other mode in which to be out of joint and therefore did not need to be put right in this. Here was the Belacqua bliss and others scarcely less precise. . . . The third, the dark [suggesting the Lacanian real], was a flux of forms, a perpetual coming together and falling asunder of forms. . . . Here there was nothing but commotion and the pure forms of commotion. Here he was not free, but a mote in the dark of absolute freedom. He did not move, he was a point in the ceaseless unconditioned generation and passing away of line" (67–68). It is well known that in discussing the issue of philosophy in *Murphy* Beckett pointed to two particular quotations, the first by Arnold Geulincx: "Ubi nihil vales, ibi nihil velis" (Where you are worth nothing, there you should want nothing); and the second by Malraux: "Il est difficile à celui qui vit hors du monde de ne pas rechercher les siens" (It is hard for someone who lives outside society not to seek out his own).[5] The first is particularly relevant to Murphy's desire for negation, which I would argue—going along with the above description of the three zones—represents for Murphy an entrance into the realm of the real. But despite his best efforts at a psychological transcendence that would allow him to enter the realm of the real, Murphy remains trapped in the imaginary.

While the mirror stage as described by Cousineau is obviously important in a Lacanian reading of *Murphy*, I would suggest that we might view it as a foundation for what might actually be a deeper Lacanian reading of the novel. In "The Subversion of the Subject and the Dialectic of Desire in the Freudian Unconscious," Lacan maintains that "man's desire is the Other's desire [*le désir de l'homme est le désir de l'Autre*] in which the *de* provides what grammarians call a 'subjective determination'—namely, that it is qua Other that man desires (this is what provides the true scope of human passion)" (*Écrits* 690). Although there are essentially two implications that stem from this oft-repeated insistence from Lacan that "man's desire is the Other's desire"—the first that the essence of desire is the desire of recognition from the other and the second that desire is directed toward the thing that the other desires—the fundamental lesson remains the same: that desire is always in some way mediated by the other and in that sense is always *social* in nature. In elaborating this point, Lacan goes on to explain:

> It should be noted that a clue may be found in the clear alien-ation that leaves it up to the subject to butt up against the ques-tion of his essence, in that he may not misrecognize that what he desires presents itself to him as what he does not want—a form assumed by negation in which misrecognition is inserted in a very odd way, the misrecognition, of which he himself is unaware, by which he transfers the permanence of his desire to an ego that is nevertheless obviously intermittent, and, in-versely, protects himself from his desire by attributing to it these very intermittences. (690–91)

The misrecognition, or *méconnaissance,* described above grows out of but extends beyond the mirror stage. It is apparent that Murphy "trans-fers the permanence of his desire" to what he believes is a stable and permanent "self" or ego, an ego that resides within the realm of the "virtual" and exists in distinction from his physical body—although, as he admits, the two are mysteriously connected in some ungraspable way. Murphy's strapping himself to his rocking chair is a symptom of this misrecognition, as he fails to realize that it is the process of desire itself that produces the very ego into which he longs to retreat. We might extrapolate this further and say that Murphy's broader dichoto-mizing of the "virtual" and "actual" itself represents a misrecognition that leads to Murphy's confusion of psychological and physical space.

In order to bring our Lacanian reading into broader focus, we might turn to David Watson's insightful *Paradox and Desire in Samuel Beck-ett's Fiction* (1991). While Watson searches for a symbolic landscape that covers the whole of Beckett's fiction, at this point we can clearly see how his delineations apply to *Murphy:* "We thus now have the ele-ments of a model containing all three of Lacan's orders: the symbolic, which for Beckett is the space of words, of the alienating *je;* the real, which lies beyond the text in silence; and the imaginary, instituted at the point occupied by the mirror, where the self in the other sees an image of the self in silence, the point which is in some way the locus of an interaction between the zones of speech and silence" (48). The other for Murphy is Celia, whose relationship with him is one of the central problems in the novel, challenging his attempt at mind/body separation. "The part of him that he hated craved for Celia," the narrator explains, "the part that he loved shrivelled up at the thought of her" (5). Despite Murphy's psychological protestations, he is unable to keep himself from desiring Celia on some "bodily" level. This reflects the paradox described above, as Murphy's fatal flaw is his inability to comprehend that these two parts of him are in fact one in the same. Katz maintains that "Celia represents not an alternative to Murphy's narcissistic scrutiny of the skies—narcissistic in that his interest in them lies in his viewing them as a text of his own life, of himself—but its continuation" (38). Beckett wryly subverts in Celia the classic love interest in a way that once again brings us back to the novel's underlying conception of desire, which holds that desire is in fact desire for the desire of the other, or ultimately recognition by the other of one's self. While Murphy seeks to perpetually escape the realm of the other, ironically he must rely upon the other for his own conception of self. "In Murphy's dialectic," Katz continues, "Celia is one stop on the path that begins with the firmament and ends with Mr. Endon, in which all acts of scrutiny are investments in self-scrutiny, and where all objects derive their interest from narcissistic projection" (38). As we have seen, despite his own obsessive investment in self-scrutiny, Murphy is nonetheless always already implicated in desire as a socially mediated phenomenon; even his narcissism, in the end, is socially mediated.

We might finally say that the part of himself that Murphy hates is the desiring subject that we all inevitably are, while the part that he loves is the solipsistic self that exists outside of the subject/object relationship; thus the central conflict in the relationship between the two. Lacan says that desire is "caught in the rails of metonymy" (*Écrits* 431). If Murphy were able escape the rails of metonymy, he could then extricate himself from the prescribed path that desire inevitably leads us down. The narrator's observation that "soon his body would be quiet, soon he would be free" (6)—which is repeated near the end of the novel—reflects the notion that it is in fact the primal nature of desire that negates any notion of a freedom that we believe ourselves to be in possession of, a freedom that is inevitably tied to the corporeal body. In an insightful psychoanalytic reading of *Murphy*, Wendy Foster suggests that

> for Murphy, social meaning, as with socialized desire, has been domesticated to a state of patterned regularity, to a kind of dogmatic fixity that is crystallized, textually, in Suk's oracle and spatially in Neary's futile cycle of bar stools around which "he sat all day, moving slowly from one stool to another until he had completed the circuit of the counters, when he would start all over again in the reverse direction" (56). Neary's "circuit," as the physical exposition of Murphy's inability to provide a verbal context for meaning, articulates that fundamental paradox of mobile immobility that is life within the boundaries of the "big world."

I would add that Murphy's fear of "domestication" extends to his troubled relationship with Celia as well and her attempts to persuade him to seek out employment. Entering the workforce would mean for Murphy capitulation to a socially constructed notion of the willing subject of the state, a position that Murphy longs to avoid. Employment would mean, ultimately, a capitulation to a socially constructed notion of subjectivity that fundamentally clashes with his ideal philosophy of being. It is this resistance to social expectation, in part, that causes Murphy to gravitate toward—and eventually obsessively embrace—the mental patients at the Magdalen Mental Mercyseat. As Phil Baker observes in *Beckett and the Mythology of Psychoanalysis*, "The hermetic sphere of Murphy's mind finds its contented correlative in the padded cell; a windowless upholstered monad which takes on the qualities of both skull and womb" (71). In the asylum, the circle of life and death is closed, the metonymic chain of desire is collapsed, and language itself breaks down.

Deconstructing the Self

In a relatively innocuous-seeming moment in the middle of the novel, Murphy experiences the following train of thought: "The Chaos and Waters Facility Act. The chaos. Light and Coke Co. Hell. Heaven.

Helen. Cecilia" (106). At work in this passage is the metonymic structure of language; Murphy's mind creates a chain of signifiers beginning with the Chaos and Waters Facility Act and ending with Celia. As
Foster argues, "Within the space of the 'big world' Murphy is deprived
of any kind of agency. He is acted on and spoken through his capture
within objectification—Celia's ultimatum, Suk's prophecy, the 'goal' of
Miss Counihan, et al. The language and needs of the 'big world' are not
his own, but forces to which Murphy is passively subjected." Beckett
clearly recognizes the ultimate futility of attempting to transcend our
physically grounded subjectivity in any meaningful way. In a final post-
mortem request, Murphy asks that his cremains be unceremoniously
flushed down a toilet; however, his final desire is ultimately thwarted
when a bar fight causes them to be scattered across the barroom floor,
part of the "sand, the beer, the butts, the glass, the matches, the spits,
the vomit" (165), the remains of his physical body disseminated in
space in ironic contrast to his living attempts at immobilization.

Katz emphasizes "how scrupulous Beckett is in refusing to allow
traditional philosophical, literary, historical, and psychoanalytic notions of subjectivity, consciousness, or intention to be turned into bul-
warks of meaning to orient, control, and finally recuperate the oscillations of erasure." "If the metaphysical subject remains a crucial issue
for Beckett," he argues, "it is largely because its deconstruction is necessary for the textual movements to be freed from an ideal tether that
would prohibit their flux" (181–82). I would extrapolate from this that
deconstruction is "necessary" in *Murphy* and in the other novels ana-
lyzed in this project in order to challenge the conventional notions of
subjectivity that modernist fiction reacted against. I would argue that
Beckett's *Murphy* is the ultimate deconstructionist modernist novel.
Beckett deconstructs desire in its role as the fundamental element in
structuring language and ends not by envisioning some new conception of subjectivity but by reaffirming an essential truth: That language
inevitably casts us into the process of desire. It is impossible to conceive of oneself outside desire, as desire itself is inherent in the act of
conceiving. There is no "conscious" escape from this, as Murphy would
hope; the only escape is death, or eternal negation.

While the other writers in this project distinguish themselves from
their predecessors by deconstructing conventional notions of subjec-

tivity rather than looking to supplant them, Beckett pushes the boundaries of this kind of dialectical deconstructive thinking to its breaking point. I follow here the path laid out by Richard Begam, who explains his interest "in reading Beckett through the discourse of poststructuralism but also in reading the discourse of poststructuralism through Beckett." "Such an approach reveals," he goes on to claim, "that as early as the 1930s and 1940s Beckett had already anticipated, often in strikingly prescient ways, many of the defining ideas of Barthes, Foucault, and Derrida." "Indeed," he argues, "we might begin to understand Beckett as a kind of buried subtext or marginalium in French poststructuralism, the writer who spoke most resonantly to those thinkers in France who came after Sartre and reacted against him" (4). In other words, we might think of Beckett as a sort of full-fledged proto-poststructuralist and, further, I would argue, proto-Lacanian. While this becomes more evident in his later work, *Murphy* functions as a fascinating test case that nonetheless distinguishes itself from other novels of its time. *Murphy,* as Ackerley describes it, "represents the fullest achievement of the first decade of Beckett's writing (1926–36)" and "is a culmination of one stage in Beckett's career, but equally the beginning of another, the matrix in which many later works were formed" (10). In other words, while it is firmly grounded in the modernist tradition and the influence of Joyce[6] and others, it also represents Beckett's ultimate trajectory toward the unmistakably postmodernism. Ackerley also points out, however, that *Murphy* has never quite escaped the shadow of Beckett's later work,[7] and in that sense, I would argue, it still has much to offer us, particularly as we try to better understand the post/modern divide and its problematics, as this project has sought to do.

CODA

In *Language and Materialism* (1977), Rosalind Coward and John Ellis write that "because all the practices that make up a social totality take place in language . . . man can be seen *as language,* as the intersection of the social, historical and individual" (1). While Conrad, Woolf, Joyce, Fitzgerald, West, and Huxley undoubtedly demonstrate an awareness of language and ideology as integral components of subjectivity, in Beckett we find a more radical awareness of the notion that, as Daniel Katz remarks in an echo of Coward and Ellis, "the subject *is* language" (182). Beginning with *Murphy* and expanding into his subsequent fictional and theatrical explorations, Beckett pushes this notion to its extreme. But while in this sense he brings us closer to ideas commonly associated with postmodernism, particularly as his writing career extended into the 1980s, he also brings us back around to Conrad. Both Martin Decoud and Murphy die in solitude, haunted by the inextricability of consciousness and action. Just as Conrad and Beckett can be taken to represent the beginning and the end of the modernist period, we might consider Decoud and Murphy as occupying opposing ends of the same spectrum. While Decoud experiences an existential crisis when his sense of self vanishes into the dark solitude of the void, Murphy, paradoxically, longs to inhabit this precise condition. What Decoud finds unbearable, Murphy finds liberating. Broadly speaking, this instance in Conrad shows the desire to recapture a lost sense of order, which many critics have seen as a hallmark of modernism, while Beckett revels in the chaos in classic postmodernist fashion.

But this seeming difference is belied by the underlying irony of each novel's narrative voice. Just as Beckett produces ironic tension in *Murphy* by juxtaposing the desires of the characters within the novel to the distanced narrator, in *Nostromo* Conrad devises a narrator who exists within the world of the novel and yet presents it in a near-omniscient fashion that produces a similar tension between the characters and their ideological circumstances. As critics like Fredric Jameson have observed, Conrad's movement beyond the embedded narrator of *Lord Jim* to a more complex and nearly omniscient narrator in *Nostromo* grants him a narrative posture that lays bare the psychological dramas of his characters while simultaneously maintaining a narrative distance that more panoramically frames those dramas for readers. Read this way, the intersection of Beckett's narrativity with his treatment of subjectivity is not in itself new; it is, rather, an outgrowth of a method that Conrad was already developing at the turn of the century. While Beckett thus brings us closer historically and stylistically to the moment of postmodernism, his modernist lineage is essential to an understanding of the role of modernism in shaping the ways of depicting subjectivity in fiction and of actually theorizing subjectivity as a phenomenon.

In closing, I would like to make one last gesture toward the historically oriented post/modern debate through which I have framed the more particular issue of subjectivity. In a December 20, 1897, letter to R. B. Cunningham Graham, Conrad advances a definition of history that encapsulates both the turn-of-the-twentieth-century zeitgeist and modernism as historical and artistic phenomena:

> There is—let us say—a machine. It evolved itself (I am severely scientific) out of a chaos of scraps of iron and behold!—it knits. I am horrified at the horrible work and stand appalled. I feel it ought to embroider—but it goes on knitting. You come and say: "this is all right: it's only a question of the right kind of oil. Let us use this—for instance—celestial oil and the machine shall embroider a most beautiful design in purple and gold." Will it? Alas no. You cannot by any special lubrication make embroidery with a knitting machine. And the most withering thought is that the infamous thing has made itself; made itself without thought, without conscience, without foresight, without eyes, without heart. It is a tragic accident—and it has happened. You can't interfere with it. The last drop of bitterness is in the suspicion that you can't even smash it. In virtue of that truth one and immortal which lurks in the force that made it spring into existence it is what it is—and it is indestructible! (*Selected Letters* 82)

As we have seen in our analysis of *Nostromo,* Conrad's world is a frighteningly indifferent one absent of a priori determinants or values.[1] Human existence, according to such a viewpoint, is distinctly messy; despite our best efforts to construct historical events into a narrative that fits them into whatever value systems we have adopted, the situation on the ground, so to speak, ultimately resists meaningful representative signification. While Conrad does not directly address the issue of subjectivity here, we see that by implication it is interpenetrated by the processes of history. We might say, in keeping with his metaphor, that human consciousness is woven into the fabric of history's knitting; it is not distinctly visible in its individuality from a panoramic view, but it is nonetheless integral. After all, what is history without human consciousness to experience and record it? This interrelationship between the unfolding of history and the individuals caught up in its unfolding encapsulates Conrad's narrative project and, as we have seen, *Nostromo*'s exploration of both personal and historical dramas. As I have shown in chapters 1 and 2, Conrad's approach forecasts that of other modernist writers, who similarly deconstruct conventional notions of subjectivity and show that while humans are actively engaged in the process of "making" history in the form of narrative, our own (self-)identities are simultaneously implicated in these same processes.

I would like to close by juxtaposing Conrad's knitting machine metaphor to one of the most important passages from Thomas Pynchon's *The Crying of Lot 49* (1966), widely viewed as a seminal postmodern novel, and one that led Brian McHale to "favor 1966 as year zero of postmodernism" ("What Was Postmodernism?"). In it, the narrator describes a trip taken by the heroine, Oedipa Maas, and her now deceased ex-boyfriend, Pierce Inverarity, to Mexico City: "They somehow wandered into an exhibition of paintings by the beautiful Spanish exile Remedios Varo: in the central painting of a triptych, titled 'Bordando el Manto Terrestre,' were a number of frail girls with heart-shaped faces, huge eyes, spun-gold hair, prisoners in the top room of a circular tower, embroidering a kind of tapestry which spilled out the slit windows and into a void, seeking hopelessly to fill the void: for all the other buildings and creatures, all the waves, ships and forests of the earth were contained in this tapestry, and the tapestry was the world" (20–21). The work described, known in English as *Embroidering*

Earth's Mantle, was painted late in Varo's career, in 1961, just two years before her death. The obvious primary influence of the work is surrealism, a movement that coincided with modernism in the 1920s but remained popular beyond World War II and into the 1960s. The painting becomes a centerpiece in the novel, much like Tod's *The Burning of Los Angeles* in West's *The Day of the Locust.* What is initially striking about the painting in a most general sense is that Varo's choice of metaphor closely resembles Conrad's. But whereas Conrad is embroiled in a historical moment marked by the growth of modernity and thus imagines a "machine," Varo imagines a tapestry that is human made. And while Conrad's machine can only knit—suggesting that history unfolds chaotically rather than neatly—Varo's women embroider a remarkable tapestry that billows from their tower and comprises the landscape around them. McHale explains that the painting "produces a visual equivalent of the kind of ontological paradoxes that one finds in postmodernist novels—paradoxes based on the running-together, in a logically impossible way, of different levels of reality. . . . Pynchon calls our attention to this paradox in Varo's painting, and builds it into his heroine's experiences of entrapment in a world of strange loops." Although Varo's painting and its use by Pynchon depart metaphorically from Conrad's image in various ways, Conrad's fiction similarly represents the "paradoxes based on the running-together, in a logically impossible way, of different levels of reality." He does this in *Nostromo,* for example, by taking us into the psyches of various characters and showing how their unique circumstances affect their consciousness and perception of the "real" events that occur in the novel. He does this earlier in *Lord Jim* as well, where fragments of the narrative are slowly pieced together as they are recalled by various characters. And like Joyce and Woolf, he also engages the void, as we have seen.

Looked at another way, Varo's painting might be seen as a metaphor for the way in which the void of each individual's subjectivity is populated by the world of the symbolic. As Lacan tells us, that which we experience as "reality" is in fact only our illusory relationship to the real as it is mediated through the realm of the symbolic. As she stands in front of the painting, Oedipa begins to weep as she experiences a moment of epiphany, realizing that the painting symbolizes her own condition of existence:

She had looked down at her feet and known, then, because of a painting, that what she stood on had only been woven together a couple thousand miles away in her own tower, was only by accident known as Mexico, and so Pierce had taken her away from nothing, there'd be no escape. What did she so desire to escape from? Such a captive maiden, having plenty of time to think, soon realizes that her tower, its height and architecture, are like her ego only incidental: that what really keeps her where she is is magic, anonymous and malignant, visited on her from outside and for no reason at all. Having no apparatus except gut fear and female cunning to examine this formless magic, to understand how it works, how to measure its field strength, count its lines of force, she may fall back on superstition, or take up a useful hobby like embroidery, or go mad, or marry a disk jockey. If the tower is everywhere and the knight of deliverance no proof against its magic, what else? (21–22)

Oedipa's name, which is of course derived from *Oedipus,* suggests the inescapability of fate. The "anonymous and malignant" magic that is "visited on her from outside and for no reason at all" evokes the indifference of time in Conrad's knitting-machine metaphor. The glibness of the choices afforded her—"fall back on superstition, or take up a useful hobby like embroidery, or go mad, or marry a disk jockey"—testify to the absurdity of living in a world without inherent meaning, one in which the ego is "only incidental" and the tower in which one is imprisoned is one's own creation. While Oedipa is unable to escape her own subjectivity, history marches on indifferent to her plight.

While McHale and others view *The Crying of Lot 49* as a prototypical postmodern text, I wonder if Pynchon's treatment of ontology is really so different from Beckett's, or even Conrad's? On the contrary, I would argue that the primary difference between Pynchon's exploration of ontological questions in *The Crying of Lot 49* and Conrad's in *Nostromo* and elsewhere is more than anything merely stylistic. As is typical in the postmodern novel, Pynchon pulls readers into the drama that his characters are experiencing in a way that Conrad does not. Conrad maintains an ironic distance in his narrative posture the likes of which Pynchon has rejected entirely. But despite certain undeniable stylistic differences, I have tried to show that as far back as Conrad we see writers working through the notion that our "reality" is in fact a construction of our own subjective consciousness. The examples from Conrad and Pynchon above *do* reflect changes in both historical perspective and stylistic conventions, but they are in essence promoting the same ontological worldview.

I would thus reiterate that rigid distinctions like McHale's—especially given his explicit use of Pynchon—rely too heavily upon an oversimplified view of the modernist project. Certainly historical evolutions and major historical events—namely, World War II—have produced scientific, technological, social, economic, and other changes that justify the practice of demarcating epochal changes. So my goal is not the rejection of postmodernism as a historical, artistic, or theoretical category. Such distinctions as those between modernism and postmodernism can be both useful and necessary in helping us understand historical progression and social evolution. But as the eminent modernist scholar Robert Scholes remarks in his conclusion to *Paradoxy of Modernism* (2006), "the Modernists were grappling with the same modernity which we inhabit, though ours is a more extreme case of it, to be sure" (276). Just as Scholes breaks down the critical tendency to draw distinctions within the modernist period between "high" and "low," "old" and "new," and ultimately "good" and "bad," we must resist the impulse to view postmodernism as an overcoming of modernism's limitations. Rather, we ought to view postmodernism, particularly on the pivotal subject of ontology, as carrying on the project of the modernist writers who were already speaking the language of postmodern theory. Doing so will allow for a more robust appreciation of modernism's contribution in shaping one of the central philosophical and artistic preoccupations of the twentieth century, and one that despite our best efforts we still have not quite moved beyond.

INTRODUCTION

1. It is worth noting that Nancy ultimately defends subjectivity, offering the following explanation: "That which obliterates is nihilism—itself an implicit form of the metaphysics of the subject (self-presence of that which knows itself as the dissolution of its own difference). There is nothing nihilistic in recognizing that the *subject*—the property of the *self*—is the thought that reabsorbs or exhausts all possibility of *being in the world* (all possibility of *existence,* all existence as being delivered to the possible), *and* that this same thought, never simple, never closed upon itself without remainder, designates and delivers an entirely different thought: that of the *one* and that of the some *one,* of the singular existent that the subject announces, promises, and at the same time conceals" (4).

2. In a follow-up to their 2006 book *Bad Modernisms,* Douglas Mao and Rebecca Walkowitz remark that "were one seeking a single word to sum up transformations in modernist literary scholarship over the past decade or two, one could do worse than light on *expansion*" ("New Modernist Studies" 737). In tracing this expansion, they address the insular focus of twentieth-century modernist criticism:

> Meanwhile, interrogations of the politics, historical validity, and aesthetic value of exclusive focus on the literatures of Europe and North America have spurred the study (in the North American academy) of texts produced in other quarters of the world or by hitherto little-recognized enclaves in the privileged areas. In addition to these temporal and spatial expansions, there has been what we are calling here a vertical one, in which once quite sharp boundaries between high art and popular forms of culture have been reconsidered; in which canons have been critiqued and reconfigured; in which works by members of marginalized social groups have been encountered with fresh eyes and ears; and in which scholarly inquiry has increasingly extended to matters of production, dissemination, and reception. (737–38)

The article quoted here, "The New Modernist Studies," provides an excellent survey of the ever-changing landscape of modernist studies in the early twenty-first century.

3. Although it should be mentioned that the general notion of modernisms in varying contexts dates back at least to Frank Kermode's use of the term in *The Sense of an Ending*.

4. Ross closes by arguing that "our task now is to explore the occulted relationship between modernism and theory as aspects of the twentieth century's massive cultural upheavals. We must approach the problematic of modernism/theory from a range of perspectives, including the institutional, historical, and discursive constructions of them as distinct fields. Additionally, we must push beyond disciplinary squabbles to ask not just what modernism can tell us about theory and what theory can tell us about modernism, but also what the nexus modernism/theory can tell us about the twentieth century's preoccupations, tendencies, triumphs, and failures" (*Modernism and Theory* 15). As subjectivity was certainly one of the preoccupations, if not the central one, of twentieth-century intellectual and artistic culture, it is imperative that we shed a new light on this nexus.

5. Friedman's explanation of why Joyce's work lends itself particularly well to post-structuralist readings is also useful: "First, as Sigmund Freud frequently stated, poets often 'discover' what philosophers and others come to theorize many years later. Post-structuralist theory is, in the eyes of many, an extension into philosophy, psychoanalysis, and linguistics of what writers such as Gertrude Stein and Joyce forged in literary discourse" (3). The present volume operates on the same premise, arguing that post-modern theories of subjectivity are extensions of ideas forged in modernist fiction.

6. I borrow here from Julia Kristeva's concept of the "subject-in-process": "It is poetic language that awakens our attention to this undecidable character of any so-called natural language, a feature that univocal, rational, scientific discourses tend to hide—and this implies considerable consequences for its subject. The support of this signifying economy could not be the transcendental ego alone. If it is true that there would unavoidably be a speaking *subject* since the signifying set exists, it is nonetheless evident that this subject, in order to tally with its heterogeneity, must be, let us say, a questionable *subject-in-process*" (135).

7. According to Roudinesco,

During the First World War, as a pupil at the Collège Stanislas, Lacan thought of embarking on a political career, happily regarding himself as a twentieth-century Rastignac. He was interested in everything: new literature, the work of James Joyce, Maurras' style, Léon Bloy's desperate imprecations, libertinism, extreme experiences, the philosophy of Nietzsche. And he had a horror of his family origins: a bigoted mother, a father who was a sales rep crushed by the omnipotence of his own father, and ancestors who were vinegar merchants. In a sense, he rejected the chauvinistic *France profonde* from which he hailed. Hence his attraction to Parisian intellectual elites, avant-garde movements

(Dadaism and surrealism), sartorial eccentricity, unusual food, the centres of European culture (London and Rome), and, finally, women who did not resemble his mother, who were not "maternal." (11–12)

Chapter 1
THE INTERPELLATED SUBJECT

1. By my count, Nostromo himself references the parable four times, and there are two additional descriptions of Nostromo's thoughts in which he compares himself to the enslaved specters. There are, additionally, many other implicit references and connections to the parable throughout the novel that do not name it explicitly.

2. For an exemplary account of how spiritualism and the occult influenced such imagery in late nineteenth-century writers, and Conrad in particular, see Stephen Ross's "*The Nigger of the 'Narcissus'* and Modernist Haunting."

3. Robert Caserio's 1981 essay "Joseph Conrad, Dickensian Novelist of the Nineteenth Century" is a notable exception. Caserio argues that Conrad's fiction can be characterized as "a reflective medium . . . whose objects and forms are likened best to spectral emanations" (340). Conrad's particular type of novel, which Caserio calls "a spectral mirror," uniquely captures "what is—like a ghost—visible and invisible, substantial and shadowy, natural in origin and preternatural in manifestation or effect" (340) and, in doing so, "challenges the authority of history, sociology, philosophy, and science" (339). Caserio's essay offers a workable foundation for considering the nature and importance of Conrad's spectral narrativity, but like many Conrad critics, he stops short of what might be a more fruitful engagement with the intersection of the personal and political that informs so much of Conrad's fiction.

4. Derrida's book was originally published in 1993 as *Spectres de Marx* but was first published in English in 1994 by Routledge.

5. "The Spectre of Ideology" was subsequently reworked and appeared in *Interrogating the Real* (2006) as "Between Symbolic Fiction and Fantasmic Spectre: Towards a Lacanian Theory of Ideology." My references throughout will be to the former.

6. Cedric Watts gives a useful account of the novel's "narratorial mobility," relating it specifically to the narrator's "spectral mobility of fictional 'omnisciences'" (77).

7. Jameson says of the role of the Monterist Revolution in the novel: "The hold of conventional notions of presence, both physical and narrative, leads us to assume that it is only at this second point in the novel that the event in question 'really' happens at last. Yet it would surely be more adequate to suggest that in that sense it never really happens at all, for the initial discursive reference to it—not as scene but as fact or background—dispenses Conrad from having to 'render' it in all its lived presence later on. This central event is therefore present/absent in the most classic Derridean fashion, present only in its initial absence, absent when it is supposed to be most intensely present" (*Political Unconscious* 270). This absent presence illustrates just one of the many ways in which Conrad's narrative style anticipates a poststructuralist understanding of language, narrative, and interpretation.

8. Žižek's point recalls Blanchot's concept of "permanent revolution," which for Derrida "supposes the rupture of that which links permanence to substantial presence, and more generally to all onto-logy" (*Specters of Marx* 39).

9. Benita Parry, for example, argues that because "the central figures are represented as individual products and victims of historical circumstances, pressing against the frontiers of their given situation and destroyed by their presumption, 'history' as the collective project of human agents is itself the principal protagonist in *Nostromo* and the destiny of an entire social order its subject" (101–2). Guerard, who for his part is more attuned to the importance of focusing on the psyche of the individual in the novel (but still undervalues the complexity of its psychodynamics), argues that it "recognizes unconscious motives and self-deceptions (Charles Gould's especially) but its treatment of them—its psychology, in a word—is classical rather than Freudian. Reason and folly play a larger part than unconscious or half-conscious compulsion; reasoning on political affairs occupies more pages than solitary introspection" (177). And Ian Watt is similarly out of step in *Conrad in the Nineteenth Century* (1979), remarking that "Conrad did not continue to develop the subjective aspect of the disjunction between the individual consciousness and everything outside it; or at least it was in the phase of intense experimentation which began in 1896 and ended in 1900 that Conrad was most deeply involved in presenting the obdurate incompatibility of the self and the world in which it exists" (357). Cedric Watts is a notable exception in this regard. He maintains that "*Nostromo* is a powerfully psycho-political novel. By 'psycho-political' I mean that Conrad conceives human psychology largely in terms of political history, and political history largely in terms of human psychology" (85).

10. In addressing such a suggestive misreading of this scene, Stephen Ross fittingly turns to the language of "gaps" that we have encountered across the works of Eagleton, Jameson, and Žižek: "Seeing both the world around him and his own existence as permeated with gaps, perplexing spaces of nothing, Nostromo becomes a fully modern, proto-Imperial subject. With this reconfiguration, Nostromo steps out of the spurious social role he has occupied (as merely a structural feature of the emergent Imperial order) and determines to take charge of his destiny, supplementing his earlier ethic of action with the calculation of ideological consciousness in a concerted effort to 'gain a sense of mastery over the fates'" (*Conrad and Empire* 138).

11. Jameson makes a similar observation regarding the disconnect between Nostromo's actions and the mythology that is spawned from the people's misunderstanding of them:

> The central act, the heroic expedition of Decoud and Nostromo, which ought to have grounded their status as heroes, as ultimate legendary forms of the individual subject, is appropriated by collective history, in which it also exists, but in a very different way, as the founding of institutions. In classical Sartrean language, we can say that the historical act of Decoud and Nostromo has been alienated and stolen from them even before they achieve it; or in a more Hegelian terminology, their action can be characterized as that of structural ephemeral mediation. They stand indeed in the Weberian place of the "vanish-

ing mediator," of the prophetic or charismatic individual term whose historical but transindividual function, according to the "ruse of history," is merely to enable the coming into being after him of a new type of collectivity. Decoud's and Nostromo's is the moment of the action of the individual subject, but one which is at once reabsorbed by the very stability and transindividuality of the institutions it is necessary to found. (*Political Unconscious* 278–79)

That such an "action of the individual subject" should be so cynically co-opted by the very forces that have set the annihilation of Nostromo and Decoud in motion shows the inextricability of the ideological and subjective registers in the novel.

12. Cedric Watts makes a similar point, writing that "Conrad's oblique method [of time shifts as a narrative strategy] could almost have been designed to induce in the reader the very flexibility that most of the main figures in the novel lack, and suffer from lacking. Thus, while demonstrating the political infancy of men, the novel embodies its own political maturity in techniques which entail for the reader an education in that maturity. By delaying the decoding of events, Conrad forces us to share the myopia of his characters; but, by provoking the decoding, he provides a therapy which helps us to share his own keen vision" (82). I view this "decoding" as another way of describing the ideology critique in which the novel's narrative voice engages. I would only add my belief that despite the characters' undeniable myopia, this decoding *is* available within the world of the novel to anyone who would truly attempt to understand the layers of ideological mystification at work.

Chapter 2
THE VOID OF SUBJECTIVITY

1. For a compelling comparative study of Conrad and Joyce, see Szczeszak-Brewer. Citing Adolf Nowaczyński, who "called the Irish the Poles 'of the Western world'" (9), Szczeszak-Brewer examines the two writers as like-minded exiles who developed a skepticism toward the religious authority and colonial past of their respective homelands and points to the ways in which Conrad and Joyce used their fiction to critique traditional power structures and ideologies in favor of a more individualized form of self-determination.

2. The most well known example comes from Fredric Jameson's *Political Unconscious,* which examines the influence of popular- and mass-culture genres like romance and adventure tales on Conrad's fiction: "This emergence is most dramatically registered by what most readers have felt as a tangible 'break' in the narrative of *Lord Jim,* a qualitative shift and diminution of narrative intensity as we pass from the story of the *Patna* and the intricate and prototextual search for the 'truth' of the scandal of the abandoned ship, to that more linear account of Jim's later career in Patusan, which, a virtual paradigm of romance as such, comes before us as the prototype of the various 'degraded' subgenres into which mass culture will be articulated (adventure story, gothic, science fiction, bestseller, detective story, and the like)" (206–7).

3. The commentary of Mary Ann Doane is also very instructive in this regard:

In Lacan's account of the concept, sublimation is the result of a crisis concerning the object; it is motivated by the void which signals the relation between the real and the signifier—"In all forms of sublimation the void will be determinant." Art is perhaps the pre-eminent form of sublimation and the most primordial artistic activity may very well be that of the potter who produces the vase which, for the archaeologist, is the irrefutable sign of a human presence. For Lacan, the vase creates the void in its very form and through this fact suggests the perspective of fullness—"if the vase can be full, it is insofar as, in its very essence, it is empty." Given the fundamental lack or emptiness Lacan associates with the signifier, the vase deserves its archaeological prominence because it incarnates the signifying emptiness or void. Art is characterized by a certain mode of organization around the void; religion is constituted by all the means of avoiding the void (or, perhaps, as Lacan later amends it, "respecting" the void); and the discourse of science simply rejects the void in favor of a realistic discourse which is adequate to the object. (256)

4. Lacan says of *das Ding* that because it is in fact located at the level of the unconscious *Vorstellungen* (mental image), "the Thing only presents itself to the extent that it becomes word" (*Ethics of Psychoanalysis* 55), or only as a function of external signification.

5. For an excellent account of scholarship on Conrad's skepticism, see Peters, chap. 5.

6. J. Hillis Miller, for example, maintains that "the special place of Joseph Conrad in English Literature lies in the fact that in him the nihilism covertly dominant in modern culture is brought to the surface and shown for what it is" (5). John Peters points to William W. Bonney and Roy Roussel as critics with similar views of Conrad's nihilism.

7. It is important to properly contextualize Conrad's preface, and indeed all of the commentary that appears outside Conrad's fiction, as he was often susceptible to emotional reaction, hyperbole, and otherwise provocative statements that cannot always be said to represent his actual sentiments with full accuracy. Apropos of his preface to *The Nigger of the "Narcissus,"* Ian Watt tells us in a 1974 essay that "doubts about the Preface actually began very early; indeed, with Conrad himself" ("Conrad's Preface" 101). Indeed, in a letter to Edward Garnett Conrad seemed unusually reticent about the preface, and his editor, Sidney Pawling, rejected it for the initial publication of the novel. After appearing alongside the serialized version in the *New Review*, it was not included with the novel again until the 1914 Doubleday Page edition. Although the preface was criticized by some both in Conrad's time and after, Watt maintains that while such criticisms "are largely justified if we try to read it as an analytic exposition of a theory of fiction," in fact, "in any rigorous sense of the word, Conrad had no such theory, and did not want to have." "But since as Conrad wrote no other inward account of his creative aspiration," he goes on to explain, "the Preface to *The Nigger of the 'Narcissus'* remains by default the most reliable, and the most voluntary, single statement of Conrad's general approach to writing" (103).

8. Of course, we must also recognize that as on so many occasions, Conrad offers

contradictions on the point of his religious beliefs. In Zdzisław Najder's seminal biography, for example, Conrad is quoted as saying that "I was born a R.C. [Roman Catholic] and though dogma sits lightly on me I have never renounced that form of Christian religion. The booklet of rules is so, I may say, theological that it would be like renouncing the faith of my fathers" (535).

9. We might also take the opportunity here to recall Hassan and McHale's insistence on epistemology, rather than ontology, as the defining mode of modernism. This is just one instance from the modernist canon of the overriding importance of ontological concerns. Paul Armstrong is also attuned to this fact in this particular scene:

> The world is social to such a radical degree that "reality" exists only through the intersubjective recognition of objects. Things themselves become ephemeral to a single consciousness. Decoud's sense of his own identity slips as well because who we are for Conrad depends on the way others see us. . . . Decoud finds that the self loses substance when the gaze of others no longer objectifies it. Decoud's longing for another's "face" and "sight" emphasizes that one's identity is constituted by the regard of others and threatened by its absence. Deprived of a field of interpersonal differences against and within which to define himself, Decoud feels pulled into amorphous oneness with the natural world—a terrible rather than rejuvenating experience because this loss of self is pure destruction and not a reabsorption into a higher unity. (165–66)

Although he does not explicitly mention Lacan, certainly Armstrong's use of quotation marks around the word *reality* and his reference to concepts of intersubjectivity and the gaze invite a more overt comparison.

10. For another recent treatment of the issue of religion in Joyce, see Van Mierlo.

11. Although the final form of the theory appeared in 1916, it would take several years before Einstein gained general notoriety.

12. For some representative treatments of Woolf's relationship with religion, see Knight; Graham and Lewis; Griesinger; and Gay.

13. A few recent examples include Henry; Alt; and Crossland.

14. For a useful overview of competing critical positions, see Mackin.

15. Toril Moi is especially astute on this point:

> *To the Lighthouse* illustrates the destructive nature of a metaphysical belief in strong, immutably fixed gender identities—as represented by Mr and Mrs Ramsay—whereas Lily Briscoe (an artist) represents the subject who deconstructs this opposition, perceives its pernicious influence and tries as far as is possible in a still rigidly patriarchal order to live as her own woman, without regard for the crippling definitions of sexual identity to which society would have her conform. It is in this context that we must situate Woolf's crucial concept of androgyny. This is not, as Showalter argues, a flight from fixed gender identities, but a recognition of their falsifying metaphysical nature. Far from

fleeing such gender identities because she fears them, Woolf rejects them because she has seen them for what they are. She has understood that the goal of
the feminist struggle must precisely be to deconstruct the death-dealing binary
oppositions of masculinity and femininity. (13–14)

16. This is a view shared by James Martel: "One could say that, as a failed artist, Lily
is also able to access her failure as a subject; she has a sense that parts do not always
cohere, that beauty and dazzle are not the same as truth, and that there is no inherent
destiny of telos that demands that, in the end, we all will be complete and whole subjects (or at least those of us who rate such a happy ending)" (188).

Chapter 3
THE SUBJECT IN PROCESS

1. For an excellent overview of Joyce's influence on Fitzgerald, see Thomas.

2. Robert Emmet Long was the first to meaningfully explore the Conrad-Fitzgerald
connection in his essay "*The Great Gatsby* and the Tradition of Joseph Conrad." Long's
study is broad in scope and traces *Gatsby*'s influence through a number of Conrad's novels. His was also the first sustained analysis of the similarities between *Heart of Darkness*
and *The Great Gatsby*.

3. These include, to name a few, the influential collection *Female Subjects in Black
and White: Race, Psychoanalysis, Feminism* (1997), edited by Elizabeth Abel, Barbara
Christian, and Helene Moglen; Claudia Tate's *Psychoanalysis and Black Novels: Desire
and the Protocols of Race* (1998); Barbara Johnson's *The Feminist Difference: Literature,
Psychoanalysis, Race, and Gender* (1998); Christopher Lane's collection *The Psychoanalysis of Race* (1998); Kalpana Seshadri-Crooks's *Desiring Whiteness: A Lacanian Analysis of
Race* (2000); Mikko Tuhkanen's *The American Optic: Psychoanalysis, Critical Race Theory,
and Richard Wright* (2009); and various contributions from Slavoj Žižek, Homi Bhabha,
Joan Copjec, Judith Butler, and others.

4. For an excellent interpretation of the novel's internal contradictions, see John
Hilgart's essay, which "resist[s] the conclusion that contradiction in the novel defines
Nick's limitations, arguing on the contrary that contradiction is very much Nick's overt
technique, serving not only to undercut his critique of commodity culture but to mount
it" (88).

5. "The French word [*jouissance*], given its indissoluble relationship to all the rest
of Lacan's teaching, including his mathemes or his logical and topological formulae, is
difficult to translate into English. Lacan himself was aware of the problem and favored
a combination of 'enjoyment' and 'lust'; however, all translators have noted the con-
ceptual loss that is sustained in the use of these terms, and therefore the great majority
prefer to keep the French word, without italics, as a word already recognized by the
OED and as a psychoanalytic contribution to the English language" (Braunstein 103).

6. "Objet 'a' designates the lost object as an abject remnant and uncanny revenant
of the Real. Its lower-case 'a' stands for *autre* or little other in order to distinguish it
from the Big Other of the general language system. In French *objet a* was pronounced

by Lacan as *objet petit a,* 'object small a,' both in order to preserve its quasi-algebraic character as an abstract symbol for the absence of the lost object and also to sound like *objet petit tas,* 'a little pile of shit'" (Levine 67). Lacan maintained that the term should remain untranslated, wishing it to resemble an algebraic sign. As a result, it is represented by English translators as *objet petit a, objet a,* and at times simply *objet.* It is also—against Lacan's wishes—often translated as "object a," "little object a," and so on. For this reason, the reader may assume that the various terms are used interchangeably in this essay and refer to the same concept.

7. For some of the most lucid explications of Lacan's work, see Fink's *The Lacanian Subject* (1995), *A Clinical Introduction to Lacanian Psychoanalysis* (1997), *Lacan to the Letter* (2004), and *Fundamentals of Psychoanalytic Technique* (2007).

8. See Godden, "A Diamond Bigger than the Ritz," for more on Daisy's voice.

Chapter 4
SPATIALIZED SUBJECTIVITY

1. The geographical and temporal proximity of West's and Fitzgerald's deaths reflects a number of parallels between their career trajectories. Edmund Wilson points out that "both men had been living on the West Coast; both had spent several years in the studios; both, at the time of their deaths, had been occupied with novels about Hollywood" (*Classics and Commercials* 51–52).

2. While Fitzgerald and West died in 1940, well before critics began debating postmodernism, Huxley lived until 1963 and went on to write novels like *Island* (1962), which could arguably be classified as postmodern. Because the bulk of Huxley's writing occurred before World War II—and in fact stretched back as far as 1916—most of his writing can be classified as modernist.

3. *The Love of the Last Tycoon* was originally published in 1941 under the title *The Last Tycoon* and edited by Edmund Wilson, but Matthew Bruccoli's 1993 edition, which uses Fitzgerald's preferred title, *The Love of the Last Tycoon,* and more faithfully maintains the portion of the novel that Fitzgerald had actually completed, has become the preferred version.

4. Notable works include Thomas Strychacz's *Modernism, Mass Culture and Professionalism* (1993), Susan Hegeman's *Patterns for America Modernism and the Concept of Culture* (1999), Allison Pease's *Modernism, Mass Culture, and the Aesthetics of Obscenity* (2000), David Seed's *Cinematic Fictions* (2009), and Scott Ortolano's *Popular Modernism and Its Legacies* (2017).

5. Matthew J. Bruccoli writes of Fitzgerald's *Last Tycoon:* "Fitzgerald was writing a western—a novel about the last American pioneers, immigrants, and sons of immigrants who pursued and defined the American dream in the last western frontier" (introduction to *Tycoon* v). The same could be said of Nathanael West's *The Day of the Locust,* a novel that is clearly informed by both the immigrant and the frontier experience. Born Nathan Weinstein, West was himself born of an immigrant Jewish family and initially came to California chasing the dream of seeing his novel *Miss Lonelyhearts* (1933) adapted to the big screen, this only after the publisher of his book declared bank-

ruptcy and America sank deeper into the Depression. Thus both Fitzgerald and West were acutely aware of the power of the American Dream (although it was only with the publication of James Truslow Adams's 1931 book *The Epic of America* that the term entered the lexicon, the idea was pervasive *avant la lettre*) not only as a positive projection of possibility but as an idea frantically clung to by the desperate.

6. Wilson, incidentally, did not care for Huxley's *After Many a Summer*. He wrote in a 1944 *New Yorker* review of Huxley's next novel, *Time Must Have a Stop* (1944), that "Huxley's peculiar version of the life of contemplation and revelation was expounded in *After Many a Summer* by a boring non-satirical character who read homilies to the other characters with an insufferable air of quiet authority and who constantly made the reader feel that it would have been better if he, too, had been satirically treated as a typical California crank" (*Classics and Commercials* 209–10). He did give Huxley some credit, however, conceding that "the one thing that was imagined with intensity in Aldous Huxley's novel, *After Many a Summer Dies the Swan,* was the eighteenth-century exploiter of the slave-trade degenerating into a fetal anthropoid" (43).

7. Wilson wrote favorably of West's depiction of this fact, saying that "Mr. West has caught the emptiness of Hollywood; and he is, as far as I know, the first writer to make this emptiness horrible" (*Classics and Commercials* 54).

8. Wilson wrote in 1932 that "Americans still tend to move westward and many drift southward towards the sun. San Diego is the extreme southwest town of the Unites States; and since our real westward expansion has come to a standstill, it has become a veritable jumping-off place. On the West coast to-day the suicide rate is twice that of the Middle Atlantic coast, and since 1911 the suicide rate of San Diego has been the highest in the United States" (*American Jitters* 257). He does not cite a source for his claim, but later writes that "in 1926 there were fifty-seven suicides in San Diego. During nine months of 1930, there were seventy-one, and between the beginning of the January and the end of the July of 1931 there have already been thirty-six. Three of these latter are set down in the coroner's record as due to 'no work or money'; two to 'no work'; one to 'ill health, family troubles and no work'; two to 'despondency over financial worries'; one to 'financial worry and illness'; one to 'health and failure to collect'; and one to 'rent due him from tenants.' The doctors say that some of the old people who have been sent out here by their relations but whose source of income has recently been cut off, kill themselves from pride rather than go to the poorhouse" (259).

9. In Fitzgerald's case we have only his working notes. There are suggestions about how he had planned to end the novel, including outlines that he had created and an account by Sheilah Graham, with whom Fitzgerald was romantically involved at the time of his death. It appears that Fitzgerald had intended for Stahr to be killed in a plane crash and for the novel to end with the scene of his funeral, which according to Graham's account would have included "all the Hollywood hypocrites" (qtd. in Bruccoli, introduction to *Tycoon* xix). Bruccoli stresses, however, that "Graham's account does not necessarily provide Fitzgerald's final plot." "It is unlikely that he had decided how the novel would continue," he explains, for "as late as 2 November 1940—less than two months before his death—he wrote to his wife, Zelda, that the novel 'is still in the early

character-planning stage'" (xix). We can only speculate about how Fitzgerald would
have actually ended the novel, which leaves us with the incomplete draft that Bruccoli
assembled for Scribner as the most coherent and accurate version of the novel.

10. Regarding *Tycoon's* narrative perspective, Fitzgerald once again acknowledges
his debt to Conrad. He writes the following in a 29 September 1939 prospectus to *Col-
lier's* editor Kenneth Littauer: "This love affair is the meat of the book—though I am
going to treat it, remember, as it comes through to Cecilia. That is to say by making
Cecilia at the moment of her telling the story, an intelligent and observant woman, I
shall grant myself the privilege, as Conrad did, of letting her imagine the actions of the
characters. Thus, I hope to get the verisimilitude of a first person narrative, combined
with a Godlike knowledge of all the events that happen to my characters" (qtd. in Bruccoli, introduction to *Tycoon* ix).

11. Wilson's insight into this final scene is worth mentioning as well: "The America
of the murders and rapes which fill the Los Angeles papers is only the obverse side of
the America of the inanities of the movies. Such people—Mr. West seems to say—dis-
satisfied, yet with no ideas, no objectives and no interest in anything vital, may in the
mass be capable of anything. The daydreams purveyed by Hollywood, the romances that
in movie stories can be counted on to have whisked around all obstacles and adroitly
knocked out all 'menaces' by the time they have run off their reels, romances which
their fascinated audiences have never been able to live themselves—only cheat them
and embitter their frustration. Of such mobs are the followers of fascism made" (*Classics and Commercials* 54).

12. *Tycoon* mentions Hearst in passing, as Stoyte and Kathleen are stopped at a red
light and a newsboy nearby yells, "Mickey Mouse Murdered! Randolph Hearst declares
war on China!" (79).

Chapter 5
THE NEGATION OF SUBJECTIVITY

1. For two exemplary accounts of how Beckett has been classified in relation to
modernism and postmodern, see Connor; and Beloborodova, Van Hulle, and Verhulst.

2. Critics have noted here the similarity to Joyce, who published a book of poetry
and a book of short stories prior to *A Portrait of the Artist as a Young Man*.

3. As an alternative to *erasure*, which I find preferable, others commonly focus instead on the notion of *silence* in Beckett's work. Anthony Cronin, for example, writes
the following:

> Beckett was a perfectionist. Most artists are; and indeed perfectionism, à la
> Eliot and Joyce, was a feature of modernism, which rejected both the jour-
> neyman's code of "needs must" and the slapdash, hit-and-miss methods of the
> great Victorians. But he was a perfectionist to a degree which was unusual and
> obsessive even among the modernist masters. He yearned for silence, the blank
> white page, the most perfect thing of all. As an artist he had had more false
> starts and false beginnings than most. The principal failing of his earlier work,

so knowing but also so self-revealing in all the wrong ways, is the failure to achieve a form and a tone of voice which would allow him to express his particular truths. Perhaps this repeated failure made him feel more acutely than most the torment of marred utterance, of false utterance, of would-be significant utterance; and to feel also more intensely than others that the object of the true, achieved and necessary utterance is silence—in some sense or other, a permission to be silent, whether granted by one's daemon or by one's creator. (376)

4. Andrew Gibson, in a similar vein, writes that "Murphy commits himself to an extreme version of apagogic reason whose ironical futility is clear from the start: that is, he conducts himself 'as though he were free' in a world to which he 'fondly hope[s]' he does not belong" (144).

5. Lawrence Harvey relates a statement from Beckett that 'if he were a critic setting out to write on the works of Beckett (and he thanked heaven he was not), he would start with two quotations, one by Geulincx: 'Ubi nihil vales, ibi nihil velis,' and one by Democritus: 'Nothing is more real than nothing'" (267–68).

6. Ackerley explains that "Beckett had written for his own delectation as much as anybody's, but the example of *Ulysses* could hardly be ignored. He probably believed that his novel should do for London (the dear indelible world of the 16th, 18th, and 20th centuries) what *Ulysses* had done for Dublin. It was not to be" (19).

7. "Samuel Beckett's *Murphy* is a vast, rollicking *jeu d'esprit* in the tradition that runs from Cervantes and Rabelais through Burton and Fielding to *Ulysses*," writes Ackerley, "and it maintains itself proudly in the company. Yet it has never received the attention it deserves. For all its mere 282 pages (158 in the Calder edition), it has an intricacy which justifies its place among these giants of philosophical comedy, and cries out for the kind of close scrutiny that has not yet been made of it" (10).

CODA

1. For an illustrative reading of Conrad's letter, see Schwarz: "Conrad uses this elaborate ironic trope to speak to the late Victorian belief that the industrial revolution is part of an upwardly evolving teleology; this belief is really a kind of social Darwinism. According to Conrad, humanity would like to believe in a providentially ordered world vertically descending from a benevolent God; that is, to believe in an embroidered world. But, Conrad believed, we actually inhabit a temporally defined horizontal dimension within an amoral, indifferent universe" (52–53).

WORKS CITED

Abel, Elizabeth, Barbara Christian, and Helene Moglen, eds. *Female Subjects in Black and White: Race, Psychoanalysis, Feminism.* Berkeley: U of California P, 1997.

Ackerley, Chris. *Demented Particulars: The Annotated "Murphy."* Edinburgh: Edinburgh UP, 2010.

Adams, James Truslow. *Epic of America.* Boston: Little, Brown, 1931.

Adams, Rachel. "The Ends of America, the Ends of Postmodernism." *Twentieth-Century Literature* 53.3 (2007): 248–72.

Alt, Christina Marie. *Virginia Woolf and the Study of Nature.* Cambridge: Cambridge UP, 2010.

Althusser, Louis. "Ideology and Ideological State Apparatuses." *Lenin and Philosophy and Other Essays.* Trans. Ben Brewster. New York: Monthly Review, 1971. 127–86. First published in 1968 by Francois Maspero as *Lénine et la philosophie.*

Aristotle. "On Sense and Sensible Objects." *Aristotle: On the Soul. Parva Naturalia. On Breath.* Trans. Walter Stanley Hett. Cambridge, MA: Harvard UP, 1957. 207–86.

Armstrong, Paul. *The Challenge of Bewilderment: Understanding and Representation in James, Conrad, and Ford.* Ithaca: Cornell UP, 1987.

Baker, Phil. *Beckett and the Mythology of Psychoanalysis.* Basingstoke: Macmillan, 1997.

Baudrillard, Jean. *America.* London: Verso, 1998. First published in 1986 by Bernard Grasset as *Amérique.*

———. *Simulacra and Simulation.* Ann Arbor: U of Michigan P, 1994. First published in 1981 by Éditions Galilée as *Simulacres et simulation.*

Beach, Sylvia. *Shakespeare and Company.* 1956. Reprint, Lincoln: U of Nebraska P, 1991.

Beattie, Tina. *Theology after Postmodernity: Divining the Void—A Lacanian Reading of Thomas Aquinas.* Oxford: Oxford UP, 2013.

Beckett, Samuel. *Dream of Fair to Middling Women.* 1992. Reprint, New York: Arcade, 2012.

————. *Echo's Bones and Other Precipitates*. Paris: Europa, 1935.

————. *More Pricks than Kicks*. 1934. Reprint, New York: Grove Press, 1970.

————. *Murphy*. 1938. Reprint, New York: Grove Press, 1957.

Begam, Richard. *Samuel Beckett and the End of Modernity*. Stanford: Stanford UP, 1996.

Beloborodova, Olga, Dirk Van Hulle, and Pim Verhulst, eds. *Beckett and Modernism*. Cham: Palgrave Macmillan, 2018.

Berman, Ronald. *"The Great Gatsby" and Modern Times*. Urbana: U of Illinois P, 1994.

————. *"The Great Gatsby* and the Twenties." *The Cambridge Companion to F. Scott Fitzgerald*. Ed. Ruth Prigozy. Cambridge: Cambridge UP, 2002. 79–94.

Berman, Russell A. "British Expatriates and German Exiles in 1930s–1940s Los Angeles." *The Cambridge Companion to the Literature of Los Angeles*. Ed. Kevin R. McNamara. Cambridge: Cambridge UP, 2010. 49–58.

Best, Stephen, and Douglas Kellner. *Postmodern Theory*. New York: Guilford, 1991.

Borges, Jorge Luis. "On Exactitude in Science." *Collected Fictions*. Trans. Andrew Hurley. New York: Penguin, 1998. 325.

Braunstein, Néstor A. "Desire and Jouissance in the Teachings of Lacan." *The Cambridge Companion to Lacan*. Ed. Jean-Michel Rabaté. Cambridge: Cambridge UP, 2003.

Briggs, Julia. *Virginia Woolf: An Inner Life*. Orlando: Harcourt, 2005.

Brockelman, Thomas. "Lacan and Modernism: Representation and its Vicissitudes." *Disseminating Lacan*. Ed. David Pettigrew and François Raffoul. Albany: State U of New York P, 1996.

Brown, Paul Tolliver. "Relativity, Quantum Physics, and Consciousness in Virginia Woolf's *To the Lighthouse*." *Journal of Modern Literature* 32.3 (2009): 39–62.

Bruccoli, Matthew J. Introduction. *The Love of the Last Tycoon*. New York: Scribner, 1994. v–xxi.

————. Introduction. "Winter Dreams." *The Short Stories of F. Scott Fitzgerald*. By F. Scott Fitzgerald. Ed. Matthew J. Bruccoli. New York: Scribner, 2003. 217.

Buntin, John. *L.A. Noir: The Struggle for the Soul of America's Most Seductive City*. New York: Broadway Books, 2010.

Butler, Judith. *Bodies That Matter: On the Discursive Limits of "Sex."* New York: Routledge, 1993.

————. *The Psychic Life of Power*. Stanford: Stanford UP, 1997.

Caserio, Robert L. "Joseph Conrad, Dickensian Novelist of the Nineteenth

Century: A Dissent from Ian Watt." *Nineteenth-Century Fiction* 36.3 (1981): 337–47.

Chesney, Duncan McColl. "Beckett, Minimalism, and the Question of Postmodernism." *Modernism/Modernity* 19.4 (2012): 637–55.

City of Los Angeles Planning Department. "La Fayette Square Preservation Plan." *Office of Historic Resources*. Los Angeles Department of City Planning, 25 Sept. 2008. Web.

Coleridge, Samuel Taylor. "Kubla Khan." *Selected Poetry*. Oxford: Oxford UP, 2009. 101–2.

Collits, Terry. "Anti-Heroics and Epic Failures: The Case of *Nostromo*." *Conradian* 29.2 (2004): 1–13.

Connor, Steven. *Beckett, Modernism and the Material Imagination*. Cambridge: Cambridge UP, 2014.

Conrad, Joseph. *Almayer's Folly*. 1895. Reprint, New York: Penguin 1991.

——. *The Collected Letters of Joseph Conrad*. Ed. Frederick R. Karl and Laurence Davies. 9 vols. Cambridge: Cambridge UP, 1983–2007.

——. *Heart of Darkness and Other Tales*. Oxford: Oxford UP, 2008.

——. *Letters from Conrad 1895 to 1924*. Ed. Edward Garnett. London: Nonesuch, 1928.

——. *Lord Jim*. 1900. New York: Norton, 1996.

——. *The Nigger of the "Narcissus" and Other Stories*. London: Penguin Classics, 2007.

——. *Nostromo*. 1904. Reprint, Oxford: Oxford UP, 2009.

——. *An Outcast of the Islands*. 1896. Reprint, New York: Penguin 1990.

——. *The Selected Letters of Joseph Conrad*. Ed. Laurence Davies. Cambridge: Cambridge UP, 2015.

Cousineau, Thomas J. "Descartes, Lacan, and *Murphy*." *College Literature* 11.3 (1984): 223–32.

Coward, Rosalind, and John Ellis. *Language and Materialism: Developments in Semiology and the Theory of the Subject*. London: Routledge & Kegan Paul, 1977.

Cronin, Anthony. *Samuel Beckett: The Last Modernist*. 1997. Reprint, New York: Da Capo, 1999.

Crossland, Rachel. *Modernist Physics: Waves, Particles, and Relativities in the Writings of Virginia Woolf and D. H. Lawrence*. Oxford: Oxford UP, 2018.

Decker, Jeffrey Louis. "Gatsby's Pristine Dream: The Diminishment of the Self-Made Man in the Tribal Twenties." *Novel* 28.1 (1994): 52–71.

Derrida, Jacques. *Specters of Marx: The State of the Debt, the Work of Mourning and the New International*. Trans. Peggy Kamuf. New York: Routledge, 1994. Originally published in 1993 by Éditions Galilée as *Spectres de Marx*.

———. *Writing and Difference.* Trans. Alan Bass. London: Routledge, 2002. First published in 1967 by Éditions du Seuil as *L'écriture et la différence.*

Doane, Mary Ann. *Femmes Fatales: Feminism, Film Theory, Psychoanalysis.* New York: Routledge, 1991.

Drouin, Jeffrey S. *James Joyce, Science, and Modernist Print Culture: "The Einstein of English Fiction."* New York: Routledge, 2015.

Eagleton, Terry. *Criticism and Ideology: A Study in Marxist Literary Theory.* 1976. Reprint, London: Verso, 1978.

Einstein, Albert. "On the Electrodynamics of Moving Bodies." *Annalen der Physik* 17 (1905): 891–921.

———. *Out of My Later Years.* 1950. Reprint, New York: Citadel, 1956.

Eliot, T. S. *The Waste Land.* 1922. Reprint, Ed. Michael North. New York: Norton, 2000.

Ellmann, Richard. *James Joyce.* 1959. Reprint, Oxford: Oxford UP, 1982.

Eysteinsson, Astradur. *The Concept of Modernism.* Ithaca: Cornell UP, 1990.

Fink, Bruce. *A Clinical Introduction to Lacanian Psychoanalysis.* Cambridge, MA: Harvard UP, 1997.

———. *Fundamentals of Psychoanalytic Technique: A Lacanian Approach for Practitioners.* New York: Norton, 2011.

———. *The Lacanian Subject: Between Language and Jouissance.* Princeton: Princeton UP, 1995.

———. *Lacan to the Letter: Reading "Écrits" Closely.* Minneapolis: U of Minnesota P, 2004.

Fitzgerald, F. Scott. "Confessions." *F. Scott Fitzgerald on Authorship.* Ed. Matthew J. Bruccoli and Judith S. Baughman. Columbia: U of South Carolina P, 1996.

———. *The Great Gatsby.* 1925. Reprint, New York: Simon & Schuster, 1995.

———. *The Love of the Last Tycoon: A Western.* New York: Simon & Schuster, 1994. First published in 1941 by Scriber as *The Last Tycoon.*

———. "10 Best Books I Have Read." *F. Scott Fitzgerald on Authorship.* Ed. Matthew J. Bruccoli and Judith S. Baughman. Columbia: U of South Carolina P, 1996.

———. *Tender Is the Night.* 1934. Reprint, New York: Scribner, 1962.

———. *This Side of Paradise.* 1920. Reprint, New York: Vintage, 2009.

———. "Winter Dreams." *The Short Stories of F. Scott Fitzgerald.* Ed. Matthew J. Bruccoli. New York: Scribner, 2003.

Fleishman, Avrom. "Science in Ithaca." *Wisconsin Studies in Contemporary Literature* 8.3 (1967): 377–91.

Forter, Greg. *Gender, Race, and Mourning in American Modernism.* Cambridge: Cambridge UP, 2011.

Foster, Wendy. "Murphy's Aporia: An Examination of the Spaces of Desire as Structured Absences in Samuel Beckett's *Murphy*." The Modern World, n.d. Web.

Freud, Sigmund. *Beyond the Pleasure Principle*. Trans. and ed. James Strachey. New York: Norton, 1961. First published in 1920 as *Jenseits des Lustprinzips*.

———. *The Interpretation of Dreams*. Trans. James Strachey. New York: Basic Books, 1955. First published in 1899 by Franz Deuticke, Leipzig & Vienna as *Die Traumdeutung*.

Friedman, Susan Stanford. Introduction. *Joyce: The Return of the Repressed*. Ithaca: Cornell UP, 1993.

Gay, Jane de. *Virginia Woolf and Christian Culture*. Edinburgh: Edinburgh UP, 2018.

Gebhard, David, and Harriette Von Breton. *Los Angeles in the Thirties: 1931– 1941*. Los Angeles: Hennessey & Ingalls, 1989.

Gibson, Andrew. *Beckett and Badiou: The Pathos of Intermittency*. Oxford: Oxford UP, 2006.

Gifford, Don, and Robert J. Seidman. *"Ulysses" Annotated*. 2nd ed. Berkeley: U of California P, 2008.

Giovacchini, Saverio. *Hollywood Modernism: Film and Politics in the Age of the New Deal*. Philadelphia: Temple UP, 2001.

Godden, Richard. "A Diamond Bigger than the Ritz: F. Scott Fitzgerald and the Gold Standard." *ELH* 77.3 (2010): 589–613.

———. *Fictions of Capital: The American Novel from James to Mailer*. Cambridge: Cambridge UP, 1990.

Goldsmith, Meredith. "White Skin, White Mask: Passing, Posing, and Performing in *The Great Gatsby*." *Modern Fiction Studies* 49.3 (2003): 443–68.

Gorman, Herbert. "Glimpses of F. Scott Fitzgerald." *Fitzgerald-Hemingway Annual* 5 (1973): 113–18.

Gottfried, Roy. *Joyce's Misbelief*. Gainesville: UP of Florida, 2008.

Graham, Elyse, and Pericles Lewis. "Private Religion, Public Mourning, and *Mrs. Dalloway*." *Modern Philology* 111.1 (2013): 88–106.

Griesinger, Emily. "Religious Belief in a Secular Age: Literary Modernism and Virginia Woolf's *Mrs. Dalloway*." *Christianity & Literature* 64.4 (2015): 438–64.

Griffin, Roger. *Modernism and Fascism: The Sense of a Beginning under Mussolini and Hitler*. Houndmills: Palgrave Macmillan, 2010.

Guerard, Albert J. *Conrad: The Novelist*. Cambridge, MA: Harvard UP, 1958.

Haines, Christian P., and Sean Grattan. "Life after the Subject." Introduction. "What Comes After the Subject?," special issue of *Cultural Critique* 96 (2017): 1–36.

Harvey, Lawrence. *Samuel Beckett: Poet and Critic*. Princeton: Princeton UP, 1970.

Hassan, Ihab. *The Postmodern Turn: Essays in Postmodern Theory and Culture*. Columbus: Ohio State UP, 1987.

Hegel, Georg Wilhelm Friedrich. *Phenomenology of Spirit*. Oxford: Clarendon, 1977. First published in 1807 by Goebhardt as *Die Phänomenologie des Geistes*.

Hegeman, Susan. *Patterns for America Modernism and the Concept of Culture*. Princeton: Princeton UP, 1999.

Henry, Holly. *Virginia Woolf and the Discourse of Science: The Aesthetics of Astronomy*. Cambridge: Cambridge UP, 2003.

Hilgart, John. "*The Great Gatsby*'s Aesthetics of Non-Identity." *Arizona Quarterly* 59.1 (2003): 87–116.

Huyssen, Andreas. *After the Great Divide: Modernism, Mass Culture, Postmodernism*. Bloomington: Indiana UP, 1986.

Huxley, Aldous. *After Many a Summer Dies the Swan*. Chicago: Ivan R. Dee, 1993. First published in 1939 by Chatto & Windus as *After Many a Summer*.

———. *Brave New World*. 1932. Reprint, New York: Harper Perennial, 2006.

———. *Island*. 1962. Reprint, New York: Harper Perennial, 2009.

———. *Time Must Have a Stop*. 1944. Reprint, Chicago: Dalkey Archive, 2001.

Jameson, Fredric. *The Political Unconscious: Narrative as a Socially Symbolic Act*. Ithaca: Cornell UP, 1982.

———. *Postmodernism, or, The Cultural Logic of Late Capitalism*. 1991. Reprint, Durham, NC: Duke UP, 2005.

Johnson, Barbara. *The Feminist Difference: Literature, Psychoanalysis, Race, and Gender*. Cambridge, MA: Harvard UP, 1998.

Joyce, James. *Finnegans Wake*. 1939. Reprint, New York: Penguin, 1999.

———. *The Letters of James Joyce*. Ed. Stuart Gilbert and Richard Ellmann. 3 vols. New York: Viking, 1966.

———. *A Portrait of the Artist as a Young Man*. 1916. Reprint, New York: Penguin, 1993.

———. *Ulysses*. 1922. Reprint, New York: Vintage Books, 1990.

Kane, Julie. "Varieties of Mystical Experience in the Writings of Virginia Woolf." *Twentieth Century Literature* 41. 4 (1995): 328–49.

Katz, Daniel. *Saying I No More: Subjectivity and Consciousness in the Prose of Samuel Beckett*. Evanston: Northwestern UP, 1999.

Kermode, Frank. *The Sense of an Ending: Studies in the Theory of Fiction*. 1967. Reprint, Oxford: Oxford UP, 2000.

Kirshner, Lewis A. "The Man Who Didn't Exist: The Case of Louis Althusser." *American Imago* 60.2 (2003): 211–39.

Klein, Norman M. *The History of Forgetting: Los Angeles and the Erasure of Memory*. London: Verso, 1997.

Knapp, Eloise Hay. "*Nostromo*." *The Cambridge Companion to Joseph Conrad*. Ed. J. H. Stape. Cambridge: Cambridge UP, 1996. 81–99.

Knight, Christopher J. "'The God of Love Is Full of Tricks': Virginia Woolf's Vexed Relation to the Tradition of Christianity." *Religion & Literature* 39.1 (2007): 27–46.

Knighton, Andrew Lyndon. "Hollywood Panoramics: Nathanael West's Baroque Modernity." *LIT: Literature Interpretation Theory* 21.3 (2010): 145–62.

Knowlson, James. *Damned to Fame: The Life of Samuel Beckett*. New York: Grove, 1996.

Kristeva, Julia. *Desire in Language: A Semiotic Approach to Literature and Art*. New York: Columbia UP, 1980.

Lacan, Jacques. *Écrits*. Trans. Bruce Fink. New York: Norton, 2006.

———. *The Ethics of Psychoanalysis: The Seminar of Jacques Lacan, Book VII*. Trans. Dennis Porter. New York: Norton, 1997. First published in 1986 by Éditions du Seuil as *L'éthique de la psychanalyse, 1959–1960*.

———. *The Four Fundamental Concepts of Psychoanalysis: The Seminar of Jacques Lacan, Book XI*. Trans. Alan Sheridan. New York: Norton, 1998. First published in 1973 by Éditions du Seuil as *Le séminaire de Jacques Lacan. Livre XI. Les quatre concepts fondamentaux de la psychanalyse*.

Laing, R. D. *The Divided Self: An Existential Study in Sanity and Madness*. 1955. Reprint, New York: Penguin, 1990.

Lane, Christopher, ed. *The Psychoanalysis of Race*. New York: Columbia UP, 1998.

Larsen, Nella. *Passing*. 1929. Reprint, New York: Penguin, 2003.

Lawtoo, Nidesh. *The Phantom of the Ego: Modernism and the Mimetic Unconscious*. East Lansing: Michigan State UP, 2013.

Lehan, Richard Daniel. "*The Great Gatsby*": *The Limits of Wonder*. Boston: Twayne, 1990.

Lernout, Geert. *Help My Unbelief: James Joyce and Religion*. London: Continuum, 2010.

Lester, John. *Conrad and Religion*. Basingstoke: Macmillan, 1988.

Levenson, Michael H. *A Genealogy of Modernism: A Study of English Literary Doctrine, 1908–1922*. Cambridge: Cambridge UP, 1984.

Levine, Stephen Z. *Lacan Reframed*. London: I. B. Tauris, 2008.

Long, Robert Emmet. "*The Great Gatsby* and the Tradition of Joseph Conrad." *Texas Studies in Literature and Language* 8.2 (1966): 257–76.

Mackin, Timothy. "Public Minds: Woolf, Russell, and Photographic Vision." *Journal of Modern Literature* 33.3 (2010): 112–30.

188

WORKS CITED

Mallios, Peter Lancelot. *Our Conrad: Constituting American Modernity*. Stanford: Stanford UP, 2010.

Mao, Douglas, and Rebecca Walkowitz, eds. *Bad Modernisms*. Durham, NC: Duke UP, 2006.

———. "The New Modernist Studies." *PMLA* 123.3 (2008): 737–48.

Martel, James R. *The Misinterpellated Subject*. Durham, NC: Duke UP, 2017.

Martell, Jessica, and Zackary Vernon. "'Of Great Gabasidy': Joseph Conrad's *Lord Jim* and F. Scott Fitzgerald's *The Great Gatsby*." *Journal of Modern Literature* 38.3 (2015): 56–70.

Marx, Karl. *Capital*. 3 vols. New York: Penguin, 1992–93. First published in 1867 by Verlag von Otto Meisner as *Das Kapital: Kritik der politischen Oekonomie*.

———. "Contribution to the Critique of Hegel's *Philosophy of Right:* Introduction." *The Marx-Engels Reader*. Ed. Robert C. Tucker. 2nd ed. New York: Norton, 1978.

Marx, Karl, and Friedrich Engels. *Communist Manifesto*. London: Penguin Classics, 1985. First published in pamphlet form in 1848 as *Manifest Der Kommunistischen Partei*.

Matthews, John T. "What was High about Modernism? The American Novel and Modernity." *A Companion to the Modern American Novel, 1900–1950*. Ed. John T. Matthews. West Sussex: Blackwell, 2013. 282–305.

McGowan, Todd. *Capitalism and Desire: The Psychic Cost of Free Markets*. New York: Columbia UP, 2016.

McHale, Brian. *Postmodernist Fiction*. New York: Routledge, 1987.

———. "What Was Postmodernism?" *Electronic Book Review*, 17 Sept. 2012. Web.

McWilliams, Carey. *Southern California: An Island of the Land*. New York: Duell, Sloan & Pearce, 1946.

Mellard, James M. "Oedipus against Narcissus: Father, Mother, and the Dialectic of Desire in Fitzgerald's 'Winter Dreams.'" *Arizona Quarterly* 58.4 (2002): 51–79.

———. *Using Lacan, Reading Fiction*. Urbana : U of Illinois P, 1991.

Michaels, Walter Benn. *Our America: Nativism, Modernism, and Pluralism*. Durham, NC: Duke UP, 1995.

Miller, J. Hillis. "'Material Interests': Conrad's *Nostromo* as a Critique of Global Capitalism." *Joseph Conrad: Voice, Sequence, History, Genre*. Ed. Jakob Lothe, Jeremy Hawthorn, and James Phelan. Columbus: Ohio State UP, 2008. 160–77.

Miller, Jacques-Alain. Translator's note. *The Four Fundamental Concepts of Psychoanalysis: The Seminar of Jacques Lacan, Book XI*. By Jacques Lacan. New York: Norton, 1998.

Minow-Pinkney, Makiko. *Virginia Woolf and the Problem of the Subject: Feminine Writing in the Major Novels.* Edinburgh: Edinburgh UP, 2011.

Mizener, Arthur. *The Far Side of Paradise: A Biography of F. Scott Fitzgerald.* Boston: Houghton Mifflin, 1951.

Moi, Toril. *Sexual/Textual Politics: Feminist Literary Theory.* 2nd ed. London: Routledge, 2002.

Najder, Zdzisław. *Joseph Conrad: A Life.* Trans. Halina Najder. 2nd ed. Rochester, NY: Camden House, 2007. First published in 1983 by Rutgers University Press as *Joseph Conrad: A Chronicle.*

Nancy, Jean-Luc. Introduction. *Who Comes after the Subject?* Ed. Eduardo Cadava, Peter Connor, and Jean-Luc Nancy. New York: Routledge, 1991.

Naremore, James. "A World without Self: The Novels of Virginia Woolf." *NOVEL: A Forum on Fiction* 5.2 (1972): 122–34.

The New Oxford Annotated Bible. Ed. Michael D. Coogan. 4th ed. Oxford: Oxford UP, 2010.

Nicholls, Peter. *Modernisms: A Literary Guide.* Houndmills: Macmillan, 1995.

Ortolano, Scott. *Popular Modernism and Its Legacies: From Pop Literature to Video Games.* New York: Bloomsbury, 2017.

Parry, Benita. *Conrad and Imperialism.* London: Macmillan, 1983.

Paulson, A. B. "*The Great Gatsby:* Oral Aggression and Splitting." *American Imago* 35 (1978): 311–30.

Pease, Allison. *Modernism, Mass Culture, and the Aesthetics of Obscenity.* Cambridge: Cambridge UP, 2000.

Pendleton, Thomas A. *I'm Sorry about the Clock: Chronology, Composition, and Narrative Technique in "The Great Gatsby."* Selinsgrove, PA: Susquehanna UP, 1993.

Peters, John. *Conrad and Impressionism.* Cambridge: Cambridge UP, 2001.

Pilling, John. "Beckett's English Fiction." *The Cambridge Companion to Beckett.* Ed. John Pilling. Cambridge: Cambridge UP, 1994. 17–42.

Pynchon, Thomas. *The Crying of Lot 49.* 1966. Reprint, New York: Perennial, 1990.

Rabaté, Jean-Michel. *Joyce upon the Void: The Genesis of Doubt.* New York: Palgrave Macmillan, 1991.

Rajchman, John. "Lacan and the Ethics of Modernity." *Representations* 15 (Summer 1986): 42–56.

Rée, Jonathan. "Subjectivity in the Twentieth Century." *New Literary History* 26.1 (1995): 205–17.

Rice, Thomas Jackson. *Joyce, Chaos, and Complexity.* Urbana: U of Illinois P, 1997.

Rogers, Martin. "Monstrous Modernism and *The Day of the Locust.*" *Journal of Popular Culture* 44.2 (2011): 367–84.

Ross, Stephen. *Conrad and Empire.* Columbia: U of Missouri P, 2004.

———, ed. *Modernism and Theory: A Critical Debate.* New York: Routledge, 2009.

———. *"The Nigger of the 'Narcissus'* and Modernist Haunting." *NOVEL: A Forum on Fiction* 44.2 (2011): 268–91.

Roudinesco, Élisabeth. *Lacan: In Spite of Everything.* London: Verso, 2014.

Said, Edward. *Beginnings: Intention and Method.* 1975. Reprint, New York: Columbia UP, 1985.

Salecl, Renata. *The Spoils of Freedom.* London: Routledge, 1994.

Scholes, Robert. *Paradoxy of Modernism.* New Haven: Yale UP, 2006.

Schreier, Benjamin. "Desire's Second Act: 'Race' and *The Great Gatsby*'s Cynical Americanism." *Twentieth-Century Literature* 53.2 (2007): 153–81.

Schwarz, Daniel R. *Rereading Conrad.* Columbia: U of Missouri P, 2001.

Seed, David. *Cinematic Fictions: The Impact of the Cinema on the American Novel Up to World War II.* Liverpool: Liverpool UP, 2009.

Seshadri-Crooks, Kalpana. *Desiring Whiteness: A Lacanian Analysis of Race.* London: Routledge, 2000.

Shoop, Casey. "Corpse and Accomplice: Frederic Jameson, Raymond Chandler, and the Representation of History in California." *Cultural Critique* 77 (2011): 205–38.

Snyder, Michael. "Premonitions of the Postmodern: Aldous Huxley's *After Many a Summer Dies the Swan* and Los Angeles in the Thirties." *Aldous Huxley Annual* 5 (2005): 167–92.

Starr, Kevin. *The Dream Endures: California Enters the Forties.* Oxford: Oxford UP, 1997.

Strychacz, Thomas. *Modernism, Mass Culture and Professionalism.* Cambridge: Cambridge UP, 1993.

Szczeszak-Brewer, Agata. *Empire and Pilgrimage in Conrad and Joyce.* Gainesville: Florida UP, 2011.

Tate, Claudia. *Psychoanalysis and Black Novels: Desire and the Protocols of Race.* New York: Oxford UP, 1998.

Thiher, Allen. *Fiction Refracts Science: Modernist Writers from Proust to Borges.* Columbia: U of Missouri P, 2005.

Thomas, J. D. "F. Scott Fitzgerald: James Joyce's 'Most Devoted' Admirer." *F. Scott Fitzgerald Review* 5 (2006): 65–85.

Tomšič, Samo. *The Capitalist Unconscious: Marx and Lacan.* London: Verso, 2015.

Tuhkanen, Mikko. *The American Optic: Psychoanalysis, Critical Race Theory, and Richard Wright*. Albany: State U of New York P, 2009.

Turner, Timothy G. "Architect Wright Doesn't Like This City and Bluntly Says So." *Los Angeles Times* 20 Jan. 1940: 1.

United States Census Bureau. Population Division. "Population of the 100 Largest Cities and Other Urban Places in the United States: 1790 1990." Washington, DC: US Census Bureau, June 1998. Web.

Van Mierlo, Chrissie. *James Joyce and Catholicism: The Apostate's Wake*. London: Bloomsbury Academic, 2017.

Watson, David. *Paradox and Desire in Samuel Beckett's Fiction*. New York: St. Martin's, 1991.

Watt, Ian. *Conrad in the Nineteenth Century*. 1979. Reprint, Berkeley: U of California P, 1981.

———. "Conrad's Preface to *The Nigger of the 'Narcissus.'*" *NOVEL: A Forum on Fiction* 7.2 (1974): 101–15.

Watts, Cedric. *Joseph Conrad: "Nostromo."* London: Penguin, 1990.

West, Nathanael. *The Day of the Locust*. 1939. *The Complete Works of Nathanael West*. New York: Farrar, Straus & Cudahy, 1957.

———. *Miss Lonelyhearts*. 1933. *The Complete Works of Nathanael West*. New York: Farrar, Straus & Cudahy, 1957.

Wilson, Edmund. *The American Jitters: A Year of the Slump*. 1932. Reprint, Freeport, NY: Books for Libraries, 1968.

———. *Classics and Commercials: A Literary Chronicle of the Forties*. New York: Farrar, Straus, 1950.

Woolf, Virginia. "Character in Fiction." *The Essays of Virginia Woolf, Volume Three: 1919– 1924*. Ed. Andrew McNeillie. San Diego: Harcourt Brace, 1988.

———. *The Letters of Virginia Woolf*. Ed. Nigel Nicolson and Joanne Trautman. 6 vols. New York: Harcourt, 1975.

———. *To the Lighthouse*. 1927. Reprint, San Diego: Harcourt Brace Jovanovich, 1981.

Yeats, W. B. *The Collected Poems of W. B. Yeats*. Ed. Richard J. Finneran. New York: Scribner, 1996.

Zima, Peter. *Subjectivity and Identity: Between Modernity and Postmodernity*. London: Bloomsbury, 2015.

Žižek, Slavoj. *Interrogating the Real*. Ed. Rex Butler and Scott Stephens. London: Continuum, 2010.

———. "The Spectre of Ideology." Introduction. *Mapping Ideology*. Ed. Slavoj Žižek. London: Verso, 1994. 1–33.

———. *The Sublime Object of Ideology.* London: Verso, 1989.

———. "The Thing from Inner Space." *Angelaki: Journal of the Theoretical Humanities* 4.3 (1999): 221–30.

Zolotow, Maurice. *Billy Wilder in Hollywood.* 1977. Reprint, New York: Limelight Editions, 1996.

INDEX

Ackerley, Chris, 147, 155, 162, 180n6,
    180n7
acting, 133, 139
action, 58
adiaphane, 65
Adler, Alfred, 147
Adorno, Theodor, 144
adventure fiction, 23, 35, 48, 173n2
aesthetics, 6, 11, 25, 70, 73, 80–81, 96,
    111–12, 115–16, 138, 169n2
affect, 42
affect studies, 1
Africa, 86, 115
After Many a Summer Dies the Swan (Hux-
    ley), 20, 106, 108, 113–115, 138–144,
    178n6
alienation, 20, 98, 135, 156, 158, 172n11
Almayer's Folly (Conrad), 23
Althusser, Louis, 15–16, 18, 21, 25–27,
    51, 148
American landscape, 19, 103, 128
American Dream, 123, 177n5
American exceptionalism, 138
aporia, 104. *See also* Derrida
architecture, 20, 100, 111–15, 118, 121,
    124, 131
Aristotle, 65, 67
art, 18, 21, 46, 48–57, 59, 62, 64, 66, 69–
    70, 79–80, 82–83, 117, 134, 136, 169,
    174n3; categories of, 8, 168; creation
    of, 10, 19, 50, 61, 64, 69–70, 83–84;
    forms of, 1, 48; process of, 48 57, 59,
    69, 80–82; and vision, 84
artificiality, 16, 115, 133–35, 139, 144, 156
artist, the, 48, 55–56, 61–62, 64, 68, 81,
    83–84, 175n15, 176n16, 179n3
arts, the, 2, 48; visual, 17

atheism, 68, 82
authoritarianism, 25, 76
autopoiesis, 90

Badiou, Alain, 2, 16
Barnes, Djuna, 17
Barth, John, 10
Barthes, Roland, 162
Baudrillard, Jean, 20, 111, 116–17
Beach, Sylvia, 86
Beckett, Samuel, 20–21, 145–48, 154–64,
    167, 179nn1–3, 180nn5–7; *Dream of*
    Fair to Middling Women, 146; *Echo's*
    Bones and Other Precipitates, 146;
    More Pricks Than Kicks, 146; *Murphy,*
    20–21, 145–163, 180n4, 180n7
Berkeley, George, 63, 65, 67
Berman, Ronald, 93, 95
Berman, Russell, 144
Bible, 54–56, 67
Bion, Wilfred, 147
Borges, Jorge Luis, 14, 111, 117
Bosch, Hieronymus, 111
Brave New World (Huxley), 138
Brecht, Bertolt, 108
Bruccoli, Matthew J., 91, 123, 177n3,
    177n5, 178n9, 179n10
Butler, Judith, 12–13, 16, 18, 25–26, 44,
    176n3

California, 20, 106, 108, 113, 118, 120–22,
    131, 133, 144, 177n5, 178n6. *See also*
    Southern California
Calvino, Italo, 14
Capec, Karl, 133
capitalism, 15, 20, 24–25, 38, 40, 42, 87,
    112, 121, 145
Cartesian dualism, 4, 58, 147, 151–52,
    154–55
Caserio, Robert, 46–47, 171n3
castration, figurative, 89, 92, 101–102
Catholic Church, 61–62; faith of, 67, 175
celebrity, 69, 124, 129, 135

chaos, 19, 34, 81, 122, 160–61, 163–64
Chamson, André, 86
Chamson, Lucie, 86
Chandler, Raymond, 108
Chaplin, Charlie, 133
chora, 91. *See also* Kristeva, Julia
Christ (Jesus), 54–56, 62, 67
Christianity, 24, 26, 55–56, 62, 133, 140,
    142, 175n8
civilization, 30, 77, 100, 103, 135
class: ruling, 27–28, 38, 40; social, 27
class struggle, 34, 37–41
Claver, Peter, 142
cognition, 65, 88–89
cognitive studies, 1
Coleridge, Samuel Taylor, 142
collective unconscious, 99, 119
colonialism, 24, 173n; and colonization, 78
commodity, 91, 95, 139, 176n4; and fe-
    tishism, 89, 95
communism, 16, 25
Conrad, Joseph, 18–19, 21, 23, 25–26,
    28, 31, 34–36, 38, 41–44, 46–49,
    51–62, 64–65, 67–71, 77, 79, 83–87,
    129, 145, 163–68, 171nn2–3, 171n7,
    172n9, 173n12, 173nn1–2, 174nn5–7,
    174n8, 175n9, 176n2, 179n10, 180n1;
    Almayer's Folly, 23; *Heart of Darkness,*
    23, 56–57, 59–60, 86, 176n2; *Lord*
    Jim, 23, 36, 52–53, 60, 86, 164, 166,
    173n2; *The Nigger of the "Narcissus,"*
    23, 54, 57, 59–60, 67, 171n2, 174n7;
    Nostromo, 18, 23–47, 57, 85, 87, 153,
    163–67, 171n1, 172–73nn9–11; *An*
    Outcast of the Islands, 23
consciousness, 1, 18, 27, 62–63, 75, 84,
    94, 143, 149, 154, 161, 163, 165–66,
    168, 172nn9–10, 175n9; group, 69;
    self-, 125; social, 32. *See also* ideol-
    ogy: as false consciousness; stream
    of consciousness; subconscious;
    unconscious
Cooper, Gary, 138

corporeality, 21, 154, 160

Coward, Rosalind, 163; *Language and Materialism*, 163

critical theory, 2, 6, 10–13, 17, 25, 170n4. *See also* postmodernism: theory of; queer theory

Criticism and Ideology (Eagleton), 35–36

Crying of Lot 49, The (Pynchon), 20–21, 165–68

cult of personality, 123–24

cynical subject, 28

Dadaism, 7, 16, 170–71n7

Darwinism, 68; social, 180n1. *See also* evolution, theory of

Dawson, Warrington, 53

Day of the Locust, The (West), 20, 106, 108, 113, 115, 120–21, 130–40, 166, 177n5

death, 34, 40, 45, 66, 136, 140, 142, 146, 148–49, 155, 160–61, 166, 177n1, 178n9; of the subject, 2; symbol of, 103; symbolic, 108

Debord, Guy, 116

decentering, 20, 36, 116, 127; and geography, 110, 116–17, 127; and spatiality, 116; and subjectivity, 8, 14, 51, 127.

Decker, Jeffrey Louis, 87–89

deconstruction, 1, 7, 14, 22, 35, 39, 41, 127, 147, 154, 160–62, 165, 175–76n15

defense mechanism, 49

dehumanization, 133

Deleuze, Gilles, 15

Derrida, Jacques, 14, 16, 18, 23, 26, 29, 31, 36, 97, 104, 162, 171n4, 171n7, 172n8; *Specters of Marx*, 18, 23, 26, 29, 172n8; *Writing and Difference*, 97

Descartes, René, 4, 58, 147

desire, 6, 12, 14, 19, 21, 27, 33, 37–41, 44, 49–51, 55, 66, 70, 72–73, 75–76, 81–82, 85–86, 89–102, 122, 125–27, 129, 132, 134–35, 139, 143, 147–50, 152–61, 163, 167; collective, 96; dialectic of, 91, 98, 157; negation of,

147, 154, 156–57; object of, 19, 75–76, 92, 98 (see also *objet a*); object manifestation of, 95; Oedipal, 76, 102; of the other, 93, 157–59; repressed, 135; subconscious, 156; surplus, 98, 100

dialectic, 36, 71, 91, 98, 159, 162

diaphane, 65

Dickens, Charles, 46

disability studies, 1, 13

discourse, 29, 48–49, 78, 87, 147, 154, 162, 170n5, 173–74n3; philosophical, 78; scientific, 48, 170n6

disillusionment, 20, 119, 122, 131

displacement, 14, 19, 36, 39, 42–43; psychological, 12

Divided Self, The (Laing), 71

doubt, 35, 40, 48–49, 53, 57, 61–62, 68. *See also* skepticism

Dream of Fair to Middling Women (Beckett), 146

dystopia, 138

Eagleton, Terry, 35–37, 172n10; *Criticism and Ideology*, 35–36

Echo's Bones and Other Precipitates (Beckett), 146

economics, 10, 13, 31, 33, 36, 168

ecstasy, 70–71, 83–84, 125

ego, 4, 19, 22, 42–44, 51, 76–77, 143, 158, 167, 170n6. *See also* Freud

egoism, 55

egotism, 70, 82

Einstein, Albert, 2, 48–49, 63, 66, 69, 175n11

Eliot, T.S., 5–6, 140, 148, 179n3; *The Waste Land*, 6, 148

Ellis, John, 163; *Language and Materialism*, 163

Ellmann, Richard, 62

empire, 41, 43

Enlightenment, the, 58, 144

enslavement, 26–29, 31, 41–42, 121, 130, 171n1, 178n6

environmental studies, 1

epiphany, 43, 45, 83–84, 166

epistemology, 9, 175n9

ephemerality, 84, 144, 172n11, 175n9

epoch, 23, 60, 168

ethereality, 73, 77

ethnicity, 30, 87, 102

ethnic studies, 13

ethnology, 94

evolution, theory of, 53

existentialism, 2, 11

expressionism, 4

Eysteinsson, Astradur, 14

façade, 114–15, 118, 121–122, 134, 139–40

Fanon, Frantz, 88

fantasy, 19, 43, 49, 58, 90, 92–93, 96,
    100, 115, 127, 130–31, 133, 136–37,
    153–54; collective, 103, 111; sexual,
    131. *See also* fundamental fantasy

fascism, 138, 179n11

fatherhood, 39, 52, 61, 69, 76, 91–92,
    101–2, 105, 133, 146, 170n7, 174–
    75n8. *See also* paternity

Faulkner, William, 17, 108; *The Sound
    and the Fury*, 14

Felman, Shoshana, 12

feminism, 11, 13, 175–76n15, 176n3

fetish, 25, 135, 153. *See also under*
    commodity

film, 17, 107, 113, 117, 119–21, 126

film industry, 109, 115–19, 124, 126, 138

Fink, Bruce, 94, 96, 177n7

Finnegans Wake (Joyce), 14, 63–64, 108,
    146

Fitzgerald, F. Scott, 8, 20, 85–88, 91,
    95, 100, 106–10, 115, 117–19, 122,
    125–27, 129–31, 133, 138–40, 143–45,
    163, 176nn1–2, 177–78nn1–5, 178n9,
    179n10; *The Great Gatsby*, 8, 19,
    85–106, 117, 119, 122–26, 128, 130,
    147, 156, 176n2; *Lipstick*, 107; *The
    Love of the Last Tycoon*, 20, 106–8,

115, 117–18, 122–131, 133, 136, 138,
    177n3, 177n5, 178–79nn9–10, 179n12;
    Tender Is the Night, 106–7; *This Side
    of Paradise*, 86; "Winter Dreams,"
    91–92, 98

Fitzgerald, Zelda, 107, 178n9

Fleishman, Avrom, 63

floating signifier, 104

Forster, E. M., 68

Forter, Greg, 88, 100

Foster, Wendy, 160–61

Foucault, Michel, 15–16, 20, 44, 162

fragmentation: *See under* identity

France, Anatole, 85

Franklin, Benjamin, 92

free indirect discourse, 48, 77

French Communist Party, 16

Freud, Sigmund, 2, 4, 15–16, 19, 49–51,
    76, 95–97, 99, 102, 125, 147, 157,
    170n5, 172n9; *Beyond the Pleasure
    Principle*, 96; *The Future of an Illusion*,
    49; *Interpretation of Dreams*, 2; *Three
    Essays on the Theory of Sexuality*, 96

Friedman, Susan Stanford, 12, 170n5

fundamental fantasy, 19, 89, 101

Future of an Illusion, The (Freud), 49

future anterior, 104

futurism, 4

Galsworthy, John, 52, 85

Garnett, Edward, 36, 56–57, 174n7

gender, 50, 78, 83; and identities, 175n15;
    and roles, 83

gender studies, 3, 13

Genealogy of Modernism, A (Levenson), 5

geography, 24, 110, 117, 148

Geulincx, Arnold, 157, 180n5

Gifford, Don, 67

globalization, 25

God, 7, 19, 51, 54, 62, 68, 82, 90, 94–95,
    140, 142–43, 180n1

Godden, Richard, 88, 95, 177n8

gothic, 31, 114, 173n2

Graham, R. B. Cunningham, 164
Great Depression, 119, 177–78n5
Great Gatsby, The (Fitzgerald), 8, 19, 85–106, 117, 119, 122–26, 128, 130, 147, 156, 176n2
Greek skeptics, 63
grotesque, 99, 122, 131, 134, 142
Guerard, Albert J., 41, 172n9
guilt, 19, 61–62, 68, 109

Haggard, Rider, 23
Harrow, Susan, 2
Harvey, David, 3, 20
Hassan, Ihab, 6–10, 22, 109–10, 175n9
Hearst, William Randolph, 138, 179n12
Heart of Darkness (Conrad), 23, 56–57, 59–60, 86, 176n2
Hegel, Georg Wilhelm Friedrich, 15–16, 21, 58, 102, 172n11
hegemony, 15, 23, 27, 40
Heidegger, Martin, 50
Hilgart, John, 88, 94–95, 176n4
historicity, 111, 113, 116, 118, 144
history: as academic discipline, 2, 4, 24, 27, 82, 140, 171n3; as narrative process, 18, 21, 31, 36, 45–46, 94, 104, 109–12, 164–166, 172n9, 172n11, 173n11
Hollywood, 107–9, 115–21, 123–25, 127–31, 133, 135, 138, 177n1, 178n7, 178n9, 179n11
Horkheimer, Max, 144
Hume, David, 63
Huxley, Aldous, 20, 106, 108, 110, 113–15, 122, 138–45, 163, 177n2, 178n6; *After Many a Summer Dies the Swan*, 20, 106, 108, 113–115, 138–144, 178n6; *Brave New World*, 138; *Island*, 177n2; *Time Must Have a Stop*, 178n6
Huyssen, Andreas, 109–10
hyperreal, 114, 117
hysteria, 51

identity, 1, 6, 9, 18–20, 24, 39, 42, 44, 57, 76, 87, 89, 115, 117, 122, 124, 126–27, 129, 136, 143–44, 156, 175n9; American, 89–90; fragmented, 4, 6, 8, 22, 126, 143; Jewish, 90; national, 87, 89–90; and place, 20; racial, 19, 88, 90; sexual, 175n15. *See also* personality; subjectivity
ideological state apparatus, 27
ideology, 18–19, 21, 23–30, 32–46, 51, 62, 87–88, 128, 138, 152–53, 163; American, 128, 138; bourgeois, 153; and capitalism, 25; critique of, 18, 25, 29–30, 37, 44–46, 173n12; as false consciousness, 18, 25, 41; and fantasy, 138, 153 (*see also* fantasy); and imperialism, 18, 32, 44; and mystification, 25, 29–30, 32, 37; nativist, 88 (*see also* nativism); and religion, 26–27, 33, 38, 62; of ruling class, 27, 33, 40, 45 (*see also* class: ruling); and spectrality, 23, 25, 34, 38, 44; and subjectivity, 18, 24, 27, 41, 145
imagism, 4
imperialism, 18, 24, 27, 32, 38, 40, 42, 44, 61, 172n10
imperial subject, 27, 42, 172n10
impressionism: as movement, 79; as style, 54
indeterminacy, 7–9
industrialism, 15, 112, 119, 121, 180n1; and capitalism, 112, 121
industrial revolution, 180n1
interpellation, 18, 22–23, 26, 42, 46
Interpretation of Dreams (Freud), 2
Interrogating the Real (Žižek), 171n5
Irigaray, Luce, 15–16
Irish independence, 82
Island (Huxley), 177n2

Jackson, Andrew, 128
James, William, 18
Jameson, Fredric, 3, 20, 25, 31, 36–37,

Jameson, Fredric *(continued)*
111–15, 118, 145, 164, 171n7, 172nn10–
11, 173n2; *The Political Unconscious,*
31, 36, 171n7, 171–72n11, 173n2; *Postmodernism,* 111–12
jouissance, 92, 98, 100, 103, 148, 176n5
Joyce, James, 5, 12, 18–19, 48–49, 51,
61–64, 66–70, 82–87, 108, 140, 145–
146, 149, 162–63, 166, 170n5, 170n7,
173n1, 175n10, 176n1, 179nn2–3; *Finnegans Wake,* 14, 63–64, 108, 146; *A
Portrait of the Artist as a Young Man,*
51, 62, 68, 82, 85–86, 179n2; *Ulysses,*
14, 52, 63–68, 85, 180nn6–7
Joyce, Nora, 61
Judaism, 90, 128, 177n5; and anti-Semi-
tism, 90, 100–1
Jung, Carl, 147

Kant, Immanuel, 50, 99–100
Kermode, Frank, 10, 170n3
Kierkegaard, Søren, 2
Kipling, Rudyard, 23
Kojève, Alexandre, 15
Kristeva, Julia, 15–16, 91, 170n6

Lacan, Jacques, 8, 11, 15–17, 19, 21,
34–35, 42, 48–51, 56, 58, 63, 65–66,
71, 76, 88–89, 91, 94, 98–101, 104,
141, 143, 147–48, 154–59, 162, 166,
170n7, 173–74nn3–4, 175n9, 176–
77nn5–7; and fundamental fantasy,
19, 89; and future anterior, 104; and
the imaginary, 34, 50–51, 157–58;
and Law of the Symbolic Father, 76,
91; and the mirror stage, 15, 93, 154,
156–58; and Name-of-the-Father
concept, 76, 92, 105; and *objet a,* 19,
50, 66, 76, 89, 93–95, 176–77n6;
and the real, 34–35, 37, 41, 50–51,
58, 66, 71, 75, 99, 148, 157–58, 166,
174n3, 176n6; and symbolic order,
42, 50, 89, 156, 158; and the symbolic, 34–35, 39, 50–51, 58, 65, 71,
76, 99, 104, 143, 148, 150, 157–58,
166; and the Thing (*das Ding, la
chose*), 49–50, 99–100, 174n4; and
the void, 18–19, 42–43, 49–52, 56–
59, 61, 64, 66–71, 75, 82–83, 89, 94,
143, 163, 165–66, 174–75n3
Laing, R. D., 71; *The Divided Self,* 71
Lang, Fritz, 133; *Metropolis,* 133
language, 1, 4, 9, 15, 21–22, 34, 49, 50–
51, 63, 65, 71, 75, 97, 104, 141, 148,
155–56, 160–61, 163, 171n7, 176n6;
and subjectivity, 1, 15, 21–22, 34, 49–
51, 63, 65, 75, 97, 104, 155–56, 161,
163, 170n6. *See also* linguistics
Language and Materialism (Coward and
Ellis), 163
Larsen, Nella, 12–13, 17
Lawtoo, Nidesh, 42–43
Le Corbusier, 114
Lefebvre, Henri, 20
Lehan, Richard, 87
Leibniz, Gottfried Wilhelm, 147
Lester, John, 56
Levenson, Michael, 5; *A Genealogy of
Modernism,* 5
Lévi-Strauss, Claude, 104
linguistics, 4, 13–15, 19, 54, 104, 154,
170n5. *See also* language
Lipstick (Fitzgerald), 107
Locke, John, 63
London, United Kingdom, 147–48, 170–
71n7, 180n6
Long Island, New York, 90, 99
Lord Jim (Conrad), 23, 36, 52–53, 60, 86,
164, 166, 173n2
Los Angeles, 20, 106, 108, 110–19, 121,
127, 134–35, 137–38, 140, 143–44,
179n11
lost generation, 87
lost object. *See under* psychoanalysis
Love of the Last Tycoon, The (Fitzgerald),
20, 106–8, 115, 117–18, 122–131, 133,

136, 138, 177n3, 177n5, 178–79nn9–10, 179n12

Lyotard, Jean-Francois, 3, 10

Madonna-whore complex, 125
magical realism, 4
Mallios, Peter Lancelot, 87
Malraux, André, 157
Mann, Thomas, 108
Mao, Douglas, 169n2
Mapping Ideology (Žižek), 29
Marx, Karl, 15, 25–26, 58, 98, 100, 153
Marxism, 3, 11, 13–14, 17–18, 24, 26,
    35, 41, 43, 153; neo-, 3, 11, 13, 24, 35;
    post-, 3, 11, 13, 24, 25; structuralist, 11
masquerade, 106, 121–22, 131, 133
mass culture, 109–10, 137, 173n2. *See also*
    popular culture
maternity, 19, 49, 89, 96, 103, 128, 136,
    170–71n7. *See also* motherhood
Matthews, John T., 5
McHale, Brian, 9–10, 22, 109, 165–68,
    175n9
McWilliams, Carey, 117
mechanization, 133
méconnaissance, 43, 145, 148, 156, 158
Mellard, James, 75, 88, 91–93, 98
metaphysics, 1, 7, 58, 152, 161, 169n1,
    175n15
metonymic chain, 94, 160
metonymy, 7–8, 10, 27, 29, 92, 94, 159–61
metropolis, 110, 115
Metropolis (Lang), 133
Michaels, Walter Benn, 87, 90, 92–93,
    101; *Our America*, 87, 90, 92, 101
Miller, J. Hillis, 25, 174n6
Miller, Jacques-Alain, 51
mimesis, 36, 42–43
Minow-Pinkney, Makiko, 77–78
mirror stage, 15, 93, 154, 156–58
miscegenation, 101–102
misrecognition, 39, 42–43, 45, 148, 153,
    156, 158

Miss Lonelyhearts (West), 177n5
Mizener, Arthur, 85, 107
modernism, 1, 3–17, 20–21, 23, 42, 44,
    63, 108–10, 112–14, 116, 133, 138,
    140, 143–46, 161–66, 168, 169n2,
    170nn4–5, 175n9, 177n2, 177n4,
    179n1, 179n3; and architecture, 114;
    straw-man, 6, 8; and theory, 11–12,
    170n4
modernisms, 6, 9, 11, 15–16, 18
modernist fiction, 1, 6, 9, 12, 14, 17–19,
    22, 25, 111, 144, 161, 170n5
modernist literature, 2, 12
modernist novel, 14, 17, 19–20, 47–48,
    143, 161. *See also* novel, the
modernist studies, 5–6, 10–12, 169n2;
    new, 11–12, 169n2
Modernist Studies Association, 10
modernist subjectivity, 18, 20, 111
modernity, 5, 41, 138, 166, 168
modernization, 15
Moran, Lois, 107
More Pricks Than Kicks (Beckett), 146
motherhood, 49, 66, 76, 80, 91, 93–94,
    96–97, 103, 125, 129, 142, 147, 156,
    170–71n7. *See also* maternity
Murphy (Beckett), 20–21, 145–163,
    180n4, 180n7
mysticism, 25–26, 49, 68–70, 83–84, 113
myth, 24, 32, 40, 45, 103, 124, 172n11
mythopoesis, 24, 90

nacheinander, 66
Najder, Zdzisław, 175n8
Nancy, Jean-Luc, 1
narcissism, 77, 82, 139, 143, 147, 159
Naremore, James, 70–71
narrativity, 18, 25, 35, 164, 171n3
narratology, 6, 8, 88
nativism, 19, 87–88, 100–1
nebeneinander, 65
negation, 21, 36, 145, 147, 154, 156–59,
    161

neurosis, 49, 51, 96, 147

New Historicism, 11, 88

New York City, 86, 99, 108, 110, 114, 117–18

Nicholls, Peter, 5–6, 9–11

Nietzsche, Friedrich, 2, 43, 170n7

Nigger of the "Narcissus," The (Conrad), 23, 54, 57, 59–60, 67, 171n2, 174n7

nihilism, 35, 52, 169n1, 174n6

Nordic, 89–90

Nostromo (Conrad), 18, 23–47, 57, 85, 87, 153, 163–67, 171n1, 172–73nn9–11

novel, the: as genre and form, 14 17, 19, 25, 36, 46–48, 143. *See also* modernist novel

objet a, 19, 50, 66, 76, 89, 93–95, 176–77n6.

Oedipus complex, 19, 76, 89, 91–93, 95, 98–99, 101–3, 105

Olson, Charles, 9

omniscient narrator, 163–164

ontology, 9, 19, 21–22, 144, 151, 166–68, 175

other, the, 1, 21, 42–43, 66–67, 87, 93, 102, 109, 145, 157–59, 176

Our America (Michaels), 87, 90, 92, 101

Outcast of the Islands, An (Conrad), 23

overdetermination, 30, 38, 67, 89, 94, 98, 125

paranoia, 7, 51

Paris, France, 86, 114, 170n7

Park, Josephine, 2

parody, 64, 112, 114

Parry, Benita, 27, 172n9

pastiche, 20, 114–15

paternity, 49, 76, 78, 101–2, 124. *See also* fatherhood

patriarchy, 19, 91, 175n15

Paulson, A. B., 88, 95, 102–3

perception, 3, 63, 65, 70, 152, 166

performance studies, 88

Perloff, Marjorie, 6, 8

personality, 8, 58, 71, 122, 124–25, 130, 132–33, 135, 138, 142–43; cult of, 123; as fragmented, 4, 126, 143; multiple, 130–132

Peters, John, 52, 174nn5–6

phallus, 7, 75, 89, 92, 93

phenomenalism, 63

phenomenology, 11

philosophy, 2, 46–47, 63, 70, 78, 146, 148, 157, 170n5, 171n3

Plato, 65, 90

pleasure principle, 97–100

Political Unconscious, The (Jameson), 31, 36, 171n7, 171–72n11, 173n2

political antagonism, 30

political beliefs, 36, 45

political climate, 109

political conflict, 29, 32, 38, 41

political critique, 41

political factions, 34

political influence, 33

political instability, 32

political order, 36

political power, 78

political resistance, 29

political revolution, 37

politicization, 109

politics, 13, 27, 29, 31–33, 39, 41, 44, 46, 88, 123, 138, 153, 169n2, 170n7, 171n3, 172n9, 173n12; bio-, 42; and dictatorship, 33, 123, 153; and identity, 1; awareness of, 83; and psychology, 172n9; and race, 87–88

polysemy, 91, 104

popular culture, 110, 135, 139. *See also* mass culture

populism, 25

Portrait of the Artist as a Young Man, A (Joyce), 51, 62, 68, 82, 85–86, 179n2

postcolonialism, 3, 11, 13

postimpressionism, 2, 79–80

postmodern divide, 6, 10, 20, 109–10

postmodernism, 2–11, 13–14, 17, 20–21,

46, 109–16, 118, 144–46, 162–65, 168, 177n2, 179n1; and architecture, 112, 114–15; and art, 21; and criticism, 9–10, 13, 22, 29, 116; and geography, 100, 108, 111; and literature, 9–10, 14, 20, 144, 166–67; and subjectivity, 8, 13–14, 17, 111, 143, 170n5; theory of, 1, 3, 10, 12–15, 17, 21, 168

Postmodernism (Jameson), 111–12

postmodernisms, 9

postmodernity, 5, 116

poststructuralism, 3, 11–15, 17, 24, 145, 162, 170n5, 171n7; French, 162

Pound, Ezra, 5

Proust, Marcel, 17, 69, 71, 95, 145–46

psyche, 20, 34, 41–42, 138, 152, 166, 172n9

psychic dispossession, 43

psychic loss, 50

psychic order, 6

psychic subjugation to power, 44

psychic unity, 49

psychic well-being, 61, 84

psychoanalysis, 3, 8, 11–17, 19, 24, 83, 88, 99, 143, 147, 156, 160–161, 170n5, 176n3, 176n5, 177n7; and lost object, 50, 66, 176–77n6. *See also* psychology

psychological repetition, 19, 44, 89, 91, 93–94, 96–99, 105, 124, 126, 131, 147

psychology, 2, 8, 13, 15, 18–20, 23, 25, 29, 42–43, 68, 76, 86, 97–98, 102, 105, 111, 146–50, 154, 157, 159, 164, 172n9; abnormal, 136; and crisis, 122; crowd, 43; gestalt, 147; and space, 158. *See also* psychoanalysis

Pynchon, Thomas, 14, 20–21, 165–68; *The Crying of Lot 49*, 20–21, 165–68

queer studies, 11

queer theory, 1, 3, 13, 88

Rabaté, Jean-Michel, 49, 62–63

race, 13, 19, 21, 36, 68, 87–99, 100–1, 105, 120, 130, 176n3; and identity, 19, 88, 90

racial politics, 87–88

realism: as style, 66; Victorian, 23

recognition of the other, 67, 101–2, 156–57, 159

redemption: concept of, 19, 52, 56, 59, 61–62; artistic, 62, 68; religious, 62. *See also* salvation

reification, 94–95

relativity, special theory of, 2, 63, 69

religion, 18–19, 26–27, 29–30, 32, 38, 40, 48–51, 54–57, 61–62, 64, 68–70, 82, 84, 136, 140–41, 143, 173–74n3, 174–75n8, 175n10, 175n12; and authority, 26, 173n1; and dogma, 38; and faith, 68; and ideology, 26–27, 33; and imagery, 56–57, 61–62, 67; and myth, 32; and redemption, 65

repression, 34, 37, 40, 91, 93, 97, 109, 135, 137

Rhys, Jean, 17

Romanticism, 7

Ross, Stephen, 11–12, 27–28, 41–43, 170n4, 171n2, 172n10

Said, Edward, 36, 41

Salecl, Renata, 16, 29–31

salvation, 52, 54, 140. *See also* redemption

Saussure, Ferdinand de, 15

Scholes, Robert, 168

Schreier, Benjamin, 88–89

science, 2, 3, 18–19, 47–51, 53–56, 58, 61, 63–64, 68–69, 72, 77–78, 80, 81–82, 84, 140–41, 143, 151, 164, 168, 171n3; and discourse, 48, 170n6, 173–74n3

science fiction, 138, 173n2

scientific method, 80

scientific truth, 64

sensory experience, 54, 65–67, 79, 116, 152–154

signification, 35, 42, 50–51, 165, 174n4.
    See also metonymy
signified, 7, 9, 50, 78
signifier, 3, 7, 9–10, 14, 42, 50, 78, 94–95,
    104, 161, 173–74n3
signifying chain, 92
simulacrum, 116–17, 127
skepticism, 2, 18, 26, 35, 48, 51–52, 54,
    62–64, 68, 70, 77–78, 89, 147, 173n1,
    174n5. *See also* doubt
Skinner, B. F., 20
Sloterdijk, Peter, 28
social antagonism, 45–46, 87
social order, 27, 35, 44, 71, 172n9
social reality, 28, 33, 37, 153
sociology, 2, 47, 171n3
Soja, Edward, 20, 111
solipsism, 42, 52, 71, 151, 159
solitude, 43, 57–58, 74, 147, 149–150,
    163
Sound and the Fury, The (Faulkner), 14
Southern California, 113, 117, 138
spatiality, 20–21, 23, 63–64, 66, 71, 106,
    111–12, 116–17, 148–49, 152, 155, 158,
    160–61, 169n2
spatial turn, 20
Specters of Marx (Derrida), 18, 23, 26,
    29, 172n8
spectral imagery, 24–25, 33–34, 38, 44,
    60, 74, 100, 171n3
spectrality: ghost-like, 24–26, 28, 32, 38,
    45, 100, 171n1; and ideology, 23, 25,
    34, 38, 44; as narrative device, 18, 25,
    35, 37–38, 44, 171n3, 171n6
Spinoza, Baruch, 147
Stein, Gertrude, 170n5
Steinbeck, John, 108
Stevenson, Robert Louis, 23
stream of consciousness, 6, 48, 65, 70
structuralism, 11, 15
subconscious, 122, 156
subject formation, 27, 44–46, 76, 88, 93
subject-in-process, 14, 19, 170n6

subjection, 28, 44
subjectivity, 1–4, 6, 8, 12–24, 27–28, 36,
    40–46, 49–51, 57–58, 60, 63, 66–70,
    75–76, 83–84, 86–89, 92–94, 97,
    104–5, 108, 110–11, 115–16, 127, 132,
    143, 145, 147–49, 151–52, 154–55,
    157–62, 164–68, 169n1, 170n4, 170n6
    172n9, 172–73n11, 175n15, 176n16;
    as decentered, 8, 14, 51, 127; and de-
    sire, 93, 147, 159; as fragmented, 22;
    and ideology, 18, 24, 27, 41, 145; as
    interpellated, 22–23; inter-, 42, 129,
    175n9; and language, 1, 15, 21–22, 34,
    49–51, 63, 65, 75, 97, 104, 155–56,
    161, 163, 170n6; and perception, 3;
    postmodern, 8, 13–14, 17, 111, 143,
    170n5; and race, 19, 88; and space,
    20; and temporality, 104–5; void of,
    18–19, 56, 83, 89
subjugation, 18, 44, 78
sublimation, 48–51, 56, 143, 173–74n3
Sublime Object of Ideology, The (Žižek),
    28, 98, 100, 153
surrealism, 16, 166, 170–1n7
symbolic order, 42, 50, 89, 156, 158

temporality, 63, 98, 104, 111, 169n2,
    177n1, 180n1
Tender Is the Night (Fitzgerald), 106–7
terror, 52, 71
Theosophical Movement, 68
This Side of Paradise (Fitzgerald), 86
Three Essays on the Theory of Sexuality
    (Freud), 96
Time Must Have a Stop (Huxley) 178n6
Titanic, RMS, 98–100, 103
Tolstoy, Leo, 63
To the Lighthouse (Woolf), 52, 68–84,
    175n15
tragedy, 40, 44–45, 97–99, 101, 111, 122,
    133, 136, 138, 154, 164
transcendence, 7, 21–22, 54, 69, 74, 82,
    99, 147, 152, 157

trauma, 30, 34, 41, 96, 146
Trumbo, Dalton, 108

Ulysses (Joyce), 14, 52, 63–68, 85, 180nn6–7
unconscious, 2, 15–16, 27, 34, 42–43, 93, 153, 172n9, 174n4
utopia, 44–45, 147

Varo, Remedios, 21, 165
Venturi, Robert, 114
Victorian era, 4, 18, 54, 79, 179n3, 180n1
Victorian literature, 23
Victorian religiosity, 54
Victorian style, 48
violence, 32–33, 101, 111, 122, 131, 133–38
void, 18Ð19, 42–43, 49–52, 56–59, 61, 64, 66–71, 75, 82–83, 89, 94, 118–19, 143, 163, 165–66, 174–75n3
Voyage Out, The (Woolf), 71

Waste Land, The (Eliot), 6, 148
Waves, The (Woolf), 14
wealth, 27–28, 78, 91–92, 100, 130, 135, 139
West, Nathanael, 20, 106; The Day of the Locust, 20, 106, 108, 113, 115, 120–21, 130–40, 166, 177n5; Miss Lonely-hearts, 177n5
West Coast, 117–18, 177n1, 178n8
whiteness, 19, 89–90, 101–2
Wilder, Billy, 107
Williams, Raymond, 4
Wilson, Edmund, 113, 115–16, 118–19, 177n1, 177n3, 178nn6–8
"Winter Dreams" (Fitzgerald), 91–92, 98
womb, 136, 150, 154, 156, 160
Woolf, Virginia, 2, 18, 19, 48; To the Light-house, 52, 68–84, 175n15; The Voyage Out, 71; The Waves, 14
World War I, 88, 116, 145
World War II, 2, 4, 10, 17, 108–110, 112, 116, 138, 144–45, 166, 168, 177n2
Wright, Frank Lloyd, 113
Writing and Difference (Derrida), 97

Yeats, W. B., 116

Žižek, Slavoj, 2, 16–18, 25, 28–29, 32, 34–35, 37–40, 43–46, 98–100, 103, 152–53, 172n8, 172n10, 176n3; In-terrogating the Real, 171n5; Mapping Ideology, 29; The Sublime Object of Ideology, 28, 98, 100, 153

www.ingramcontent.com/pod-product-compliance
Lightning Source LLC
Chambersburg PA
CBHW030251100426
42812CB00002B/390